mystery man

mystery man

William Rhodes Davis
American Nazi Agent of Influence

Dale Harrington

Brassey's
Washington, D.C.

Library of Congress Cataloging-in-Publication Data

Harrington, Dale.
    Mystery man : William Rhodes Davis, American Nazi agent of influence / Dale Harrington.
        p.   cm.
    Includes bibliographical references (p.   ) and index.
    1. Davis, William Rhodes, 1889–1941.   2. World War, 1939–1945—Collaborationists—United States Biography.   3. World War, 1939–1945—Collaborationists—Germany Biography.   I. Title.
    D810.S8D294   1999
    940.53'163—dc21   99-29911
                                                                              CIP

ISBN 1-57488-338-0 (alk. paper)

Printed in the United States of America on acid-free paper that meets the American National Standards Institute Z39-48 Standard.

Brassey's
22883 Quicksilver Drive
Dulles, Virginia 20166

First Edition

10 9 8 7 6 5 4 3 2 1

To my father

'Tis strange—but true;
for truth is always strange;
Stranger than fiction.
—Byron

Contents

Preface

In the 1980s the third in Steven Spielberg's series of adventure movies on Indiana Jones called *Indiana Jones and The Last Crusade* reached the film screen. Set in the 1930s, the movie centers on Indiana's efforts to defeat a plot by the Nazis. The main villain of the movie is a wealthy American businessman, William Donovan. Indiana Jones first meets Donovan at the villain's elegant New York office located high up in a Manhattan skyscraper. Donovan comes across as a sophisticated and highly cultured man who conceals his evil intentions from Indiana. Later in the movie, Indiana Jones discovers that Donovan is working for the German government and is the leader of a Nazi plot. After many thrilling exploits, the movie concludes when Indiana Jones defeats Donovan by tricking him into drinking a cup of poison. Donovan is the epitome of the Hollywood-style sinister Nazi villain. Amazingly, there was a real person who closely resembles the movie's fictional villain.

This is the story of that American, William Rhodes Davis, who was the paramount agent of influence for Adolf Hitler in the United States. As an agent of influence, Davis was not a spy in the classic sense. A spy's primary goal is to obtain secret information for a foreign power, whereas an agent of influence's aim is to further the long-term interests of a foreign power. Unlike a spy, an agent of influence is hard to stop legally, at least in democracies. Only rarely do these operatives commit criminal acts and it is difficult to prove when they do break the law. For example, there were three attempts to charge Davis with breaking U.S. laws, but none were successful.

Compounding the enigmatic nature of agents of influence is the ambiguity of their actions. It is not always apparent when or if an agent of influence is working at the behest of a foreign power. It is often difficult to tell if Davis was working for the Germans or just furthering his own interests. As the U.S. ambassador to Mexico, Josephus Daniels, said, "Some people regarded Davis as a profiteer; others, as a man who would furnish needed markets for Mexican oil; and others as a . . . Nazi agent or as a crook. In reality, he was a composite of each of these descriptions."

There are many contradictory stories about Davis and the truth of these stories will almost certainly remain equivocal. The author's quest for the Davis story was beset with many biographical hazards strewn like misleading signposts from New York to Berlin, London to Mexico City, Washington to Stockholm, Boston to Lima, and Houston to Rome. To trace Davis's life is to grope in the dark and find after much searching a maze of contradictions. Davis, himself, created a mystery about his life, quite often with the deliberate intention of making a virtue out of obscurity. With his own conflicting stories and those of his friends and enemies, he remains a sketchy, shadowy figure more than a half a century after his death.

I know the facts of certain events in his career and I will focus on these episodes, but of the steps between these episodes I can only make educated guesses. As written in the *New York Times* in 1941, "in the last war [World War I] it was intrigue in munitions that dominated the scene back-stage and the elderly Sir Basil Zaharoff, with his black hat and cape, was the so-called 'mystery man' of international politics. This time it has been oil, the new 'mystery man' [is] William Rhodes Davis." Davis was the epitome of a mysterious international entrepreneur, wearing elegant suits, smoking a cigarette European style held with two fingers, and standing with one hand half in his suit jacket pocket.

Much of his life is veiled in mystery, but there are certain facts of notoriety that are undeniable. What is important about Davis is that he had a significant impact on government strategies. The following list of a few of Davis's activities indicates why he is such a fascinating and important figure:

- He built the largest oil refinery in Nazi Germany with money from a U.S. bank and supplied the German navy with fuel from the refinery.
- He obtained the assistance of John L. Lewis, president of the CIO, and the acquiescence of Franklin D. Roosevelt, to provide 24 million barrels of oil to Nazi Germany. This oil was a key element in Adolf Hitler's ability to start World War II.
- He attempted to stop World War II in 1939 to the benefit of Nazi Germany.
- He donated more than $5 million to the Republican Party in 1940 in an effort to prevent Roosevelt from being reelected president. The money came from the German government.

These are only a few of the many important events in which Davis was a key player. His commercial and political activities encompassed the world with significant operations in Great Britain, Germany, Ireland, Mexico, Peru, Sweden, and the United States. Through these ventures he developed connections with such important political leaders of the period as Mexican president Lazaro Cárdenas, Reichsmarshall Hermann Goering, U.S. senators Joseph Guffey and Burton Wheeler, Adolf Hitler, Secretary of War Patrick Hurley, Secretary of Commerce Jesse Jones, CIO Chairman John L. Lewis, President Franklin Roosevelt, presidential advisor Adolf Berle, president of the Reichsbank Hjalmar Schacht, leader of the Mexican labor movement Vincente Toledano, and Republican presidential candidate Wendell Willkie.

Despite his importance, little has been written about Davis. None of America's leaders wanted their association with Davis to be public knowledge. Much like links to Mafia bosses today, public ties to the Nazis could destroy an American politician in the 1940s. President Roosevelt, John L. Lewis, Senator Wheeler, and others discouraged publication of their friendly association with a known Nazi sympathizer and possible German espionage agent. Nor did the British and U.S. intelligence communities want Davis's story in the spotlight. They discouraged for many years the release of government documents about Davis because they wanted their roles in sabotaging Davis's business empire to remain secret.

Uncovering Davis's biography will add a new exciting element to our understanding of the 1930s and early 1940s. This book will establish how Davis's early years as an oil wildcatter and shady businessman, his international connections, and his superb salesmanship were all experiences that made him an outstanding Nazi agent of influence.

The biography will then focus on Davis's business manipulation and political intrigue to gain oil for Germany and power and wealth for himself. Concurrently, the biography will tell how powerful U.S., British, and Mexican business and political leaders aided and abetted Davis's services to Adolf Hitler. The book will end by describing his strange death and the attempts to cover up the part that prominent American leaders played in Davis's activities.

I want to thank Neil Moore and Rina DePaoli Austin for providing insightful comments about early drafts of this book and Hayward Blake for his assistance in tracing people. I also want to thank my editor, Don McKeon, for taking a chance on a new author. Finally, I want to thank Libby Pannwitt and my wife, Carrie Austin, for encouraging me to reach for the stars.

The Davis Corporate Empire
as of March 1, 1938

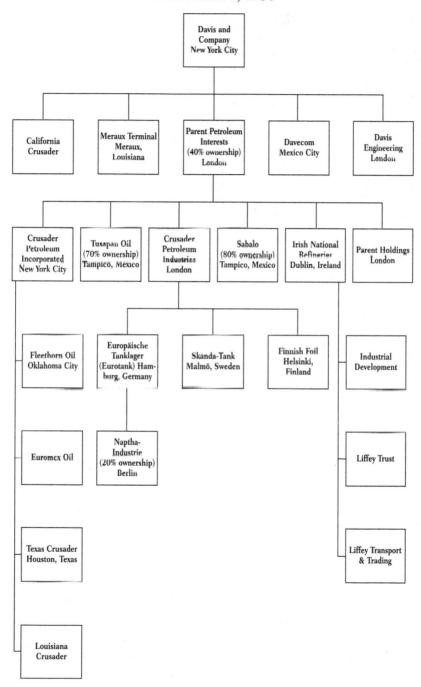

Davis and Company
New York City

California Crusader

Meraux Terminal
Meraux, Louisiana

Parent Petroleum Interests
(40% ownership)
London

Davecom
Mexico City

Davis Engineering
London

Crusader Petroleum Incorporated
New York City

Tusapan Oil
(70% ownership)
Tampico, Mexico

Crusader Petroleum Industries
London

Sabalo
(80% ownership)
Tampico, Mexico

Irish National Refineries
Dublin, Ireland

Parent Holdings
London

Fleethorn Oil
Oklahoma City

Europäische Tanklager
(Eurotank) Hamburg, Germany

Skanda-Tank
Malmö, Sweden

Finnish Foil
Helsinki, Finland

Industrial Development

Euromex Oil

Naptha-Industrie
(20% ownership)
Berlin

Liffey Trust

Texas Crusader
Houston, Texas

Liffey Transport & Trading

Louisiana Crusader

Personae

Almazán, Juan Andreu—Conservative pro-fascist candidate for Mexican presidency in 1940. Attempted coup against Mexican president Cárdenas with assistance from Davis.

Benedum, Michael Late—Pittsburgh oilman. Davis's employer in 1920s and major backer of Roosevelt in 1932.

Berle, Adolf Augustus—U.S. assistant secretary of state. Advisor to Roosevelt on espionage and security matters. Ordered surveillance of Davis by the FBI.

Burgess, Thomas Clarkson J.—British managing director of Thames Haven oil storage company and member of board of directors of Davis's Parent Petroleum Company.

Camacho, Manuel Avila—Handpicked by Cárdenas to be president of Mexico, 1940–1946.

Camacho, Maximinio—Brother of Manuel and governor of the Mexican state of Puebla. Business partner of Wenner-Gren and Davis.

Cárdenas, Lazaro—Left-wing president of Mexico from 1934 to 1940. Nationalized the Mexican oil industry in 1938.

Childs, Marquis—Reporter for the *St. Louis Post-Dispatch*. First reporter to write about Davis's pro-fascist activities.

Daniels, Josephus—U.S. ambassador to Mexico from 1933 to 1940. Close friend of President Roosevelt.

Davis, William Rhodes—President of Davis and Company oil company and member of board of directors of Parent Petroleum Company. Involved in German peace overtures in 1939. Contributed funds and provided other assistance to Roosevelt's 1932 and 1936 election campaigns and to Willkie's 1940 campaign. Built major oil refinery in Germany in 1933 and obtained Mexican oil for Germany in 1938 and 1939.

Fetzer, Friederich—Ministerial director of the German navy. Handled Davis's oil contracts with the German navy.

Goering, Hermann—Head of German air force and number two man in Nazi Party. Negotiated peace plan with Davis in 1939.

Gray, Walter Latimer—Vice president of First National Bank of Boston. Bank's main contact with Davis from 1933 to 1941.

Guffey, Joseph Francis—U.S. senator from 1934 to 1946. Pittsburgh oilman who worked extensively for Roosevelt in 1932. Good friend of Benedum and a major player in Davis's Mexican oil deals.

Hansell, Nils V.—Swedish-American engineer and longtime friend of Davis. Officer of Davis and Company and manager of construction of Davis's German refinery. Involved in Davis's Peruvian land concession.

Hertslet, Joachim Adolf Gustav—Economist on Goering's staff. Liaison to Davis on Mexican oil deals and on the 1939 peace plan. Smuggled oil out of Mexico to Germany in 1940 and 1941 and worked with Davis on Willkie's election campaign.

Inverforth, Lord—Member of British cabinet in early 1920s. Member of the board of directors of Thames Haven and Parent Petroleum Company. One of the richest men in England. Involved in the German peace overtures in 1939.

Jones, Walter Adelbert—Pittsburgh oilman and former confidential secretary of Michael Benedum. Democratic Party activist in 1930s, with access to Roosevelt. Conduit for Davis to Roosevelt.

Kauffman, James Lee—Corporate attorney for Davis and Company. Davis's primary business adviser.

Lee, Bertram—American oil speculator. Originator of Davis's Peruvian oil concession.

Lewis, John Lewellyn—Head of the Congress of Industrial Organizations (CIO) from 1937 to 1940, as well as head of United Mine Workers. Interceded for Davis in Mexico oil purchases for Germany. Worked with Davis on 1939 German peace plan and on Willkie's presidential campaign.

Lindbergh, Charles—Famous aviator and major isolationist leader. Selected Verne Marshall to lead militant isolationist organization.

Marshall, Verne—Isolationist newspaper editor. Major backer of Willkie and in 1940 leader of a militant isolationist organization that was funded by Davis.

Morgenthau, Henry—U.S. treasury secretary under Roosevelt.

Pryor, Sam—Willkie's campaign manager in 1940. Brought Davis into Willkie's campaign.

Roosevelt, Franklin Delano—President of the United States from 1933 to 1945.

Smith, Bernard E.—Stockbroker and Davis business associate. Partner in Davis's syndicate to acquire Mexican oil in 1938. Involved in German peace overtures in 1939 and 1940.

Stephenson, William—Head of British intelligence in North America from 1940 to 1945. Coordinator of British efforts to counter Nazi espionage in the Americas.

Suárez, Eduardo Aransolo—Mexican finance minister in 1930s and early 1940s. Negotiated oil deal with Davis.

Von Clemm, Karl F.—German banker in Berlin. Hired by Davis to be a liaison with German government on Eurotank transactions. Member of board of directors of Davis's Crusader Petroleum Industries. Connected to the German SS (Schutzstaffel).

Von Clemm, Werner C.—Twin brother of Karl. U.S. citizen living in New York. Vice president of Davis and Company and owner of import business used as a cover for diamond smuggling. Supported American isolationist movement.

Wehrle, Erna Frieda—Davis's personal secretary and close friend from 1934 and president of Davis and Company after Davis's death.

Wenner-Gren, Axel—Swedish industrialist and wealthiest man in the world in 1941. Go-between for peace negotiations between British and German governments. Friend of Duke of Windsor and business associate of Davis.

Wheeler, Burton Kendall—U.S. senator from Montana. Major isolationist leader backed by John L. Lewis for Democratic presidential nomination in 1940.

Willkie, Wendell—Republican presidential candidate in 1940.

Wilson, Henry Warren—Davis employee. Managed development of Eurotank and later was president of all of Davis's European operations and vice president of Davis and Company. Worked on Roosevelt's election campaign in 1936.

Wohlthat, Helmuth—German economist on Goering's staff. Negotiated the German part of Davis's Mexican oil deal.

one

High Roller

WILLIAM RHODES DAVIS was a gambler, or, as his personal secretary Erna Wehrle said, "a high roller." The risk involved in business ventures did not scare him; he would go the limit when he liked a deal. At one point he financed twenty-seven dry hole oil wells, and yet kept right on drilling. This behavior made him several fortunes during thirty years of business, but also lost him several fortunes as well. He was not always a high roller, however; the first half of his life was more conventional.[1]

Born in Montgomery, Alabama, on February 10, 1889, he was the son of Alice Rhodes Davis and John Wesley Davis. He had two younger brothers, Lynwood and George, and a younger sister, Lillie. His father was a policeman and the family lived in a rented home. The polite term of the period would describe them as being *in reduced circumstances*. Given his family names, Davis often claimed to be a descendant of Jefferson Davis and the grandson of the first cousin of Cecil Rhodes, the British Empire builder. Whether these alleged family relations were true or just the vanities of a self-made man is not known.[2]

His family's difficult financial situation forced Davis to leave school at age sixteen because his family could not afford to educate him further. In 1905, he left home and got a job as a newspaper boy on a small Mississippi railroad. A hard worker and a clever man, he quickly worked his way up to better railway jobs during the next thirteen years. He became a locomotive fireman and then in 1910 an engineer on a railroad in Oklahoma. He remained in this position for the next eight years. Davis was evidently happy with his years on the railroad because Austin Taylor, a vice president in the Davis organization, said that Davis "always kept his union card showing that he once was a railroad man."[3]

In 1909, with his economic circumstances improving, Davis supposedly married May Tankin, the first of his three wives, in Boston, Massachusetts. She bore him his first son in the same year, William Rhodes Junior. Little is known of May Tankin, or why Davis was in Boston or how he met her. In fact, it is not clear that Davis ever legally married May Tankin because there is no record of the marriage in the Massachusetts records. If Davis had continued with the railroads, his life might have been the conventional life of a working-class American family man.[4]

Possibly because of his new family responsibilities, the railway engineer job did not satisfy Davis's ambitions, for soon after his marriage, he became involved in the booming Oklahoma oil fields. Davis discovered a new talent within himself, an uncanny sense for business promotions, and he became consumed by an addiction to high-stakes speculation. Under the stress of his single-minded devotion to business, his marriage collapsed.

In Oklahoma, he worked as a laborer and driller on the oil rigs. After learning the oil business from the ground floor up, he decided to start his own wildcat company. His career as a business promoter began in 1913, when, at the age of twenty-four, he organized the Best Test Oil and Gas Company of Muskogee, Oklahoma. He invested a few hundred dollars in this venture and made thousands, an investment that changed his life. For the rest of his life, he would make and lose fortunes as he invested in one risky business venture after another.[5]

In 1915, he organized the Gotham Mining and Milling Company of Joplin, Missouri, followed by the Malcona Zinc Corporation, also of Joplin. He sold these mining companies in 1917 and received a considerable sum for the mines. However, he soon lost the money through new investments in oil wells. Although he had kept his job with the railroad, his business ventures took more and more of his time. Even if World War I had not intervened, Davis would no doubt have soon quit his railway job anyway.[6]

After the United States entered World War I in 1917, Davis enlisted in June 1918 as a private in the army to avoid being drafted. The skills he had acquired in business quickly got him promoted through the ranks and by the end of the war he would be a lieutenant.[7]

Sent to France late in the summer of 1918, Davis was in combat with the 27th Engineers and participated in several offensives, including the bloody Meuse-Argonne battle. He alleged that he received a bad leg wound and that he lost his teeth as the result of a German bayonet thrust. However, like many other events in his life, Davis's story of his war wounds was a fabrication. Army records show that he incurred his injuries while jumping from a moving train in France in October 1918. At the end of the war he returned to the United States and spent six months in a military hospital recovering from his injuries, which left him with a slight limp for the rest of his life.[8]

Released from the army in 1920, he returned to Oklahoma and resumed his business career. There was an oil boom in progress and he saw an opportunity to make millions. He became a drilling contractor and operated from Tulsa under the name of W. R. Davis Company. Through his contracting business he met Michael Late Benedum and Joe Clifton Trees, whose Pittsburgh oil business was internationally famous and who was reputed to have discovered more oil than any other group or individual in history. Benedum first viewed Davis as just another Oklahoma wildcatter trying to get oil leases on the cheap. However, Benedum soon became aware of Davis's vision and ability, and was impressed with his ideas and business creativity. As he later said, "Major Davis can get in anywhere."[9]

Benedum could see that Davis was a man of instinct, not of intellect, and that he relied on his intuition. He was always optimistic, was not the type of person who got mad, had a magnetic personality, and was a natural-born actor who could change character to suit the occasion. He could be an ungrammatical southerner or, when occasion demanded, he could play the polished cosmopolitan. With his personality and acting talents, he could "sell himself" to banks, and Davis lived on borrowed money. As he would later tell his personal secretary, "if you were able to borrow large sums of money, you were a successful business man."[10]

The borrowed money sometimes led to trouble; although apparently not an intentional criminal, Davis was often overenthusiastic about a business venture to curry the favor of investors. He would convince himself of the soundness of a deal and make expansive promises. Too often, the deals were not successful, for himself or for those who financed him. Another of his flaws was that he would go where he saw the best opportunity, regardless of previous commitments to undertake a now less attractive venture, thus disappointing those who counted on him. These unscrupulous business methods led many investors to claim that he had stolen their money.[11]

Davis's business methods and failed ventures left a trail of angry investors and partners and numerous lawsuits. Between 1925 and 1928, twenty-one lawsuits were filed against him concerning his business transactions. For example, in 1922, Benedum and Trees helped Davis form the Malcona Petroleum Company, which failed in 1924 and gave rise to a series of legal actions. Davis was eventually found guilty of fraud, gross neglect, breach of trust, and fraudulent mismanagement. A judgment of $169,000 was brought against him. Lawyers hounded him for many years, but this judgment eventually collapsed due to the statute of limitations.[12]

After this failure, a flat-broke Davis was forced to get a regular job. He found employment in 1924 with British-Mexican Petroleum Company of London, which primarily transported and marketed Mexican oil. His willingness to become an employee was no doubt spurred by his new family burdens, because in 1921 Davis had married Pearl Peters, who bore him two sons, Joe Graham Davis and Currie Boyd Davis, born in 1922 and 1925, respectively.[13]

Not surprisingly, Davis's promotional skills made him a great salesman, and he was paid $50,000 per year for his efforts in the development and sale of oil properties. He traveled to Europe and Mexico for the company and became a good friend of the director of the company, Sir James B. Currie. In fact, Davis named his second son after Sir James. Despite his success as a salesman, Davis yearned to return to operating his own business. In June 1925, after he had saved sufficient capital, he resigned from British-Mexican Petroleum Company to start up the Crusader Oil and Pipe Line Company.[14]

With his new company, Davis soon entered the Smackover Arkansas oil boom, intending to transport oil from the Smackover fields through his company's pipeline. However, when the pipeline was completed, no oil was available to transport because Standard Oil had blocked oil going to Davis's company. Crusader Oil and Pipe Line Company failed in 1927. Davis swore vengeance and began what was to be a lifelong war against the major oil companies.[15]

Davis's fortunes quickly turned around. Acting as a go-between in arranging the transfer of a Benedum and Trees company to another oil company, Davis reaped a small fortune as the commission for his services. He then borrowed $500,000 from Old Colony Trust Company of Boston, Massachusetts, through a banker named Philip Stockton. He used the money to organize the Arkansas Natural Gas Corporation, which he sold in early 1928 for $1.5 million. While in Arkansas, he met and became friends with Austin B. Taylor, a twenty-five-year old lawyer, who soon joined forces with Davis and would remain with him until Davis died. With his fortunes renewed and his ambitions to become an oil tycoon whetted, Davis was drawn into his first foray in international business.[16]

In 1922, Bertram Lee, a railroad engineer who had been in Peru for the previous twenty years, secured a tentative concession from the Peruvian government to exploit the Peruvian tablelands beyond the Andes. He went to New York and interested one of the largest banking groups in the country in his concession. A syndicate was formed and various consultants investigated the project from every angle, including the possibility of securing immigrants to develop the land. In the summer of 1923, a Swedish-American engineer, Nils V. Hansell, representing the syndicate, went to Peru and organized an expedition to the site to investigate the agricultural and economic possibilities. Hansell said that he "found a region incomparably rich in natural resources." Of particular significance, Hansell said, "throughout the trip we ran across petroleum seepage." Despite the promise of these vast resources, the syndicate collapsed because it was simply too expensive to build the railroads, highways, and other infrastructure needed to exploit the concession.[17]

However, Lee did not give up. In late 1926, he obtained a formal concession through an act of the Peruvian congress to develop a large section of land in the Amazon jungle. In return for building a railway to the area, he was to receive all mineral rights in the area. In early 1927 Lee met with Mike Benedum in Benedum's Pittsburgh office and presented a plan to exploit the concession in Peru. Lee truthfully described the 100,000 square miles in western Peru as bigger than Pennsylvania and West Virginia combined. The size of the concession fascinated Benedum, and Lee was a persuasive salesman, telling of rich oil seepage, a mountain of iron ore, and gold and silver ready to be mined. As Benedum said, "He was the bewitchingest talker I ever listened to. Just with words he could make you see cities springing out of the desert, excursion trains rolling gaily over the Andes, and jungle roads as crowded as the Pennsylvania turnpike."[18]

However, Lee had no capital and he needed Benedum and Trees to develop the concession, which would cost tens of millions of dollars. Benedum and Trees sent a geologist to Peru to verify Lee's claims.

The geologist reported back after seven months that he had found 150 miles of oil seepage, the land had a fortune in timber, and the soil was fertile enough to support a population as large as Germany's. Trees said later, "After that there wasn't enough power on earth to drag Mike out of this proposition. . . . I was just as excited as he was."

Soon after receiving the geologist's report, Benedum sought out Davis, whose promotional talents he rated above those of all others. At this point, early in 1928, after the collapse of his Arkansas venture, Davis had found employment as a petroleum consultant for the Italian and Spanish governments, and he was preparing to sail for Europe. Benedum laid the Peruvian proposition before him, declaring, "This is an empire. We'll form a syndicate." Davis at first refused, saying, "I'm not in the empire-building business." After further beseeching by Benedum, however, Davis's inclination to go for the big score got the better of him. Davis agreed to talk the plan over with the ruling heads of Europe during his European oil mission. Possibly one of the European rulers would take an interest in the scheme and provide the necessary funds.[19]

While in Europe, Davis interviewed Italy's fascist dictator, Benito Mussolini, King Alfonso and Prime Minister Primo de Rivera of Spain, and President Paul Hindenburg of Germany. Davis also met with Lord Inverforth, owner of the Andrew Weir Company, the world's largest shipping line. Davis got this appointment through an introduction from his friend Sir James Currie; Inverforth was a major stockholder in Currie's British-Mexican Petroleum Company.[20]

Inverforth was to play a central role in the rest of Davis's life. The sixty-three-year-old Inverforth was one of the richest men in England and suitably well connected politically. As Mr. Andrew Weir, he had been raised to the peerage in 1919 for his service as minister of munitions during World War I, and remained in the British cabinet as supply minister through 1921. In addition to owning Andrew Weir Shipping, he was on the board of directors of thirty-six of the largest British companies, among them Lloyds Bank.[21]

Davis's promotion of the Peruvian concession to the European leaders was a great success. With an almost messianic view of the function of international trade, Davis could talk for hours about his theories with a quick, nervous brilliance. Davis said,

> I mentioned the oil seepage to Mussolini. But as much as oil reserves for Italy, it was the colonization scheme—new markets, new sources of raw materials, living space for an overcrowded population—that appealed to Il Duce. Hindenburg and King Al-

fonso were also enthusiastic. "It's magnificent and I shall give you all possible aid," said King Alfonso. Mussolini promised a million Italian colonists, Primo de Rivera talked about 500,000 Spaniards, and from Germany I was assured a million emigrants.[22]

The Europeans' enthusiasm kindled Davis's own ardor for the plan. He notified Benedum and Trees that he was "sold" and considered it one of the grandest schemes ever concocted by mortal mind. In the summer of 1928 Davis traveled to Peru with a letter from King Alfonso warmly recommending him to President Augusto B. Leguia. Davis was to assist Bertram Lee in negotiations to enlarge Lee's original concession, which was now called the Benedum and Trees concession. With Davis and Lee was Nils Hansell, who Benedum and Trees had hired to manage the Peruvian end of the project because he had such extensive knowledge of the concession. Hansell and Davis became good friends in Peru and Hansell was to become a lifelong member of Davis's business staff.[23]

Lee and Davis negotiated with Leguia for the construction of a railroad and irrigation system, colonization programs of European immigrants, and other commitments in return for the land concession. The U.S. ambassador, Alexander Moore, became a Davis ally and helped him charm President Leguia, who soon approved the concession. The size of the concession was so large (one-quarter of Peru) that it is doubtful if a democratic Peru would ever have approved it. However, the Leguia regime was a dictatorship and popular approval was not an issue. Confident that the project would start by the end of the year, Davis and Lee arrived back in New York on August 20, 1928, with the documentation allowing them to colonize and develop 12.5 million acres.[24]

To obtain the $35 million needed to start construction, Davis and Lee returned to Peru in December 1928 with a group of New York and Boston bankers representing the now-enlarged business syndicate, which included Old Colony Trust Company, Sir James Currie, Lord Inverforth, Benedum and Trees, and European companies. After the bankers agreed to fund the venture, development plans proceeded rapidly. Davis later described how "Mike and I had men all over the world studying markets, figuring crops, casting up barter schemes, dickering for old ships which would be broken up on the Peruvian coast for scrap. We even had anthropologists figuring the best ratio of Italians, Spaniards, Germans, and Scandinavians. We thought we could breed a race of supermen—the imagination of the Latin wedded to the steadiness of the Scandinavian and the logic of the

German." With the success of the project seemingly ensured, Davis received many congratulations, including from President Herbert Hoover. The president privately congratulated Davis on having the imagination to plan this new outlet for American trade.[25]

With construction ready to proceed, Davis's plans hit a snag: Bertram Lee demanded that Benedum and Trees give him $100,000 up front before development could proceed. Benedum and Davis decided it was time to get rid of Lee. Davis said, "This was a great pity but the thing had become so big that we couldn't take any chances." First, Davis pressured Lee to sign away his rights to the concession. When that failed, he persuaded Ambassador Moore to ask President Leguia to cancel Lee's concession. Leguia cooperatively declared Lee's concession forfeit in August 1929 by executive decree for breach of contract. Although it was true that Lee had failed to begin construction of a railway to the Pacific within three years as stipulated by his contract, the contract had been extended before and, with construction imminent, there was no reason it could not have been extended again.[26]

Soon after Leguia's executive decree, the concession was formally transferred to Davis and his associates, and Davis was made the sole representative of Benedum and Trees in Peru. Lee did not take the loss of his concession easily and sued in the Peruvian courts. He also hired Miles Poindexter, the former U.S. ambassador to Peru, to get the State Department to pressure the Peruvian government to arbitrate the dispute. The State Department agreed to get involved when it became apparent that Ambassador Moore had played a central role in obtaining the concession for Davis. Under pressure from the U.S. government, Peru and Davis agreed to arbitration in December 1929.[27]

Despite Lee's lawsuit, development proceeded, and Davis and another American, Henry Warren Wilson, returned to Peru in July 1929 to begin construction of the railroad over the Andes to the concession area. Wilson and Davis worked well together. They were about the same age, both were war veterans, and, like Davis, Wilson was a salesman with a background in bond sales. Davis and Wilson spent $1.6 million on the project, according to Davis, and by the fall of 1929 the empire had progressed to the point where Philip Stockton of Old Colony Trust of Boston was ready to underwrite a $60 million bond issue. At this point, however, just as the project that would catapult Davis into the ranks of the world's business tycoons was about to succeed, his plans unraveled.[28]

First, the concession became entangled in an ongoing border dispute between Peru and Ecuador. Part of the concession (with most of the potential oil fields) was in an area claimed by Ecuador. The Ecuadorian government threatened to resist any development in the disputed area, through the courts and, if necessary, with its army. Second, the plan brought Davis and his partners into conflict with Standard Oil, which had leases on part of the property in the concession and threatened lawsuits against the Davis group. Third, the syndicate's financing collapsed due to the American stock market crash.

The coup de grace came on August 25, 1930, when rebellious army officers overthrew President Leguia.[29] The new nationalist Peruvian government abrogated the Davis contract, considering the huge land concession a threat to Peruvian sovereignty.

Davis's Peruvian land boom had gone bust. Benedum said, "It was just one of those wild notions of the twenties, when a man was ready to tackle anything." The collapse of the Peruvian concession devastated Davis. He had invested all of his own funds in the business syndicate and now it was worthless. All that he had for his troubles was a fancy document weighted with the seal of Peru.[30]

With the collapse of the Peruvian scheme, Davis's fortunes had sunk low as one after another of his promotions fizzled. He had to find new employment. Despite the dearth of jobs as the Great Depression began, he used his connections with the Boston financial community to find a job as a stockbroker. Davis had employment, but he had truly come down in the world. He was no longer a big-shot wheeler-dealer, but merely an employee engaged to sell stocks. He had to be disheartened by such a lowly position after having been so high only a few years before.

The collapse of the Peruvian concession also led to more family problems for Davis. First, Davis had a falling out with his brother, Lynwood Davis, over the Peruvian affair. According to Lynwood, Davis had failed to pay him for services rendered, which left the brother destitute at a time when he was ill. Lynwood complained bitterly to the State Department in May 1930 about the treatment he had suffered at his brother's hands. Second, Davis was divorced from his second wife in 1931.[31]

At the beginning of 1932, William Davis was forty-three years old, his hair was noticeably thinning, and he was developing a double chin. He no longer had the look of a young vital man; he had become middle-aged. Like most men at this time in their life, Davis was anxious about where he had been and where he was going. He had been divorced for a second time, and he was broke again. It was the Great Depression and business opportunities were meager. After twenty years of business life, he had no more than when he had started. Like many other speculators in the early 1930s, it seemed Davis's days as a high roller were over.

Men at mid-life often will make a radical change in their careers or take major risks to change the course of their lives. These risk takers are often men who have not been great successes in their chosen fields. Davis's string of failures in the 1920s clearly placed him in this category. Davis was probably psychologically ready for a radical change in his career. No doubt his desire to return to the "big time" stimulated his subsequent actions. During the next few years, he made major decisions that would set the course for the rest of his life.

two

Eurotank

IN THE FALL of 1932, Davis's time as an employee ended as he again started his own company. Philip Stockton, Davis's banker at Old Colony Trust during the Peruvian venture, had become an officer at First National Bank of Boston (present-day Bank of Boston), a large New England bank that had purchased Old Colony Trust at the end of 1929. With the aid of Stockton and Arthur L. Hobson, an acquaintance of Davis and lawyer for Bank of Boston, Davis got backing to form a new company, Foreign Oil Company, Inc. (Foil), with headquarters in Boston, Massachusetts. Davis organized Foil to develop oil business in Latin America and Europe.[1]

Foil fit the bank's business strategy because Bank of Boston specialized in foreign transactions through a separate foreign accounts department. It had extensive overseas operations in Latin America and Europe, and European offices in London, Paris, and Berlin. With his Peruvian experience and his contacts with European political leaders, Davis convinced Bank of Boston managers that he could develop a successful oil business in Europe and Latin America.[2]

11

Davis proposed development of two oil concessions: one on the Yucatán Peninsula in Mexico and one in Nicaragua. He planned to drill five wells in the Yucatán and one deep well in Nicaragua. With the backing of Bank of Boston, Davis was able to find investors and the company became operational in February 1933. In his first move to bring his eldest son into his business, Davis sent twenty-four-year-old William Rhodes Davis Jr. to Nicaragua in 1933 to explore for oil.[3]

The trip proved both unsuccessful and tragic. Foil invested $90,000 in drilling the deep oil well in Nicaragua. It was a dry hole and the loss left Foil in desperate financial straits. It seemed Foil was about to end in bankruptcy. Even worse for Davis, his son, along with Nils Hansell's son, was killed in an airplane crash in Nicaragua. Although personally distraught from his loss, Davis was already working on a scheme to save Foil by combining his link with Bank of Boston and the new Nazi government in Germany. This new scheme changed Davis's fortunes and his life.[4]

Davis saw opportunities in Germany, where the Nazis had just come to power in late January. He was dazzled by the possibilities of obtaining an oil monopoly under the Nazi regime. Davis calculated that in a future war Germany would need huge reserves of oil to fuel its submarines, tanks, and aircraft; he wanted to be the man who provided that oil.[5]

He sent Nils Hansell, who spoke German, to Berlin to make contact with the new Nazi regime. After a few weeks in Germany, Hansell cabled Davis that the oil industry was a virtual monopoly of Shell and Standard Oil and that there was no chance for Davis. Davis telephoned Hansell and told him to stay in Germany because Davis would be arriving shortly with a new plan. While Hansell had been in Germany, Davis had devised a scheme that not only would relieve Germany's expected fuel pinch, but also would line his own pockets.[6]

After arriving in Berlin in March 1933, Davis acquired a German oil storage company, Europäische Tanklager und Transport A.G. (Eurotank), with facilities in Hamburg. In early 1933, the two-year-old company was losing money because the demand for oil had slumped in economically depressed Germany. Davis proposed converting Eurotank into an oil refinery and building one of the largest oil refineries in the world at Hamburg. He would ship in crude petroleum, refine it into fuel oil and gasoline, and sell it to the German navy. It was a good plan but the German banks refused to finance the acquisition.[7]

Davis had not soared from newspaper boy to wealthy international wheeler-dealer by accepting defeat meekly. He intently studied the new German monetary system devised by Dr. Hjalmar Schacht, president of the Reichsbank, the German central bank. Dr. Schacht had lumped together everything concerned with regulating the value of money and recognized no limitation on the powers of the government to do what it considered necessary to manage the currency. As part of this system, the new Nazi government almost immediately suspended interest payments on foreign commercial debt.[8]

Davis noted Schacht's tight controls on foreign currency exchange and the inability of foreign companies to transfer their profits out of Germany. Using this information, he developed a clever strategy to use an $8 million account of Bank of Boston to pay for construction of his proposed refinery. The money was deposited in Germany in securities denominated in reichsmarks and was, therefore, frozen in Germany.[9]

When Davis approached the bank with his proposal, Bank of Boston jumped at the chance to fund the refinery. Like most other American banks at the time, it had been under severe financial stress since 1931 because of the Great Depression. The bank's stock price had plummeted from $132.50 per share in 1930 to only $20 per share by 1933. In March 1933, when Davis appeared with his proposal, the American banking crisis was at its apex, with the entire banking system closed for days by government order. Further, due to the financial restrictions under Schacht's Standstill Agreement, the bank could not withdraw from Germany its cash dividends from German securities, except at an unfavorable depreciation. Thus, the funds could be used only in Germany, which was the intention of Schacht's restriction. Therefore, it is not surprising that the bank agreed to let Davis use the blocked reichsmarks to help rebuild the refinery. By making a multi-million-dollar loan to finance the construction and operation of the oil refinery, Bank of Boston might "unfreeze" some of its German investment.[10]

Davis's ingenious plan was to purchase crude oil outside Germany, transport it to the Hamburg refinery, and market part of the refined petroleum in free currency markets, such as those in Scandinavia. If the refinery only broke even, the German processing costs, such as labor, depreciation, and so on, would automatically be converted from the blocked German reichsmarks into a free currency. If the refinery made a profit, the profits would also take the form of free currency. Even if the refinery lost money, at least the bank's "frozen" German paper money would be converted into a physical asset—buildings and plant—that had transferable value. The bank believed that Davis's plan would enable it to get all its German credits paid. Thus, an

American bank, for profit, financed a key component of the budding Nazi war machine.[11]

During the years to come, Davis would seek financing around the world, but his regular port of call for finances would always be Bank of Boston. Despite statements from bank officials that Bank of Boston would not finance his pro-Nazi schemes, it was to this bank that Davis would always go when he needed financial sustenance.[12]

W. Latimer Gray, a thirty-nine-year-old vice president trained in credit, and manager of Bank of Boston's foreign department, was in charge of the Davis account. Philip Stockton, who was by then chairman of the bank's board of directors, and whom Gray considered his best friend in the bank, met with Gray to talk about Davis's account. Stockton asked Gray to take over the loan package because Charles Eldridge Spencer, president of Bank of Boston, did not want to be involved in the Davis transaction.[13]

It is not surprising that Spencer did not want to be involved in the loan because everyone at the bank knew that the money would be used to build up the Nazi war machine. Gray did not have Spencer's moral qualms about the loan and told Stockton he would take the account. Starting with this loan, Gray became the bank's primary link to Davis for the next eight years. He would meet many powerful Germans, including Hermann Goering, head of the German air force and number two man in the Nazi Party. During the next decade, Gray became an integral part of Davis's operations. Like the arms merchants of the 1980s and 1990s, Gray never considered his activities immoral—just "good banking business".[14]

With American financial backing confirmed, Davis prepared a prospectus for the German government, whose support he needed to clinch the deal. Searching for a German with Nazi political contacts, Davis met Karl F. Von Clemm through a recommendation from a German bank, and soon developed a close bond with him.[15] Karl and his twin brother Werner C. were just what Davis needed because they were not only bankers, but also first cousins by marriage to the leading Nazi diplomat, Joachim Von Ribbentrop.

Thirty-five years old in 1933, the Von Clemm brothers were tall, slim, thin-lipped, spoke English with a clipped elegant accent, and had an aristocratic manner. The brothers' family was Austrian nobility, which gained the twins entrée to Berlin's elite. They were connected to the powerful Schröder Bank through interlocking directorships and were well known in high-society circles in Berlin. They were both ardent supporters of the Nazi Party and had close contacts within the Nazi apparatus. For example, Karl's wife was the mistress of Rudolf

Diels, the head of the Gestapo, the German political police.[16]

While Karl was living in Berlin, his brother, Werner, had moved to New York and was active on Wall Street. Werner had immigrated to the United States in 1922 after serving as an officer in the German army during World War I. He went to the United States when he married the daughter of Harry T. S. Green, a vice president of National City Bank of New York (present-day Citicorp). He became a U.S. citizen in the early 1930s and lived on Long Island in the wealthy suburb of Syosset, New York.[17]

Werner was connected with Pioneer Import Corporation of New York City, which imported merchandise from Germany and handled Von Ribbentrop's champagne business. He was also a representative of Hardy and Company, a German international banking firm, as was his brother Karl, in Berlin. Of more than passing interest is whether Werner Von Clemm was in 1933 already an agent for German intelligence. There is no hard evidence. It is known, however, that the Abwehr, the German intelligence agency, did have undercover agents in the United States as early as 1927 and that Werner was involved in German espionage during World War II.[18]

After Davis arrived in Berlin, Karl Von Clemm arranged a reception for him to meet German businessmen, including Hermann Schmitz, chairman of the powerful chemical firm I. G. Farben, and Kurt Von Schröder, an important German banker. Davis made an immediate impression on the group when he gave the Nazi salute as he entered the banquet room at Berlin's famous Adlon Hotel. A Nazi salute was a smart gesture on Davis's part because the Nazis had the enthusiastic backing of the big financiers and industrialists at the reception.[19]

These businessmen were ardent Nazi supporters for several reasons. The Nazis offered their big companies tax concessions, government subsidies, legal restrictions on the right of stockholders to interfere with "management," and a variety of administrative concessions that could be granted by officials to anyone who had the proper inside track—in other words, supporters of the Nazi Party. With introductions from these corporate leaders, Davis made appointments with government officials.[20]

Because he needed Hitler's personal approval, Davis wrote a note to him outlining his refinery plan and sent it by special messenger. The next day two Gestapo officers, delegated by Heinrich Himmler, leader of the Schutzstaffel (SS), presented him with a note from Hitler asking him to confer with Dr. Schacht. One of Schacht's functions was to develop a relationship and level of trust between German industry and foreign businessmen.[21]

Schacht was cold and uninterested in Davis's plan and brushed the matter aside. Schacht already had deals in the works with Standard Oil and Shell, and he had no time for small operators such as Davis. After being rebuffed by Schacht and given the runaround in the Third Reich's bureaucratic maze, the furious Davis sent another note to Hitler telling him of Schacht's behavior. Hitler sent a reply for Davis to appear the following day at the Reichsbank.[22]

The next morning Davis was ushered into the directors' room, with some twenty or thirty Germans sitting around a table. Davis began presenting his oil plan to the disgruntled Dr. Schacht and other high-level German financiers. Davis could sense by their demeanor that his proposal was falling on deaf ears. Fortunately for Davis, only a few minutes into his presentation, a door opened and the führer strode into the room and everyone jumped to attention and remained standing. "Gentlemen," Hitler said evenly, "I have reviewed Mr. Davis's proposition and it sounds feasible, and I want the bank to finance it." Then Hitler gave the Nazi salute and walked out. The führer had spoken. There was not a dissenting vote to Davis's proposal.[23]

Davis always thought that his great success with Hitler resulted from the influence of his contacts with German big business. Probably more central to Hitler's decision were other factors. Hitler could have done business with Standard Oil or Shell, but he preferred to rely on Davis. Standard Oil, if pressured, would have had to harmonize its operations with the foreign policy of the U.S. government, and Shell, if pressed, would take orders from the British Foreign Office.[24]

Davis, on the other hand, was a freelancer and, therefore, in a better position to resist such government pressure. Further, Davis's operations, unlike those of Shell or Standard Oil, were small enough to be dominated by the German government. The Germans reasoned that Davis would do their bidding as long as his German business continued to be profitable. At the same time his U.S. citizenship would be useful in the Americas. As Hermann Goering said later in reference to Davis, "At the time of the American depression I was desperately looking for someone who would [be] useful to me in America in exploiting the economic situation." Although the major oil companies (Big Oil) tried to hang on to the German market, increasingly Davis became the main conduit for German oil imports.[25]

Just as interesting as the Nazi attraction to Davis is Davis's attraction to the Nazi regime. There was nothing unusual about an American businessman operating in Nazi Germany; many American and British corporations were doing business with Hitler in the 1930s. These international companies, many with major subsidiaries in Germany, saw Hitler as just another dictator with whom they could do business. However, unlike most of these businessmen, Davis had a more personal attraction to the Germans than pure profit.

There were many aspects of Davis's personality and life experiences that would attract him to the Nazis. Like many of the businessmen who became Nazi adherents, Davis was deeply resentful of the big trusts and cartels. In the nineteenth century, there had been abundant opportunities for entrepreneurs to set up in business, make money, and rise in the social scale. By the 1930s, big business was preventing the fruition of many such ambitions. It was no longer enough for a businessman to work hard, save, and thrive, because a big combine could put him out of business overnight. Thus, pro-fascist businessmen were usually in debt and chronically discontented with their lot.[26]

Like other entrepreneurs, Davis had a deep grudge against the power brokers. He saw himself as the persecuted victim of the big oil companies, "the international combine," he called it. It was easy to persuade him that the economic developments that were endangering and eliminating small and medium enterprises should be curtailed. Laissez-faire economics started to look threatening to ambitious small capitalists who had in the past benefited from it; and it became connected in many of their minds with liberal politics. They believed the old political system should be replaced with a more reliable order that was restrictive and protective, controlling private enterprise in order to protect it.

Most of these businessmen did not know how to formulate their resentments and their claims. Nor were most of them willing to take the risks involved in converting beliefs into action. Davis was different, however; he had drive, ambition, and a desire to get even that forced him to tireless, fanatical extremes beyond those of a normal man.[27]

It was the Great Depression and the collapse of his business ventures in 1930–31 that led Davis from resentment to action. The world economy based on free exchange had collapsed and the established democracies seemed unable to cope with the crisis. Further, Davis, the ambitious would-be tycoon, saw the established cartels as barring his way to the top. The Nazis offered a solution to Davis's ambitions by demanding the rejuvenation of big business with an influx of fresh blood from smart and ambitious men of action like Davis.[28]

From the Von Clemms, the Germans knew of Davis's background, which they turned to their advantage. He was the kind of person the Nazis understood. The Germans gave Davis the grand tour when he was in the "new" Germany. The Nazi government had a special organi-

zation—the Council for Propaganda for German Economic Affairs—
for courting foreign business leaders. Its main task was to use the opportunity afforded by the conclusion of trade agreements to establish
contacts with influential foreign businessmen.[29]

The handsome, healthy men in black uniforms and the pretty
blond women fascinated Davis. To Davis, the Nazi expansionist phi-
losophy sounded like American-style enterprise with its talk of a great
economic union of the Anglophile world. The booming Nazi Third
Reich seemed a far cry from the breadlines and pinched faces of
America during the Great Depression. Even the Nazi racist ideology
was consistent with Davis's own beliefs as a white man from Alabama,
and his own employees had observed his dislike for Jews. By the end
of 1933, Davis had become deeply committed to Nazism. Although he
did not become an official German agent at this time, he had become
an agent of influence for Nazi Germany.[30]

Soon after signing the Eurotank agreement with the Germans,
Davis hired the American company, Winkler-Koch Engineering of
Topeka, Kansas, to design and supervise construction of the Eurotank
refinery. Work began quickly and, using German materials and labor,
the 300,000-ton annual production refinery was completed in late
1934, just more than one year after starting construction. Construction was hastened by Davis's political connections in Germany, which
enabled him to have several adverse rulings by Hamburg's building in-
spectors overturned in Berlin.[31]

Until completion of Eurotank, Davis had been hard pressed for
ready money, but the German contracts opened the way for him to
amass a fortune during the next few years. Eurotank was situated in
the special "extra-customs" area of the Hamburg port, and products
from its refinery were not subject to customs duties. Because Davis
did not have to pay taxes on the plant's production, Eurotank's refined
oil products could be sold at below world-market prices. Not surprisingly, the refinery soon began making sales throughout Germany, Italy,
and the Scandinavian countries. With burgeoning sales, the company
expanded its tank farm capacity to 60,000 tons and installed new oil
tanks in Wilhelmshaven and in Spandau near Berlin. It also purchased a large number of railway tank cars.[32]

The German government was jubilant with the rapid completion of
the refinery. Davis's plant was a key unit in the Nazi rearmament plan,
for it was one of the few German refineries that could produce the

high-octane gasoline needed to fuel fighter planes. Naturally, Eurotank would do most of its business with the German military, which
came to depend on Davis for much of its precious fuel. Without the
plant and the huge stores of gasoline it produced, the Nazi goal of European domination would have been stymied. Thus, an American
businessman provided a key component of the Nazi war machine, an
American bank financed its construction, and an American engineering firm built the plant.[33]

The Germans were delighted with Davis, and he became well
known among Berlin's Nazi power elite. Hitler met with Davis at least
six times during the next few years. On one of these occasions Davis
took along a copy of Mein Kampf for Hitler to autograph for Mrs.
Davis. Davis also developed a personal connection with Hermann
Goering, which he would exploit in due course.[34]

To maintain his close connections with the Ministry of Economic
Affairs and the German industrial cartels, Davis made frequent trips
to Germany. He spent almost all of his time in Berlin and seldom ven-
tured to the Hamburg refinery. To maintain German good will, he
kept Eurotank's headquarters in Berlin and hired a German, Dr. Her-
man Leising, to manage the Berlin office of the company. Davis's
headquarters was near the Adlon Hotel, a large luxury hotel where he
stayed when in Berlin.[35]

To further tighten the German link, Davis gradually replaced Eurotank's American personnel with Germans, so that by 1937 all administrative and labor personnel were Germans, including the general
manager of the refinery, Erwin Bockelmann. Davis also had Eurotank
issue common stock, of which 20 percent was purchased by the German financial firm Hardy and Company, to which Werner Von Clemm
was connected, as was Leising. The connection to Hardy and Company was important because the company represented the powerful
Dresdener Bank, which was linked directly to high Nazi Party officials. With his German business well established, Davis was ready to
build the oil empire he had always envisioned and the Germans were
ready to back someone who could reduce Germany's dependence on
the British and American oil companies.[36]

The first step in his empire-building plan was to form Davis and
Company, Inc., in Boston, in April 1933.[37] Davis and Company functioned as an oil managing corporation in the producing, transporting,
and financing of petroleum and would oversee the myriad companies
that Davis would organize during the next eight years. With the company's formation and the completion of Eurotank, Davis began purchasing oil on the international market. At first, Davis bought oil from

American producers (Cities Services and Sinclair Oil), which after being refined at Eurotank, was sold to the Germans.[38] His purchases were underwritten with short-term loans from Bank of Boston that were secured by the oil cargoes. By 1935, Bank of Boston and its affiliates had loaned Davis about $10 million.[39]

Through Davis and Company, the bank was able to circumvent the German government's restrictions on exporting capital from Germany. The convoluted process was as follows:

1. Buy oil on letters of credit from Bank of Boston.
2. Ship the oil to Germany on chartered tankers.
3. Refine the oil at Eurotank.
4. Sell the resulting gasoline to German manufacturers.
5. Exchange the gasoline profits for German goods, such as oil drilling pipes and prefabricated steel plating.
6. Export the manufactured goods from Germany.
7. Sell the goods on the world market through one of the Davis and Company subsidiaries.
8. Pay the subsidiary for the goods in an exchangeable currency.
9. Convert the foreign currency to dollars.
10. Pay off Bank of Boston's letters of credit in dollars.

The bank was pleased with the relationship because the short-term loans were paid promptly and it got its money out of Germany.

Still, the system was complicated. Because the German government closely supervised all German industry, it was necessary for Davis to have a contact to facilitate the exchanges of oil and steel. Davis's key contact was Karl Von Clemm, who controlled the Berlin office of Eurotank Handelsgesselschaft (Eurohandel), a Davis and Company subsidiary, which purchased and shipped merchandise in exchange for the oil imported into Germany. Von Clemm's role in Eurohandel was to approach the Economic Ministry and present a certificate that a certain oil tanker had landed with a certain amount of oil. Von Clemm would then request that the value of the oil be applied against an outgoing steel order. The process was intricate, but it worked.[40]

Davis wanted to put together the essential elements of an integrated international oil enterprise. To do so, he needed a refinery, large-scale outlets that he controlled, and an oil supply. He already had a refinery in Eurotank and soon had a guarantee of outlets in Europe.

In July 1935, he purchased in Germany (financed by Hardy and Company) a 25-percent interest in Naphtha-Industrie und Tanklagen

A.G. (Nitag). Nitag had a large network of filling stations in northern and central Germany, and it took over the distribution of Eurotank's petroleum products in Germany. This agreement gave Eurotank a firm foothold in the German consumer market. This action was followed in 1936 by a contract with the German navy to buy much of its fuel from Davis's Eurotank refinery. This agreement was handled by Friederich Fetzer, a ministry director for the German navy, who became a central contact for Davis with the German government. Karl Von Clemm had introduced Davis to Fetzer, and the two became friends and worked closely for the next six years.[41]

Davis also entered the Danish market, forming connections with a Danish company, Aktieselskabet Gica (Gica) of Copenhagen, which supplied gasoline to 200 roadhouses and filling stations in or near Copenhagen. Gica was not inside the protected circle of the secret oil trust and thus was also interested in breaking the monopoly of Big Oil. Since 1925, three companies—Standard Oil, Shell, and Anglo-Iranian Petroleum (present-day British Petroleum)—had been in almost complete control of the Danish oil market. All three companies charged the same price throughout Denmark, and in 1930, Gica had participated in an attempt by the Soviet Union to break this monopoly. By 1933, however, the Soviet Union was out of the Danish market because increased Soviet domestic demand left little petroleum for export.[42]

In February 1935, Gica and Davis and Company entered a two-year agreement that called for Davis's company, Foil, to supply Gica with gasoline. Gica was then operating profitably and for a time the arrangement worked well. The Gica/Foil group was aggressive, expanding the number of filling stations and selling gasoline at prices well below Big Oil's monopoly price. Foil was able to sell gasoline at a lower price because of the cheap crude oil available in the United States and the proximity of the Eurotank refinery in nearby Hamburg. Oil was cheap in the United States because the deepening depression had reduced demand, causing oil price wars in the United States. Davis's colleague, Nils Hansell, had business contacts in Sweden, and Davis, through these contacts, was able to sell his Eurotank oil to the Scandinavian countries. After selling the oil in Scandinavia, Davis exchanged the sound Scandinavian currency for U.S. dollars and thereby gradually covered the credits owed to Bank of Boston for construction of Eurotank.[43]

However, a critical element was missing from Davis's organization—a secure supply of oil. To solve this problem, Davis sought out his friend, Lord Inverforth, who had a contract to purchase an oil concession in Iraq. Davis set up a partnership, British Oil Development Company, with Inverforth and another respectable gentleman, Thomas Clarkson J. Burgess, managing director and chairman of London and Thames Haven Oil Wharves, Ltd. (Thames Haven). Burgess was a handsome, gray-haired, balding man in his early sixties. An employee of Thames Haven since its founding and chairman since 1931, he was on the board of seven large British companies. Burgess knew Inverforth through Inverforth's membership on the board of directors of a Thames Haven subsidiary.[44]

In 1935–36, Davis, Inverforth, and Burgess attempted to purchase from Azienda Generale Italiana Petroli (an Italian government-controlled enterprise) its interest in an Iraqi oil field. Francis W. Rickett, a Thames Haven employee, negotiated the contract. Unfortunately, the effort to purchase the £2 million Iraqi concession failed because the partners could not raise the required cash. In desperation, Davis and Burgess tried to persuade the British government to fund their purchase of the concession by implying that the Japanese were about to obtain the oil field. The British Foreign Office turned them down because of the partners' dubious business reputations.[45]

Despite the failure of the Iraqi venture, Davis's connections with Azienda Generale Italiana Petroli enabled him to get a foothold in the Italian market. After meeting with dictator Benito Mussolini and Count Galeazzo Ciano, the Italian foreign minister, Davis contracted to sell gasoline to the Italian government during its war with Ethiopia (1935–36). At the heart of the scheme was the Vatican's desire to liquidate large credits that it held in Germany. As was the case with other international organizations, the Vatican was not permitted to withdraw funds from Germany except at ruinous depreciation. The Vatican and Mussolini's government were on good terms during the Ethiopian war, and the Vatican tacitly supported the Italian war efforts. Taking advantage of Mussolini's goodwill, the Vatican turned to the Italian government for assistance with its German financial difficulties. The plan Davis devised combined the Vatican's needs with Italy's oil requirements.[46]

Davis had the Italian government pay the Vatican in Italian lira an amount equal to the value of the German gasoline that the Italian government required. Davis was in turn paid for the gasoline refined at the Eurotank facility by taking over the credits that the Vatican held in Germany. Under this arrangement, on January 14, 1936, an Italian ship loaded 3,000 tons of gasoline at Davis's Hamburg refinery.[47]

Everyone was satisfied. Davis had made a nice profit, the Vatican had gotten its money out of Germany, and the Italian government had received its gasoline. The Ethiopian people may have had a different perspective on this arrangement, but no one seemed to care about the "natives," certainly not Davis, the Nazis, the fascists, and it seems not even the Vatican.[48]

It is not difficult to imagine Davis's emotions by the end of 1935. He was close to being able to compete with the oil titans. He could undersell them and force them to meet his terms. However, Eurotank was still almost completely dependent on Big Oil for its supply of crude oil and Big Oil had no interest in supplying an upstart like Davis. By late 1935, Big Oil, using its leverage to try to break him, was selling oil to Davis only at very high prices.

three

Big Oil and Parent

BIG OIL WAS out to stop Davis because of a secret agreement among the major oil companies to control the oil market. Oil production after World War I had increased dramatically, which led to intense competition among the world's major oil companies. To dampen the competition, the major oil companies met in Scotland in August 1928 and negotiated an agreement to divide up the world's oil markets. The result of these discussions was the "As-Is" agreement. The document's key element allocated to each company a quota in the various markets based on its share in 1928. A company could increase its actual volumes only as total demand increased, but it would always keep the same percentage of market share. In addition, the agreement set a uniform price for oil based on the price of American Gulf Coast oil. These two provisions were central to the agreement because they ended the unprofitable price competition among the major companies.[1]

The agreement, which established an informal oil cartel to ensure high profits at the consumers' expense, was kept secret because it allowed a handful of businessmen to allocate the oil trade and to fix prices. It was not fully exposed until 1952. Although never fully implemented, the agreement had intentions and principles central to the policies of the major oil companies, especially Standard Oil and Shell, throughout the 1930s.[2]

At first, the "As-Is" agreement was unsuccessful in dampening competition because only the large firms adhered to it. There were many small operators, such as Davis, who did not hesitate to steal market share from the major companies. However, in 1935, under the economic pressures brought on by the Great Depression, the "As-Is" agreement was strengthened with the establishment of a central secretariat to administer the agreement and to settle disputes among the adherents. From this point until the start of World War II in 1939, the major companies operated in relative unity. With most of the world's oil resources controlled by the big companies, the agreement succeeded in its main objectives of maintaining stable prices (the high American prices) and limiting competition inside each country.[3]

Davis tried various avenues to get around the oil cartel and obtain oil for Eurotank. Eurotank refined much of the small amount of oil that Germany was purchasing in Mexico in 1935, and also obtained the rights to refine some of the oil from the small oil fields in northern Germany. These two sources provided only a trickle of oil and Davis's primary goal was to purchase his own oil fields. Familiar with Peru from his previous work in 1929 and 1930, he looked for oil there, but nothing came of this venture.[4]

With no cheap oil supply available, Eurotank was losing money because Davis was unable to purchase oil except at prices higher than what it cost him to refine it at the Eurotank refinery. Eurotank was 16 million reichsmarks (1 reichsmark = 40 cents in U.S. currency at that time) in debt and insolvent. In August 1935, Bank of Boston refused any further advances with Davis owing $2 million to the bank. The bank's refusal of further credit rendered the Eurotank refinery derelict because no oil could be purchased for the refinery. It seemed that the Big Oil cartel had succeeded in extinguishing Davis's dream of an oil empire.[5]

Compounding Davis's woes were problems with the Gica contract. In the fall of 1935, Big Oil attacked Foil, Davis's subsidiary, by reducing its fixed price to meet Foil's competition. In addition, the price of American crude oil had stabilized because of the Roosevelt administration's intervention and the more rigorous enforcement of Big Oil's "As-Is" agreement. Because Davis did not control his own oil production, he had to buy crude oil on the open market at the new higher prices. Foil's oil contracts with Gica were at a low fixed price, which became prohibitively expensive when the price of crude oil rose in 1935. Therefore, Foil reneged on its contract and stopped deliveries of oil to its Danish distributors.[6]

Gica then sued Foil in a German court for damages. In November 1935, Gica obtained an arbitration award in Berlin against Foil. Having obtained the award, Gica management discovered that Foil had no assets in Europe. Under pressure from Bank of Boston, Foil's assets had already been transferred to Crusader Petroleum Industries, a recently formed Davis and Company subsidiary. Bank of Boston had been fearful for some time of losing its loan collateral to Gica if it, as plaintiff, won the arbitration.[7]

Under the dual pressure of the imminent collapse of Eurotank and the Gica fiasco, and before the arbitration decision, Davis had gone to his English friends, Lord Inverforth and Thomas Burgess, for assistance. They in turn set up an English company, Crusader Petroleum Industries, to obtain new capital. Formed in November 1935, the company's managing director was Davis's longtime employee, Henry Warren Wilson. The other directors included Davis and his good friend, Karl Von Clemm.[8]

The key to the new partnership was the massive cash flow available to Burgess in his capacity as chairman of Thames Haven. Thames Haven was one of the largest and best-known oil storage companies in the world, with capital of more than £2 million ($1 million). The company had an extensive oil storage reservoir at Mucking, which was downstream from London on the Thames River. The company's primary function was transporting oil and gasoline upriver to London by barge from the tankers of Standard Oil and Shell that came to Mucking. Because British safety regulations did not allow gasoline and oil to be stored nearer London than Mucking, the company enjoyed a monopoly. It was a blue chip firm that had paid a 10 percent dividend for seventeen years and was considered a sound investment.[9]

Formed in 1898, the company had a history of steady and continuous expansion. It covered some 300 acres with approximately 200 storage tanks, which could hold more than 1 million tons of oil, and had more than three miles of frontage on the Thames River. It had ample facilities for handling oil, including a power station, pumps and pipelines, deep-water jetties capable of berthing the largest tankers, and five miles of railway sidings. In 1926, one-quarter of all petroleum products entering the British market passed through this installation.[10]

Burgess was interested in a partnership with Davis because the financial stability of Thames Haven was merely a facade. In 1932, Thames Haven's revenues had begun to decline as demand for oil storage facilities dwindled during the depression. At first Burgess hid the earnings problems by manipulating Thames Haven's accounting through paper transactions with its French subsidiary. However, by 1935, these paper machinations were not sufficient to hide the losses at Thames Haven. Burgess was desperate for a new source of revenue for the company.[11]

Davis's plans fit neatly into the solution for Thames Haven's troubles. Davis proposed to Burgess and Inverforth that they create a new company that, with new investors, would solve both Eurotank's and Thames Haven's troubles. Davis, Burgess, and Inverforth embarked on a grandiose plan to transform Thames Haven through a new corporation into a vertically integrated oil company with oil fields, refineries, tankers, storage facilities, and a distribution network. Davis hoped the plan would bring to fruition his goal of an oil empire.[12]

To realize this plan, they organized Parent Petroleum Interests (Parent), in London on April 6, 1936. Parent had a capital base of £2.5 million and, as a private company, listed only Davis and Burgess as investors. Davis sold his Mexican and European oil properties to Parent for £500,000 as payment for his share of the new company. In addition to Davis, two other Davis and Company employees, Nils Hansell and Langdon Dearborn,[13] were on the seven-member Parent board of directors.[14]

The main objectives of Parent were to procure crude oil for the Eurotank[15] and Thames Haven refineries and to build tankers to transport the oil. In May 1936, Parent signed contracts to build seven 14,000-ton oil tankers in German shipyards, the construction to be financed by the delivery of crude oil to Germany. Thus, Davis had secured British investors to finance the development of the Nazi oil and shipping industries.[16]

Later in the year, Parent's capital was increased to £4.5 million as the company's operations went into high gear and were expanded into Ireland and Mexico. After this round of investment, Inverforth joined the board of directors in November. At this point, Parent was owned 40 percent by Davis, 20 percent by Inverforth, and 40 percent by Thames Haven. At first Burgess and Inverforth controlled Parent through a voting trust but, with their acquiescence, Davis took control of Parent's daily operations.[17]

Davis was entering dangerous ground in his attempt to organize a new oil company based in Great Britain. Although Big Oil never achieved complete control of the world's oil market, the big companies with local allies could construct tight monopolies in individual countries. Unfortunately for Davis, one of the most effective of these monopolies was in Great Britain, where Shell and Anglo-Iranian Petroleum collaborated with Standard Oil to fix prices and formed a joint British marketing company called Shell-Mex. With his policy of granting rebates and undercutting the cartel's prices, Davis could expect Big Oil to attempt to crush Parent.[18]

Burgess was interested in constructing an oil refinery in Ireland and distributing the gasoline there. Ireland was a closed market at the time, however, with Big Oil supplying almost all of Ireland's refined petroleum requirements (worth £1.6 million in 1935). Davis knew that the Irish government had for several years been exploring plans to build a refinery and thus break the monopoly, and he had even visited Dublin in 1935 to investigate the prospects for such a venture. Although Davis was never personally enthused about the Irish refinery and would readily have dropped the whole scheme, it was Burgess's pet project and Davis had to go along with it to gain Burgess's investment in Parent.[19]

Through Burgess's connections, a deal was negotiated that gave a virtual monopoly of all sales in the country to Parent in June 1936. As part of the deal, Parent was given the right to erect an oil refinery in Dublin. In return, Parent agreed to return half of the refinery's profits to the Irish government. This project was one of the largest developments in Ireland in many years.[20]

Because the completed Irish refinery would need 500,000 tons of oil per year, a secure source of crude oil was required. (As described in chapter Four, this requirement led to Parent's investment in Mexican oil fields.) To finance the construction of the refinery, Burgess proposed that Thames Haven issue new stock and invest the proceeds in the refinery, but this proposal fell apart under pressure from Shell and Standard Oil. Instead, Parent, in November 1937, took over the liability to build the Dublin refinery. As the stock proposal indicates, the link between Parent and Thames Haven was solidifying. Burgess had already invited Inverforth to join the board of directors of Thames Haven in March 1937.[21]

Parent also looked to the United States for possible oil sources. During 1935–37, using Parent money, Davis organized five American oil subsidiaries: Texas Crusader, Fleethorn Oil, Louisiana Crusader, California Crusader, and Meraux Terminal. These companies controlled oil fields and storage facilities in California, Louisiana, Oklahoma, and Texas.[22]

Davis began accumulating oil holdings in Texas in February 1936, when he organized Texas Crusader with headquarters in Houston, where he took over an entire floor of a downtown office building. By the end of 1936, this company had opened oil fields in southern Texas. He also organized Louisiana Crusader, which, during the period 1937–38, drilled wells in Louisiana. In July 1937, Davis purchased, for $5 million, Fleethorn Oil, an Oklahoma oil production company. The purchase was funded with loans from Bank of Boston and First National Bank of Oklahoma City. His business in the Southwest was developing rapidly, and he frequently flew to Houston from New York to oversee operations.[23]

To run most of these various operations, Davis chartered a new holding company, Crusader Petroleum Incorporated, and made Henry Wilson president of the new company. Wilson had negotiated the acquisition of the oil properties that made up the new company and had made some sharp deals that fleeced the former owners of their properties.

Thus, by March 1938, Davis controlled a vast international oil empire of twenty-one affiliated companies (see chart on page xiii). His main American holding was Crusader Petroleum Incorporated, with extensive holdings through subsidiaries in Alabama, Louisiana, Texas, and Mexico, with offices in Houston. Overseas, Davis owned, through Parent, terminals and distribution facilities in Denmark, Germany, Norway, and Sweden. His holdings included the Eurotank refinery and gas stations in Germany, an oil terminal at Malmö, Sweden, and an oil storage and distribution facility in Finland serving Estonia, Latvia, and Lithuania. His overseas business carried out an extensive oil trade in Europe and Africa. This rapid expansion was based primarily on the money invested by Inverforth and Burgess. Davis's vast oil empire was directed from a plush suite of offices on the fifty-fourth floor of 30 Rockefeller Plaza, a building in New York's Rockefeller Center, where Davis had moved his operations in 1934.[24]

The officers of Davis and Company in 1938 were all longtime Davis associates, as follows:

William R. Davis, President
Pierce B. Watson, Vice President and General Manager
Austin B. Taylor, Vice President
Henry W. Wilson, Vice President
Werner C. Von Clemm, Vice President
Nils V. Hansell, Vice President
James Lee Kauffman, Secretary
W. W. Van Allen, Treasurer and Assistant Secretary[25]
Morris Geye, Assistant Treasurer

Davis now had both Von Clemm brothers working for him, one in New York (since September 1935) and one in Europe. Kauffman was the company's attorney and a close adviser on all of Davis's business deals. Davis's personal secretary said that "Kauffman knew everything going on." Despite his influence, Kauffman kept behind the scenes while Davis was alive, and his name only rarely appeared in the newspapers.[26]

Davis's employees were extremely loyal to him, and most of his top employees stayed with the company until it dissolved. This loyalty derived from two of Davis's traits. As his long-serving vice president Austin Taylor said about Davis, "Whether it was his office boy or his partner, he was interested in that individual's welfare. He was one of the hardest working men I have ever known." As Davis's secretary told the author, "He worked all the time. He never had a holiday." His hard work gained the respect of all his employees. With this respect came a willingness to carry out Davis's orders even when many people would consider those orders treasonous.[27]

In his new role as international oil tycoon, Davis was living the high life of the nouveau riches, spending a great deal of money on expensive cars, homes, and other extravagances. At the Davis and Company Christmas party of 1936, his wife wore $500,000 worth of diamonds. His palatial mansion in fashionable Scarsdale, New York, was considered the third best house in that section of wealthy Westchester County. A stately white wooden structure of Georgian architecture, it was set back from the road on a plot of several acres, and was surrounded by a stone wall with iron gates. A Finnish couple took care of the house—the man was Davis's chauffeur, the woman cooked and cleaned. Despite the stately home, Davis seldom entertained guests at his residence. The house was his private place where he could forget the business world.[28]

He also purchased a home for his first wife, Pearl Davis, and his two sons, Joe and Currie, in the nearby New York suburb of Bronxville. Davis and Pearl got along amicably and saw each other on a regular basis when she needed money for the children. Several summers Davis took the children to Germany on his business trips.[29]

Davis had become widely known throughout Europe and the Western Hemisphere among prominent oilmen as an international entrepreneur of the most flamboyant, impressive, and dangerous kind: a promoter with both personal magnetism and unscrupulous methods. He was also well known in political circles and probably had easier access to the heads of governments than any other oilman of the period.[30]

Davis looked every bit the respected executive with his expensive clothes, graying hair, and southern courtesy. He was riding high and everything seemed to be going his way. Befitting his new wealth, he hired a "personal secretary" in 1934, Erna Frieda Wehrle, to work in his New York office. A beautiful woman with dark brown hair and brown eyes, Wehrle was twenty-three years old when she met Davis. Born in Grand Rapids, Michigan, she was of German extraction, spoke German, and her father had not become a U.S. citizen until 1920. Wehrle had lived in Germany with relatives for a year in the late 1920s.[31]

She first came to Davis's attention because she could read and write German, skills Davis needed to assist with his German business. Wehrle was perfect for Davis—intelligent, shrewd, and hard working. Davis found her irresistible, and Wehrle soon became Davis's constant companion, traveling with him on his trips around the globe, nearly always accompanying him to Nazi Germany. Whether she was more than just his secretary is unknown, but her relationship to him was very close; they usually stayed in the same hotel suite.[32]

Blessed with a good memory, Wehrle handled all the details of Davis's business transactions. As she told the author, "I was the one who watched all the pennies and fussed and fumed." Because Davis did not keep notes and did not try to keep track of details, Wehrle soon knew more about Davis's business than any other individual. Over the years Davis became very dependent on her and he was said to have paid her a salary of $1,000 per month, which was an unbelievable sum to pay "just" a secretary in the 1930s. She was affectionately called "the boss" by Davis and his associates.[33]

At this high point in Davis's life, Big Oil became alarmed at the potential of what Davis had put together: European refineries, extensive European outlets, a tanker fleet, storage facilities of Thames Haven, and oil wells in the United States and Mexico. He was no longer a small-time operator they could ignore, he was a serious threat to the cartel. They decided to strike back on several fronts. Under their relentless counterattack, Davis's empire-in-construction began to crumble.[34]

Big Oil viewed the Dublin refinery as a direct threat to its control of the Irish petroleum market. In response to this threat, several of Thames Haven's large clients, including Shell, Anglo-Iranian Petroleum, Standard Oil, and Texaco gave notice in April 1937 that they would cancel their long-term storage contracts with Thames Haven at the end of the year. This was a serious loss for Thames Haven because these companies represented 80 percent of Thames Haven's storage business.[35]

Shell and Anglo-Iranian Petroleum had already announced in March that they would not use the proposed Dublin refinery to process their oil, and they threatened to close down all of their Irish operations, which would put 2,000 workers out on the street. Big Oil also delayed construction of the Irish refinery by instigating a six-month strike by the building trades. The Irish unions saw Parent as a threat because many workers would be laid off by Big Oil if Parent gained a monopoly over the Irish oil market. There were a series of Irish newspaper attacks on Davis. The *Irish Labor News*, a small paper, carried on a long campaign against Davis, reprinting extensive extracts from American legal records involving Davis. This material could have come only from the British Foreign Office or from British oil companies.[36]

Thames Haven began to hurt financially as it began to starve for oil. In addition, Burgess had arranged with Davis to finance the Dublin refinery construction from American sources, but the Davis financing never came through. Moreover, unknown to the board of directors of Thames Haven, Burgess gave a guarantee to Parent that if Parent could not finance the Dublin refinery that Thames Haven would secure the financing. No doubt due to pressure from Shell, Burgess's efforts to find the necessary funds were not successful and Thames Haven became massively overdrawn at its bank.[37]

To staunch the financial crisis, Inverforth, through his company, Inver Tankers, purchased the seven tankers under construction in Germany from Parent for £1.2 million in November 1937. Under attack from the Thames Haven board of directors, Davis was forced to resign as managing director of Parent in February 1938. Simultaneously, Hansell and Dearborn, the two Davis employees on Parent's board, resigned.[38]

Next, Bank of Boston became nervous about the potential negative publicity that could result from openly financing what could only be seen as German rearmament. It closed its Berlin office in 1937 and conducted its European business through its London office. In addition, it wanted to remove its name from all its German loan papers. Under pressure from the bank's management, Davis persuaded the Schröder Bank branch[39] in London to take the place of Bank of Boston. From that point, Bank of Boston was making loans only to German banks, thus no longer directly linking the bank to Hitler's war efforts.[40,41]

Big Oil's most important attack was on Thames Haven's monopoly of London's oil storage facilities. Ten years before, Anglo-American Oil Company, a Standard Oil subsidiary, had made serious efforts to have the limiting line moved from Mucking farther up the Thames and nearer London to Purfleet, which would include its own oil depot. This change would have meant the end of Thames Haven's comfortable monopoly. A royal commission was appointed and, after taking volumes of testimony and considering at length the safety of the great mass of the people in the London dock area and the danger of a collision of an oil tanker in the narrow reaches of the Thames, the commission found against changing the limiting line.

Now, ten years later, in retaliation for Thames Haven's poaching in Ireland, the effort to change the limiting line was revived by Standard Oil. In February 1938, the London Port Authority proposed to move the limiting line to Purfleet. By March, as the likelihood that it would lose its monopoly became public, Thames Haven's credit dried up and it was in serious financial trouble with a bank overdraft of $688,213. As a result, the company reduced its annual dividend for the first time in many years.[42]

About the same time, Sir Thomas Inskip, British minister of defense, asked the London Port Authority to change the limiting line because he felt that storage tanks in central London would be easier to defend against air attack. There was public opposition from the local urban and district councils in the affected Thames River districts to the proposed change. The British Ministry of Health threatened to cut off these councils' financial subsidies if they did not back down, and so they acquiesced. In addition, several critics pointed out that for just £250,000 a pipeline could be laid from Thames Haven to the London wharf area, which would avoid the risk of a huge oil fire in central London. Despite these valid safety concerns, the regulatory change was approved.

Mr. Burgess was forced to explain to his indignant directors and stockholders why it happened:

> It was a most extraordinary position. On the one side you have had a government department appointing a commission to look into the question from a safety point of view. You have an official report in the archives of that department pointing out the almost certain coming of a calamitous disaster should petroleum ships be allowed up the Thames River. In spite of this you now have another government department (Defense) insisting upon the necessity of this danger being disregarded and of plums being handed out to a foreign-owned company (Standard). For what? For a mere trifle of supposed safely stored petrol in a region so close to the heart of the City of London that the government com-

missioners had already reported, in the event of an accident, the
London docks and Woolwich Arsenal would probably be involved.
. . . they are thereby imperiling numberless lives, and property
amounting to many millions of pounds. . . . At Thames Haven
there are no other interests involved in a disaster due to air raids,
and the passage of ships to Purfleet is an incentive for enemy aircraft to drop their bombs in a thickly populated area. . . .[43]

Burgess's protests were to no avail. The London Port Authority for-
mally proposed the change on March 21 and Minister of Defense
Inskip announced final approval of the change on June 23, 1938. In
reaction, Thames Haven's dividend shrank and the stock price fell.
Inverforth and Burgess sent batteries of lawyers to New York and
Washington, D.C., but it did not help.[44]

A key element in the destruction of Parent was the complicity of
the British government. Without the assistance of the Defense and
Health Ministries, Burgess might have prevented the change in the
limiting line and thereby kept his position at Thames Haven. Why the
British government took an active role in the destruction of Parent
and Burgess is unknown. It may have simply been a result of pressure
from Shell and Anglo-Iranian Petroleum, since both had significant
influence within the British government. However, the British government may also have felt that it was important that the Germans be denied an independent oil system outside the British and American orbit.

Under pressure from the Thames Haven board of directors and his
own determination that it was time to get out, Davis sold all of his
shares in Parent to British shareholders in late June 1938 and resigned from Parent's board of directors. The determining factor in his
decision to bail out rather than fight was related to his activities in
Mexico, which will be discussed in chapter Four. Davis's friends also
sold their shares to British shareholders. After these transactions,
Thames Haven owned 66 percent of Parent and, therefore, Parent became a subsidiary of Thames Haven. Lord Inverforth owned the remainder of the company.

In return for his interest in Parent, Davis received complete ownership of the Scandinavian and German operations of Parent and retained a 40-percent interest in the Mexican oil properties. Davis was
paid generously for his interest in Parent (estimated value of the stock
shares was £2.5 million). The value of the remainder of Parent was
written down by more than 50 percent within less than one year.
These favorable terms were no doubt because of his continuing
friendship with Lord Inverforth. Also playing a key role in the negotia-

tions was Edward Joseph Flynn, "boss" of the Democratic Party in New York City and a key supporter of Franklin Delano Roosevelt. Whether Flynn's role indicates that Roosevelt was aiding Davis is unknown. As discussed in chapter Four, Roosevelt's involvement is a distinct possibility because Davis was a major financial supporter of Roosevelt.[45]

By September 1938, Thames Haven had an overdraft of £978,000 at its bank, and the company announced it was suspending its dividend. In this critical situation, the Thames Haven board of directors decided to abandon the company's attempt to break free of the grip of Big Oil. The board went to its former customers, Shell and Standard Oil, to ask for terms for renewal of their business. Shell responded that it would not resume business with Thames Haven unless Burgess was out of the company and demanded that Thames Haven not proceed with construction of the Dublin refinery.[46]

Acquiescing to Shell's demands, the Thames Haven board forced Burgess to resign on October 10, 1938, and Burgess's resignation was soon followed by that of Lord Inverforth on November 25, 1938. The fiasco in Ireland and the loss of the Mexican oil fields resulted in a write-off of £730,887 of Thames Haven's investment in Parent in March 1939. More losses were to follow, with an additional write-off of £520,000 by the end of 1939. These losses led to the discharging of many employees and to salary cuts by Thames Haven. Eventually, as Thames Haven deteriorated, Inverforth bought the company's shares and merged it into one of his companies in July 1940. The Irish project also ended poorly, as Irish National Refineries was eventually dissolved in April 1940.[47]

In June 1938, it looked as if Big Oil had finished Davis. Parent was crumbling and Davis was getting out. The Irish refinery would never be finished. Davis was being sued by the Danish company, Gica. Bank of Boston was backing away from his operations. Everything looked bleak for Davis's future, but he was actually on the verge of his greatest successes.

Despite the loss of Parent, Davis had gained much during the past five years. He owned the largest oil refinery in Germany. He owned petroleum distribution systems in Finland, Germany, and Sweden. He owned oil fields in the United States and Mexico. He had important political and business connections in Italy, Germany, Mexico, and the United States. And, best of all, most of his new properties had been purchased with other people's money. Even the loss of Parent was not a complete disaster. Davis used the money from the sale of his interest in Parent to pay off some of his loans with Bank of Boston and, thus, placed himself in a strong financial position for new business ventures.[48]

The irony of Davis's acquisitions was that they were funded by American and British business. In the long run, the development of an independent German oil industry through Davis would be a direct threat not only to the Anglo-American oil monopoly but also to the world balance of power—tilting it toward Germany. American and British capitalists were funding the effort to weaken their countries' control over the world economy.

These businessmen did not view Germany as the threat that it was and justified their actions as good business. On a more fundamental level, the capitalist economic system has an inherent anarchic dimension. Greed and short-term individual interests rather than the long-run stability of the system often dominate decisions. There were always those who were willing to make a quick profit despite the long-term effects of their actions.

Notwithstanding Davis's gains, Big Oil would still have destroyed him if Davis had not been planning ahead. Since 1934 he had been developing business and political relationships in Mexico. Just as Big Oil was about to crush him, he was in a unique position to parlay his Mexican relationships and his European facilities and political connections into his greatest business coup and a great victory for Nazi Germany.

four

Mexico—
Preparing the
Way for Germany

FOR EUROTANK TO succeed, Davis needed a steady supply of crude oil for his Hamburg refinery. Using his knowledge of Mexico, Davis quickly found a Mexican oil concession to purchase in 1934. From this simple origin developed a contest for control of Mexico's oil. This bitter struggle for Mexican oil went on behind the scenes both before and after the Mexican government's nationalization of foreign oil companies. The struggle ended in one of the most important economic victories of Nazi Germany.

Dominating Davis's Mexican venture was the power politics of oil involving many players. The American, British, German, Italian, and Mexican governments; Mexican and American trade unions; the major American and British oil companies; and Davis all had distinct and often conflicting interests in the Mexican intrigue. The story is one of strange bedfellows, political mistakes, duplicity, betrayal, and, above all, greed.

Davis's Mexican operations started in 1934 when he purchased a 75-percent interest in Tusapan Oil Company (Tusapan Oil) in the Ojital area of southern Mexico. Tusapan Oil owned oil land with a potential value estimated at $25 million, but only limited development had been done on the property. To exploit this oil property, Davis organized in 1935 a Mexican subsidiary, Davecom Company (Davecom), in Tampico, a port city on the Gulf of Mexico in northeastern Mexico in the heart of the Mexican oil fields. The focus of Davecom's operations was the sale of German petroleum equipment and the purchase of Mexican oil for export to Germany.

Davis and Wehrle went to Mexico in 1935 to personally survey the potential of the new oil properties.[1] Davis followed this visit with a trip to the Poza Rica oil field (south of Tampico) in February–March 1936. He had been contacted by Sam Katz, an American living in Tampico, who owned oil concessions in the Poza Rica fields. Katz's company owned a small warehouse, oil drilling equipment, and a few operating oil wells, just what Davis needed to start up operations in Mexico. Although Katz owned oil land, he could not get funding to start up full oil production because Shell also claimed part of Katz's oil concession. Davis, with his hatred of Shell, was willing to take on the oil giant.[2]

Because the Germans were closely linked to Davis's operations, Otto Probst, a geological adviser from the Institute for Petroleum Geology, a subdivision of the German geological survey, the Landesanstalt, accompanied him. Probst appraised Davis's concessions as well as Katz's Sabalo properties, and told Davis that the concessions held enormous oil wealth. Having verified that oil could be acquired in Mexico, Davis was ready to proceed with his plan to get the oil to his German refinery.[3]

Soon after his trip to Mexico, Davis tried to forge a three-cornered deal between Mexico, Germany, and the United States to provide oil for his Hamburg refinery. The proposed plan was a complex barter deal with the following steps:

1. Bank of Boston would purchase surplus cotton owned as collateral for farm loans by the Federal Surplus Commodities Corporation, an agency of the U.S. government.
2. Bank of Boston would export the cotton to Germany, which had an acute need for cotton. The bank would be paid for the cotton with $8 million worth of German railroad equipment.
3. Bank of Boston would sell the railroad equipment to the Mexican government and be paid with oil products from the Mexican national oil company.
4. Bank of Boston would sell the oil to Davis, who would then sell the oil on the world market after refining it at his German refinery.

Bank of Boston played a central role in this trading scheme, as it had in the Eurotank refinery deal with Nazi Germany.[4]

Because the plan involved the participation of the U.S. government, Davis strengthened his links to the Democratic Party. In 1932, he had played a small role in Roosevelt's run for the presidency. His connection to Roosevelt's campaign came through his friendship with Mike Benedum, his friend and former Pittsburgh employer.

Benedum, with a gift of $22,500,[5] and loans totaling $20,000, became one of the largest contributors to Roosevelt's 1932 campaign. Every week until election day, a $2,500 check bearing his signature was presented to the Democratic Party treasurer, Benedum's confidential secretary, Walter Adelbert Jones, often delivered the checks.[6] Through his own small part in Roosevelt's 1932 campaign and, more important, from watching Mike Benedum, Davis learned how to operate in American party politics.[7]

Another political link that Davis forged during the 1932 campaign was a friendship with Joseph Francis Guffey, a Pittsburgh oilman and aspiring politician who traveled extensively throughout the United States to secure delegate pledges of support for Roosevelt's nomination. At the 1932 Democratic National Convention, he had held the Pennsylvania delegation firm for Roosevelt. Guffey met Davis through an introduction by Benedum, who knew him from their association in oil and gas enterprises during the 1920s. Guffey's Pittsburgh office was in the Benedum and Trees Building.[8]

Through Walter Jones, an oil operator and a Pittsburgh Democratic Party activist, Davis arranged a meeting with President Roosevelt in 1936. The sixty-two-year-old bespectacled Jones was trim and still had almost a full head of dark brown hair, which gave him a youthful appearance. Jones, like Davis, was one of the handful of independent oilmen who supported Roosevelt. His ties to Roosevelt came from his work for Mike Benedum in Roosevelt's 1932 campaign, and he had easy access to the White House and was supposedly on a first-name basis with the president. This friendship paid dividends for Jones when Roosevelt appointed him to the Coal Code Authority in 1933. He was also named to a committee to raise funds to build the Roosevelt Presidential Library at Hyde Park, New York, in 1939. Jones also enjoyed the confidence of Secretary of the Interior Harold L. Ickes, the government watchdog of the oil industry. He knew Ickes from Ickes's work as the New Deal Federal Oil Administrator.[9]

Davis described in a letter to Bernard E. Smith, a business associate, how he and Walter Jones, now a Davis employee, called on President Roosevelt at the White House in May 1936 to seek the president's approval of Davis's three-cornered trade plan. Davis said that Roosevelt:

> agreed that I would work out some three-cornered trade whereby we would be able to move a considerable amount of the United States agricultural products abroad, using Germany and Mexico in the three-cornered agreement. The President asked me to use my best efforts to accomplish such an arrangement and stated to me that I would have the support of the Administration. He afterward informed Mr. Jesse Jones,[10] of the Reconstruction Finance Corporation, of the matter, and instructed him to work with me on it. In my discussions with Mr. Jesse Jones, he expressed himself fully in accord with the program and agreed to support it.[11]

Davis was neither a powerful politician nor a corporate leader at this time, but he had a private meeting with Roosevelt and obtained the president's personal assistance on his business plans. Why was Roosevelt willing to meet Davis and why was he so amenable to Davis's plan?

Roosevelt was seeking an outlet for the government's huge surplus of cotton. The New Deal's farm commodity law was proving unworkable because not enough farmers would cooperate voluntarily to limit production. A huge 18-million-bale cotton crop required large government subsidies under a New Deal law. The Roosevelt administration was desperate to dump the surplus cotton overseas. Why Roosevelt picked Davis to solve the surplus problem is unknown, but soon after the meeting Davis made a huge monetary contribution to the Democratic Party.[12]

Davis claimed to have "made available" $225,000 to elect Roosevelt and certain U.S. senators in the fall of 1936. Walter Jones delivered the contributions, but Davis's name never appeared on the donor list. Davis said he contributed $175,000, of which about $100,000 paid for Democratic Party radio broadcasts. The remaining $75,000 went to various U.S. senators who supported the Roosevelt administration. In addition, Davis loaned the services of his employee, Henry Warren Wilson, to work with Jones on the election campaign and loaned the Democratic Party an additional $50,000. The entire contribution was the largest donation to the Democratic Party in 1936.[13] According to John L. Lewis, "Franklin Delano Roosevelt knew that every nickel . . . came from Davis."[14]

Davis's claims about his political contributions were probably true because Walter Jones was listed by the Democratic Party as having contributed $102,000 in 1936 and providing a $50,000 loan. It is unlikely that this was Jones's own money because Ickes was surprised by the size of the contribution and he thought Jones was just an employee of Benedum and Trees. What did Jones get for his political assistance to Davis? Davis said that he paid Jones a salary for acting as a go-between with the Democratic Party. Jones may also have been a silent partner in Davis's Mexican operations because by mid-1939 Jones had vastly increased his wealth to an estimated $2 million.[15]

In recognition of this major campaign contribution, Davis received a photograph of President Roosevelt signed: "To Major W. R. Davis from his friend, Franklin Delano Roosevelt." Davis kept the photograph prominently displayed on his New York office mantelpiece. John L. Lewis said later that the salutation was one of "the warmest and strongest written personal statements" that he had ever seen on a Roosevelt photograph. After this major contribution, Roosevelt readily accepted Davis's telephone calls to the Oval Office. Davis considered asking Roosevelt to appoint his attorney, James Lee Kauffman, to be U.S. attorney general as a reward for his contributions.[16]

Having laid the political groundwork for his three-cornered trade, Davis turned his attention to acquiring Mexican oil fields. First, he attempted to buy Standard Oil's Mexican holdings, but Standard Oil backed out of the negotiations under pressure from Shell because the Davis deal would violate Big Oil's monopoly agreement. As Shell's chairman Sir Henri Deterding stated in a letter to Standard Oil protesting the Davis negotiations, "We are engaged together in resistance to Davis's activities and surely it is hopelessly inconsistent with sound warfare to sell the enemy a complete set of much needed munitions with which more effectively to conduct war with us?"[17]

Having failed in the Standard Oil endeavor, Davis instead acquired Katz's Sabalo Transportation Company (Sabalo). To reduce his personal risk, he then resold Sabalo and his other company, Tusapan Oil, to his British joint venture, Parent Petroleum Interests. By March 1937, Parent had invested £1.6 million to acquire a 50-percent share in Sabalo[18] and a 75-percent interest in Tusapan Oil.[19]

With oil fields in Mexico and the political goodwill of Roosevelt, Davis was ready to proceed with his plan. Davis believed that for his campaign money he would get the aid and cooperation of the U.S. embassy in Mexico City, acting at the instruction of his friend, Franklin D. Roosevelt. However, nothing came of the proposal because Josephus Daniels, U.S. ambassador to Mexico and an old friend of Roosevelt, blocked the plan.[20]

At seventy-five, Daniels had already had a long and distinguished government career in which he exhibited a consistent populist perspective in his actions. The white-haired heavyset Daniels dressed like the North Carolina newspaper editor that he had been for most of his life. He wore old-fashioned black frock coats in winter, wrinkled white suits in summer, and string ties in every season. Despite his appearance, Daniels was a sophisticated and clever politician with a knack for making friends.[21]

He had been Roosevelt's direct supervisor as secretary of the navy in Woodrow Wilson's cabinet from 1913 to 1920. Their work together had created a special relationship between the two men. Daniels's friendship with the president allowed him a fair amount of latitude with regard to State Department directives and gave his views exceptional weight in the formulation of U.S. policy. Appointed ambassador to Mexico in 1933, Daniels became popular with the Mexican leadership for his support of Mexico's nationalist reform policies.[22]

Davis, Walter Jones, and Latimer Gray of Bank of Boston arrived in Mexico City in January 1937 to negotiate the Mexican part of the three-way deal. While they were in Mexico City, Davis and Jones called at the U.S. embassy on January 22 to outline the proposal to Daniels. Jones spoke of his close friendship with President Roosevelt and said he had the support and assistance of RFC Chairman Jesse Jones and Senator Joseph Guffey (Democrat, Pennsylvania). Walter Jones asked Daniels to arrange a meeting for the Davis group with Mexican finance minister Eduardo Aransolo Suárez and President Lazaro Cárdenas to discuss the proposal. When Daniels replied that the American embassy had a policy of not making appointments for American businessmen with Mexican officials, Jones became irritated and said the embassy would receive instructions from Washington to make an exception in this matter.[23]

And indeed, Under Secretary of State Sumner Welles sent Daniels a telegram on February 8 asking him to render assistance to Jones. Despite this request, Daniels refused to provide the embassy's support for the deal. He declared, "I cannot see that the Embassy should promote it when it would exclude the use of American-made equipment." Jones responded that both Senator Guffey and President Roosevelt had told him that the American companies affected by the Davis plan had supported the Republicans in the presidential campaign and were therefore not deserving of any consideration. He asked rhetorically, "Isn't it most important for the government to sell the cotton that is stored up and upon which the government has loaned money?"[24]

Eventually Davis and Jones did meet with Suárez and Cárdenas in early February through the intervention of the State Department in

Washington. At the request of Secretary of State Cordell Hull, who was a friend of Jones, a State Department official, Edward L. Reed, asked the Mexican ambassador in Washington to make the arrangements. At this meeting, Suárez gave his government's approval of the proposal.[25]

Suárez was to be Davis's main contact with the Mexican government for all of Davis's financial deals. The forty-two-year-old banker and lawyer had been the finance minister since 1935 and was President Cárdenas's key financial adviser. He had drafted Mexico's banking laws and was a technical adviser to Mexico's national oil company, railroad, and bank. He would continue to be the Mexican finance minister through 1945.[26]

When the Mexican press reported that Elliott Roosevelt, the president's son, was involved in the scheme, Daniels warned the president of some of the political implications. Daniels pointed out that the proposal would hurt American manufacturers, personally link the president to "a company dependent upon [German oil barter] transactions with the Mexican government," and would "tend to encourage the [Mexican] government in refusing to continue concessions to foreign oil companies in order to enlarge its own reserves."[27,28]

President Roosevelt was grateful for Daniels's information, and called off American participation in the deal. Nevertheless, Roosevelt owed Davis for his political contributions, and the time would come when Davis would need to be paid back. This episode also highlights Roosevelt's thinking about Nazi Germany in the mid-1930s. Although the president was no friend of Hitler, he did not, at this point, see American trade with Germany as a threat to U.S. national security. The consensus among American leaders during these years was to acquiesce to Axis actions and to appease Axis economic demands.[29] This position would play a role in Davis's next Mexican venture.

Davis was furious when Daniels and the State Department blocked his three-cornered deal. He felt cheated that his political contributions had not resulted in assistance from the White House. Davis later commented:

> up to today [January 14, 1938] . . . nothing has come of any of the promises made to him [Walter Jones] or to me in respect of foreign trade. . . . I thought certainly with such an amount of money advanced to a party [Democrats] that was at the time desperately in need of funds, it would be undisputed evidence of good faith and probably would go a long way toward giving me the opportunity . . . to be of assistance in the matter of foreign trade.[30]

Davis did not give up easily. Undaunted, he looked for other opportunities to link his American political connections with his Mexican and German business relationships. As late as December 1937, Davis still expected to be rewarded by Roosevelt. At that time, he told a friend that he was endeavoring to settle his many lawsuits because he expected to soon be appointed to Roosevelt's cabinet.

Despite the failure of the three-cornered plan, it was an important dress rehearsal for Davis's future use of Germany's barter system to obtain oil. The deal had taught Davis that for his barter trade to succeed he needed to become indispensable to the oil-producing country, that his assistance must be crucial for the trade deal to go through over the objections of his powerful opponents. When the next barter opportunity came, Davis was ready and in position.

When Gen. Lazaro Cárdenas became president of Mexico in December 1934, Mexico embarked on a program of nationalizing private enterprise, including the large landholders and railways. Under Cárdenas, Mexico breathed nationalism with a fierce national pride pervading the thinking of almost every Mexican leader. The foreign businessman, who had enjoyed enormous benefits in Mexico, became an object of suspicion, an intrusive force whose activities must be controlled. This attitude was based on the incredible power that foreign corporations wielded in Mexico. According to estimates made in 1914, both American and French investors owned more of Mexico than did Mexicans, and the combined total of foreign holdings was more than treble that of Mexican nationals. Under these circumstances, any wide-ranging reform program would inevitably undercut foreign interests.[31]

As part of its reform program, the new Cárdenas administration began to raise taxes on the oil industry. The oil industry was an obvious target because foreign oil companies dominated it. These large international companies had obtained title to enormous stretches of exceedingly valuable oil deposits before the Mexican Revolution of 1910. The companies had extracted huge profits from the country and Mexico was receiving very little in return. The Mexican government estimated that Shell had paid a minuscule $50,000 in taxes on a production of nearly 40 million barrels pumped through 1917. The foreign oil companies objected to the new taxes, but the new taxes were still well below those levied in the neighboring United States. Further, much of the oil companies' profits never appeared as such because the companies used accounting devices to hide their income.[32]

Cárdenas followed up the new taxes with the organization of a nationwide union of oil workers, the Syndicate of Oil Workers of the

Mexican Republic, in 1935. Although paid well by Mexican standards, the Mexican oil workers objected to foreign workers being paid better wages than Mexican nationals. The companies also refused to place Mexicans in supervisory or administrative positions, claiming that Mexicans did not have the "native aptitude" for highly technical work. In November 1936, the combative union presented the foreign oil companies with an industrywide collective contract that demanded significant wage increases.[33]

The Mexican government's next step was to announce on February 20, 1937, a law for the immediate extension of the Mexican government's activities in petroleum production and the gradual elimination of all foreign oil companies. The law created a national petroleum administration (Pemex) to handle all government oil business, and stated that all new oil leases would go to Pemex. In addition, as foreign leases expired (some were close to expiration), they would be transferred to Pemex. The foreign oil companies were much opposed to the organization of Pemex because they did not want to compete with a large-scale government operation. They were sure that Pemex was just one more step in the Mexican government's plan to boot them out of Mexico.[34]

Pemex was established on March 2, 1937, and simultaneously the prior government oil corporation, Petromex, was liquidated. Petromex had been formed in 1934, partly with private capital, to exploit the oil fields that were owned by the Mexican government. The private investor in Petromex was Sabalo. Just before the liquidation of Petromex, the crafty Davis had purchased Sabalo and agreed to work Petromex's oil fields.[35]

Davis knew that Cárdenas had decided to secure tighter control of the government-owned petroleum lands. To eliminate Sabalo's rights in Petromex, the Mexican government would dissolve Petromex and replace it with Pemex. Sabalo's owners were worried about the viability of their agreement with the Mexican government. They did not know that Davis (through his contacts in the Mexican government) had been assured that his rights to Sabalo's holdings and contracts with the Mexican government would be protected. This protection was assured because Davis had promised the Mexican government that his revenues from the Sabalo field would be used to finance $100 million in construction of railways and highways in Mexico. Using his insider information, Davis purchased Sabalo for a fraction of its true value.[36]

As a result of the Sabalo affair, Davis became convinced that President Cárdenas would soon nationalize all of Mexico's oil fields. He began preparing for this possibility. First, he sent Henry Wilson to Mexico from London to coordinate Davis's Mexican operations. Next, he began making political connections to smooth his way in the business opportunities that would arise if nationalization occurred. Davis also played up to labor in the United States and in Mexico. He made contributions to the Workers University of Mexico City through its secretary, Alejandro Marcor Carrillo, who had influence in the Cárdenas government. Davis also used his two primary Democratic Party contacts, Walter Jones and Senator Joseph Guffey, a member of the Foreign Relations Committee, to further his Mexican operations.[37]

Senator Guffey had been president of several Pittsburgh-based oil companies: Guffey-Gillespie Oil Company, Atlantic Gulf West Indies Oil Company (AGW), and the Columbia Syndicate, and an officer in various other companies. In the U.S. Senate he was an ardent supporter of Roosevelt's New Deal programs. By 1937, at the age of sixty-seven, he had become a key player in the New Deal congressional machine and had written several important New Deal laws, including the Bituminous Coal Act of 1935.[38]

Guffey was from the Pittsburgh area and had a close connection with Walter Jones, perhaps because of Jones's generous distribution of Davis's money. According to Davis, $75,000 of his 1936 political contributions was spent by Jones in Pennsylvania on radio broadcasts for the Democratic Party. Guffey later claimed that he "never knew of any such source [Davis] for Walter Jones' campaign contributions."[39]

Despite Guffey's denial of knowledge about the money's source, it should not be too surprising that in early January 1937 Guffey introduced Walter Jones to Ambassador Daniels when Daniels was in Washington. When Daniels resisted the three-cornered plan, Senator Guffey met with Secretary of State Cordell Hull to ask the State Department to persuade Ambassador Daniels to assist Davis.[40]

Senator Guffey followed this assistance in May 1937 with a trip to Mexico City with Davis and Jones, who were in Mexico to lay the groundwork for Davis's Sabalo oil deal. At the time, members of Guffey's travel group described the trip to Mexico as "just a vacation." In actuality, Guffey was in Mexico to introduce Davis and Jones to Mexican officials (including President Cárdenas) and vouch that Davis had the support of President Roosevelt and Secretary of State Hull. When the group had trouble arranging an audience with Cárdenas, Guffey (probably with Davis and Jones in tow) called on the U.S. ambassador, Josephus Daniels, in Mexico City on May 17 to demand that Daniels arrange an appointment for Guffey. Daniels, acquiescing to the request of a member of the powerful Senate Foreign Relations

Committee, dutifully arranged a meeting between Guffey and Cárdenas to promote Davis's plan. Besides meeting with Mexican officials, Guffey, Jones, and Davis met and conferred with the German ambassador, Baron Von Hollouffer, and other German officials.[41]

Guffey said he became involved in Mexico at the request of Jones. "I would do anything to help Walter Jones. He contributed largely to the election of Franklin D. Roosevelt. I never really knew Davis, but I believe he is a man of great ability." Guffey may have been seeking vengeance against the large oil companies because between 1918 and 1921 he was one of the officers of AGW, which consistently broke ranks with the rest of the oil firms in exchange for official Mexican support. In 1921, Guffey led the fight for AGW and other small oil companies to get the Mexican government to abolish the big oil companies' legal control over Mexico's oil lands. Guffey lost this fight to the big oil companies, AGW suffered tremendous losses, and Guffey was forced to sell his last interest in Mexican oil in 1928. Whatever his motivations, it is still a sad commentary on the life of a U.S. senator that such a man would aid the Nazi war machine.[42]

The trip to Mexico was not Guffey's last assistance to Davis's Mexican operations. When Mexican finance minister Eduardo Suárez was in Washington in December 1937 for meetings with U.S. treasury secretary Henry Morgenthau on the continuance of purchases of Mexican silver by the United States, Guffey hosted a luncheon for Davis and Suárez. In addition, Guffey, Jones, and Davis met with Suárez in Jones's offices at the Mayflower Hotel in Washington, D.C. No doubt they discussed Davis's role in Mexico's plans for its oil fields.[43]

On May 28, 1937, the Mexican oil workers went on strike across Mexico, seeking a wage increase and organizational changes. Acting in accordance with their plans (and probably the cooperation of the Mexican government), the workers quickly ended the strike and placed their complaint before the Mexican Board of Conciliation and Arbitration. On December 18 this labor board handed down a decision ordering the American and British oil companies to increase the wages of their Mexican workers by 33 percent and improve their pension and welfare system. The companies refused to comply with this order and appealed the decision to the Mexican Supreme Court.[44]

The appeal failed as the Mexican Supreme Court upheld the unions in the wage dispute on March 1, 1938. Negotiations between the government and the oil companies led to an impasse. The foreign oil companies refused to obey the court ruling and made an implied threat by declaring that they would not be responsible for the consequences of the dispute. In essence, they considered themselves as powerful as the Mexican government, not believing that the Mexican government would carry out its threat of nationalization. Thomas R. Armstrong, vice president of Standard Oil, boasted to the Mexican ambassador in Washington: "Cárdenas wouldn't dare expropriate us." However, this obstinacy only served to consolidate Mexican public opinion behind Cárdenas to nationalize the companies.[45]

In late 1937, as nationalization of the foreign oil companies in Mexico began to look imminent, Davis started preparations to procure the soon-to-be nationalized oil. To Davis it was obvious that when Mexico nationalized the oil fields, Big Oil would prevent tankers under their control from handling Mexican oil. To overcome this problem, Davis went to Germany and took up the matter of oil tankers with Ernst Jung, purchasing agent for the German navy and one of Davis's German partners in Eurotank. After Davis explained his concerns to Jung, Jung arranged for the Danish Maersk shipping line to have a fleet of approximately thirty vessels on call to transport Mexican oil to Germany.[46]

Next, from his joint venture, Parent, Davis brought in Francis William Rickett, a British oil operator, to negotiate with the Mexican government. Rickett was a well-known consultant to numerous oil companies and governments and had been hired in 1936 by Parent, which contracted to pay him £100,000 for his services if he could gain the rights to Mexico's oil.[47]

Rickett met with Davis in New York in December 1937 to lay the groundwork for their negotiations with Mexico. They discussed forming a syndicate to acquire the Mexican oil. The syndicate would include Bernard E. Smith, a New York stockbroker who was influential in the oil world and was later called one of the "crookedest" men on Wall Street by the U.S. State Department. Davis had Henry Wilson prepare a new plan for selling Mexican oil to Germany, a plan Davis arranged to present to the Roosevelt administration.[48,49]

While Rickett was in New York, he and Davis had informal talks with the vice chairman of the National Bank of Mexico and the Mexican finance minister, Suárez. These discussions led to the Mexicans inviting Rickett to meet with President Cárdenas in Mexico. After returning to London for further discussions with the other Parent directors, Burgess and Inverforth, Rickett left London for Mexico City in March 1938, just before the Mexican nationalization.[50]

To smooth the Mexican side of the negotiations, Davis started buying the services of high-ranking officials in the Mexican government. Davis's entree to important Mexican officials was through his employee, Fritz Flanley, the Davis and Company manager in Mexico

City. Flanley was a handsome Irish-American who was married to a Puerto Rican woman. He spoke fluent Spanish and had a permanent home in Mexico City. Because Davis did not speak Spanish, Flanley set up most of Davis's meetings with Mexican officials and attended when Davis needed a translator. It is possible that Flanley was a German intelligence operative, but the evidence is inconclusive. In any case, Davis became close to Flanley and they socialized when Davis was in Mexico City.[51]

Davis also used his close friendship with an honorary German vice consul, Gerard Maier. Maier was a merchant in Morelio, which was the native state of President Cárdenas. Maier, a rabid Nazi, had a close friendship of nearly twenty-five years with Cárdenas.[52]

Davis's best Mexican contact was Justice Xavier Icaza, a member of the Mexican Supreme Court. Davis retained Icaza for "legal services," paid him generous fees, and helped get medical assistance for his son. With this government insider as a "friend," Davis was kept well informed on the timing of the expected nationalization.[53]

In short order, Davis's preparations began to pay off handsomely. On March 17, 1938, the day before Mexican nationalization, Davis signed a contract with the Mexican government for some $3 million worth of Mexican oil. Davis paid for the oil with petroleum pipes and machinery recently brought to Mexico from Germany to work Davis's Sabalo oil field.[54,55]

Also just before nationalization, Davis contracted to purchase oil from properties that had been owned by the Mexican government prior to nationalization. Fritz Flanley reported on May 15, 1938, that the Davis contract was for 40,000 barrels per day. A spokesman for one of the American oil companies said that the Mexican government's nonnationalized oil fields produced no more than 18,000 barrels per day and that, therefore, some of the Davis and Company oil must come from the recently nationalized fields. Clearly, such a contract was impossible unless Davis knew that the oil fields were about to be nationalized.[56]

It appears that Davis had prior knowledge of the date of the nationalization, anticipating it to his own profit. He protested his innocence, pointing to his lost Sabalo subsidiary.[57] He also tried to cover his tracks by saying that his deals with Mexico were signed several months before the nationalization rather than the day before. Yet, all the evidence points to Davis having advance knowledge of the nationalization.[58]

five

Mexican Oil for Germany

WHEN THE FOREIGN oil companies refused to raise workers' wages despite the Mexican Supreme Court upholding the Labor Arbitration Board's order, the Mexican government nationalized the oil industry on March 18, 1938. It immediately took over the oil properties of the large American and British oil companies, not only the derricks, pipelines, and refineries, but also, and far more important, the vast subsurface wealth. Foreign managers and technicians were ordered to leave the country.[1]

The principal losers were Shell and Standard Oil, which together controlled 70 percent of Mexican oil production. Shell lost the most because the British had invested $20 million in the Poza Rica oil field and had not produced enough oil from the field to cover their investment before nationalization. The loss of the Poza Rica field was especially galling because the oil pool was the world's second largest and was conservatively estimated to contain 1 billion barrels. At the time of nationalization, Poza Rica was producing more than half of Mexico's oil.[2]

Following nationalization, the directors of Shell and Standard Oil, furious that their properties had been taken illegally, retaliated by instituting a worldwide blockade of Mexican petroleum. The oil companies wanted the oil fields back not only because of their intrinsic value, but also to prevent a dangerous precedent from being established: developing countries could not be allowed to unilaterally impose restrictions on Big Oil. If Mexico were allowed to nationalize its oil fields, Venezuela or Iraq might be next.[3,4]

Shell and Standard Oil used several tactics to blockade the Mexican oil. Steamship lines were warned that if their vessels refueled with the "stolen" Mexican oil, they would risk being refused refueling facilities in all other ports in the world. The oil firms also paid above-market prices to lease tankers and keep them out of Mexican hands. It was also said that Shell agents in Mexico watched the movements of all oil tankers and imposed a no-business-relations penalty on any company that violated the Mexican boycott. These threats led most shipping lines to refuse to lease tankers to Mexico.[5]

In addition, Shell pressured the British government to officially protest the Mexican nationalization. In May, after a sharp protest note to President Cárdenas, the British government recalled its ambassador from Mexico City and broke off diplomatic relations with Mexico.[6] The British government also persuaded the Scandinavian countries to discourage their many independent tankers from going to Mexico.

The blockade was very effective. It dramatically reduced the market for Mexican oil, limiting it to domestic consumption and to the small amounts that could be sold in Latin American countries, and the latter declined by at least 50 percent. The oil companies and the U.S. State Department were both involved in thwarting Mexico's initiatives.[7]

Even if the Mexican government found a buyer, it lacked the ability to ship the oil because Big Oil controlled the vast majority of the world's oil tankers, while Mexico controlled only four. Further, the Mexican government could no longer buy spare parts for its oil machinery in the United States. Big Oil intimidated the supply companies by threatening to withhold all future orders from any company selling to Mexico. Certified checks sent by the Mexican government to buy equipment were returned with the notation that the supply company dared not risk a Standard Oil blacklist.[8]

Given these obstacles, Big Oil expected Cárdenas to back down and thus refused to seriously negotiate the sale of its properties to the Mexican government. The oil companies claimed the properties were worth $450 million, while the Mexicans claimed they were worth only

$10 million. Big Oil expected its economic pressure on Mexico to cause the Cárdenas government to be overthrown if Cárdenas did not withdraw the nationalization order.[9]

Not long after nationalization, a coalition of Mexican military groups banded together to form the Mexican Constitutional Front. Although it did not openly declare against Cárdenas, this group mounted a campaign against the Confederation of Mexican Workers (CTM) and Lombardo Toledano, the leftist leader of Mexican labor, in particular. The generals leading the movement warned that Mexico's policies were too leftist and made veiled criticisms of Cárdenas's oil policy. Given this pressure, Cárdenas needed to resolve the blockade crisis quickly before the generals attempted a coup d'état.[10]

Since neither Big Oil nor Cárdenas could be budged from its position, the result was a standoff: Cárdenas had the oil wells but no markets or tankers. Mexico faced economic disaster. Yet Cárdenas did not want to give in to the oil companies. Both his nationalist ideology and his personal dealings with Big Oil militated against capitulation. In the 1920s, foreign oil company officials had attempted to bribe Cárdenas while he was secretary of government and he still felt the sting of that insult. During this moment of desperation for Cárdenas, Davis appeared with his offer of assistance, and Cárdenas leaped at the opportunity to escape his dilemma.[11]

At first, Davis was coy about his intentions. When the rumors of his German oil deal first surfaced, he issued a few statements to the press that he would deal only in nonnationalized oil. Like the other foreign oil companies, Davis's major Mexican oil production subsidiary, Sabalo (worth $11 million according to Davis), had been confiscated along with the rest. However, when the lucrative possibilities of the situation became apparent, he did not let the nationalization of his own company stand in the way of pursuing this marvelous opportunity. As he later said about his Mexican deal, "It's good business to join an opponent when you know you can't beat him." Davis was confident that his Sabalo loss could be recovered in his soon-to-be consummated Mexican-German oil contract. Over the next two years, Davis gradually liquidated the assets of Sabalo with no appreciable loss to himself.[12]

In 1938, Germany was in desperate need of oil, as was Italy. Germany was trying to amass a large stockpile of oil, of which a large proportion was coming from Romania, but the Romanian government had recently imposed a per-country quota on oil exports.[13] The Germans wanted to exploit the opportunity that the Mexican oil nationalization presented. Only three days after nationalization, the German ambassador to Mexico, Baron Freiherr Von Rüdt, sent a telegram to Berlin suggesting that the new situation offered the possibility for large German purchases of Mexican oil. Not surprisingly, a few days after nationalization, German shipping companies announced that they intended to ignore the oil boycott and carry Mexican oil.[14]

The Mexicans were also aware of the opportunities. Soon after nationalization, an intermediary, acting on behalf of Cárdenas, asked the German ambassador if Germany would be interested in arranging long-term oil purchases. About the same time Senator Guffey and Walter Jones called on the Mexican ambassador in Washington, Francisco Castillo Nájera, to lay out Davis's plans for selling the nationalized oil to Germany. These negotiations took place despite assurances from Mexican deputy foreign affairs minister, Ramón Beteta, to Ambassador Daniels that Mexico had no relations or sympathy with the fascist states and would not willingly sell oil to them.[15]

At first Davis and his partner, Lord Inverforth, entrusted the Mexican oil contract negotiations to their representatives, Francis Rickett and Bernard Smith, who met with Suárez and Eduardo Hay, minister of foreign affairs, and opened official negotiations with the Mexican government. Both Smith and Rickett, like Davis, soon reached an agreement with the Mexican government for a long-term contract.[16]

The contract allowed Parent to purchase not less than 20,000 barrels per day for a period of ten years, with the option to extend the contract for another ten years. It was agreed that Parent would immediately purchase Mexico's existing stocks of 3 million barrels. Davis formed a company in Canada called Mexint to act as the nominal purchaser from the Mexican government, which would mask the true buyer, Parent. This preliminary agreement was reached on April 13, 1938. [17]

The agreement soon fell apart under pressure from the British government, however, which used its authority over British banking to block the financing of Rickett's deal by freezing his credit at Lloyds Bank. The British Foreign Office also pressured Lord Inverforth to cancel Davis's charter of several of Inverforth's oil tankers. Rickett stopped the negotiations and left Mexico shortly after the first British note of protest was presented in Mexico City. When the British government blocked Rickett's attempt to purchase the oil for Parent, Davis decided to immediately sell his interest in Parent. By cutting loose from Parent and British government interference, Davis was able to gain the Mexican oil contract through his own American company, Crusader Petroleum Incorporated.[18]

Davis and Walter Jones rushed to Mexico as soon as Rickett's failure became apparent. Arriving in Mexico on April 19, 1938, Davis quickly began arranging to buy the nationalized Mexican oil for Germany. Davis's chances for big profits in these arrangements depended on gaining exclusive commercial rights to the nationalized oil. Because the Mexicans would naturally be reluctant to give the mysterious Davis (especially someone representing Nazi Germany) an exclusive contract, Davis's contract talks with the Mexican government were intricate, and negotiations seesawed for several months.[19]

Further complicating Davis's negotiations was strong competition from other independent oil promoters and speculators, who also recognized that Mexico would be ruined without an outlet for its oil. In fact, President Cárdenas said that he received some 200 proposals to sell the oil in the first two weeks after nationalization.[20] In fact, Mexico was already negotiating a barter deal with Sweden, and made a small deal on May 21, 1938, to trade petroleum, silver, lead, and cottonseed for newsprint worth about $125,000.

Davis had several key advantages over other promoters. First, as Davis said himself, "they [the Mexican government] will find out sooner or later we are the ones that have the ships and the markets." Davis owned seventeen tankers and had ten more under long-term contract. In addition, he had connections with a ready market, Germany. Further, Davis's Hamburg refinery was safe from the oil companies' interference, and thus he could provide Mexico with a secure outlet for its oil.[21]

Also, unlike his British and French competitors, Davis was not pressured by his government to drop negotiations. The Roosevelt administration took a hands off approach to nationalization. In fact, one of the key reasons Cárdenas went through with the oil nationalization is that he did not have to fear direct military intervention by the United States. Roosevelt had pledged not to intervene militarily in Latin America at Inter-American conferences in 1933 and 1936.[22]

This Roosevelt policy was critical to the success of Davis's negotiations; without Roosevelt's hands-off approach, Davis's plans would probably have collapsed. In contrast, not long after Davis, Monsieur Gaston Des Combes, a French banker and former president of Banco Nacional de Mexico, arrived in Mexico representing interests close to the French government's state petroleum company. He quickly signed an option for a large oil deal, but when he returned to France he found that British pressure on the French government had blocked his financing.[23]

Finally, Davis had the key advantage in that he went to Mexico City with an introduction from John L. Lewis to Vincente Lombardo

Toledano. Lewis was leader of the American labor confederation, the Congress of Industrial Organizations (CIO), and Toledano was the leader of the Mexican labor movement, the 1-million-strong CTM, which was a dominant factor behind the Cárdenas government. On the eve of nationalization, Toledano had received assurances from Lewis that the Mexican government could depend on Davis to market the oil.[24]

This assurance was critical to Toledano's decision to support nationalization and Toledano's support was critical to the success of nationalization. The Mexican labor leader was concerned that the oil workers would lose their jobs because Mexico would be unable to ship the oil. Lewis gave Toledano his personal guarantee that Davis had made arrangements to move the oil.[25]

Lewis probably gained his first knowledge of Davis through Walter Jones and Senator Guffey. Jones had become friends with Lewis while both served on the National Recovery Administration's (NRA) Coal Code Authority and was spellbound by the formidable labor leader, whom he regarded as the greatest living American. Guffey had known Lewis for many years, was one of Lewis's allies on Capitol Hill, and was a significant beneficiary of CIO political contributions. In addition, Guffey, Lewis, and Jones had all worked closely on the Coal Act of 1935. About his connection with Lewis, Davis would say only that it was arranged "through various political channels."[26]

In fact, Guffey had introduced Davis to Lewis just after Mexican nationalization. Davis and Lewis got along very well. Erna Wehrle thought it was because they had both come up from nothing and were self-made men. Lewis was impressed both by the international connections and resources Davis could command for moving the blockaded Mexican oil and by his persuasive argument that Big Oil was exploiting Mexican labor. Davis convinced Lewis that he should favor the Mexicans selling oil to Davis for resale to Germany because this transaction would end Big Oil's exploitation of Mexican labor. Enticed by this argument and the importance of Davis's international connections, Lewis used his Mexican contacts to assist Davis's purchase of oil for sale to Hitler's Germany.[27]

On April 18, 1938, exactly one month after nationalization, Lewis telephoned Vincente Toledano in Mexico City from his office at the United Mine Worker's (UMW) headquarters in Washington. When told that Toledano was not available, he asked to speak to the Secretary of the CTM's Foreign Relations Committee, Alejandro Carrillo. Lewis told Carrillo that Davis, whom he described as "a commanding figure in the oil business," would arrive the next day in Mexico City.[28]

Lewis assured Carrillo that Davis was "absolutely all right and could be depended on, other reports to the contrary notwithstanding." Lewis then told Carrillo to tell President Cárdenas that "England was canceling all [tanker] charters on Davis [Co. oil shipments] due to the pressure brought by Royal Dutch Shell" and "that Germany and Italy were the only countries with which it would be safe for Mexico to deal." Lewis asked Carrillo (who was one of President Cárdenas's closest friends) to see President Cárdenas that night with this information and make sure that Davis got the concession.[29,30]

After Davis's arrival in Mexico, Toledano introduced Davis to President Cárdenas in early May. At this meeting, Davis told Cárdenas that he would be willing to take charge of the entire nationalized oil industry. Although Cárdenas did not accept this grandiose proposal, Toledano's[31] glowing introduction enabled Davis to obtain a contract from Cárdenas to supply Germany with oil to be refined at Davis's plant in Hamburg.[32]

What Lewis was to receive in return for his assistance to Davis has never been satisfactorily determined. In 1938 Lewis was at the height of his fame and power from the organization of millions of blue-collar workers into the CIO. His leonine image, conveying power and strength, was everywhere in America: movie theaters, magazine covers, and newspapers. His presence suggested the anger, determination, and militancy of the workers for whom he spoke. Why would John L. Lewis, the militant leader of the UMW union and now head of the almost 2-million-member CIO, who had denounced the fascist states as antilabor at a major anti-Nazi rally in the previous year, assist Davis in fueling the fascist war machines? There were many reasons.[33]

Lewis's CIO lieutenants, especially those with left-wing and Communist Party connections, had encouraged contact between Lewis and Latin American labor leaders, in general, and with Vincente Toledano, in particular. The American left was attracted to Toledano because he had strong leftist views and, as leader of the CTM, was in a deadly struggle with the international oil companies. Therefore, one motivation for Lewis to help Davis swing his deal with the Mexicans was to strengthen the labor movement in Mexico.

A second motivation for helping Davis was to enhance Lewis's prestige throughout Latin America. He could emerge as the savior of Mexico and establish his own influence as an anti-imperialist throughout the Western Hemisphere. It is also possible that Lewis dreamed of a Pan-American federation of labor of which he would be the unchallenged leader. Through Davis, Cárdenas, and Toledano, Lewis would be able to consolidate the unions north and south of the border.[34]

However, the atmosphere at the UMW building during the time of the Davis-Mexican-German negotiations suggests that there may have been more involved than solidarity with Mexican workers. When newspapers and congressional investigators began to express curiosity about the Lewis-Davis operations, all files and records dealing with this subject were abruptly removed from the UMW union headquarters. Kathryn Lewis (Lewis's daughter) curtly told several office employees not to be inquisitive about these affairs. Speculation about the affair was varied and intense among Lewis's associates. This was not the only time Lewis assisted Davis in his Mexican business dealings.

When queried a decade later by Saul D. Alinsky[35] about his relationship with Davis, Lewis portrayed his link to Davis as completely proper. Lewis scorned the suggestion that Davis was an agent for the Nazis, he considered that charge Standard Oil propaganda. As we shall see later, Lewis was lying; he knew that Davis was in league with the Germans.[36]

Commenting on Davis's sale of oil to Germany, Lewis said:

> At the time when Davis was trying to make these sales to German interests, I think it only fitting and proper that inquiry be made as to what American business in this country was doing with the Nazis—whether it be Ford Motors or the working relationship between cartels such as the Farben Die [sic] Trust. This is all a matter of common knowledge today.
>
> I believe it also pertinent that one inquires into the fact that if Davis was such a democratic leper, why did Franklin D. Roosevelt give him a personally autographed photograph of himself? Also why, and of course, it is significantly related to this warm Roosevelt inscription on this photograph, did President Roosevelt gratefully accept the $400,000 contribution that Davis made, part of it directly from himself and the remainder from others acting as his fronts?[37]

In essence, Lewis believed his own behavior was acceptable because everyone else was also doing business with the Germans in the 1930s.

It is possible there was another reason for Lewis's assistance to Davis. There were persistent rumors that Lewis became involved in Davis's Mexican activities because of Davis's contributions to the Non-Partisan League (the CIO's political action committee). On a transatlantic clipper trip, Davis, in an expansive mood, boasted to a fellow passenger that he was financing the labor Non-Partisan League. If Davis actually did finance the Non-Partisan League, then this organization may have been one of the conduits Davis used in 1936 to contribute to the Democratic Party. The Non-Partisan League contributed $470,000 to the Democratic Party in 1936. Because Lewis said that Davis gave Roosevelt $400,000, while Davis reported that he personally gave $225,000 to Roosevelt, the $175,000 discrepancy may be money given by Davis to the Non-Partisan League. This would also explain where the unaccounted-for Parent money went.

The Mexican government and Davis signed a contract on June 6, 1938, to supply the Germans, Swedes, and Italians with Mexican oil. The six-month contract called for Davis to purchase $10 million of oil by December 31, 1938, and Davis was named Mexico's oil distributor for Europe.[38,39]

The $10 million was a remarkably low price, approximately one-third (excluding transportation costs) what Germany had paid for oil during the first five months of 1938. Germany could command this low price because it had tremendous leverage over Mexico, which resulted from the lack of alternative buyers.[40] During the next one and one-half years Mexican oil products were sold to the Germans and Italians at prices 12 to 15 percent below world market prices. The Mexican labor unions vociferously condemned these agreements, arguing that more advantageous terms should have been written into the contracts so that wages could be raised. However, the Mexican government had little choice but to agree to the German terms because of Big Oil's boycott. Thus, the fascists not only obtained the oil, but also paid a low price.[41]

Mexico was only partially paid in cash for its 10 million barrels of oil because the $10 million contract specified that 60 percent was to be paid in goods. The Mexicans conducted the barter portion of the contract through a specially created oil distribution agency, Distribuidora de Petroleos Mexicanos (DPM). The barter system worked as follows. When Germany received the Mexican oil, credit in German marks was established in German banks to the account of DPM. DPM selected the German goods it wished to buy for Mexico and then paid for the goods from its German bank account. This clever arrangement meant that Germany required no foreign currency to pay for the oil.[42]

In this first contract, Mexico received German machinery for its oil industry, and Sweden erected a new paper factory (valued at $500,000) in Mexico. Germany supplied approximately 75 percent of the machinery from the total agreement. The $4 million cash portion of the contract was to be provided by Swedish banking interests.[43]

The oil was shipped during the next six months with 90 percent destined for Germany, which equaled 23 percent of Germany's 1937 consumption of oil. The contracted petroleum was crude oil, most of which was refined at Davis's Hamburg plant, Eurotank, which could refine 15,000 barrels of oil per day and was being remodeled to handle the Mexican oil more efficiently. The remodeling of the refinery was completed in October 1938, and the plant operated three shifts per day to keep up with the supply of crude oil arriving from Mexico. After the oil was refined, Davis had barges available to move the oil within Germany.[44]

The comparatively small amount of cash that changed hands was not an uncommon occurrence under the barter system of trade used by Germany and Italy in the 1930s. By the end of 1937, German and Italian military expenditures had reached 24 percent and 15 percent of their respective gross national products. The intense arms buildup was placing significant strains on the fascist states' economies. One of the major strains was their acute dependence on imported raw materials. They both required vast amounts of imported metal ores, rubber, and especially petroleum. For example, even though domestic German production of fuel oils was up 700,000 tons from 1933, imports were up 1 million tons by the end of 1937.[45]

The massive armaments buildup had drained the fascist countries of virtually all foreign currency, and Germany was in the midst of a severe currency crisis. By March 1938, Germany was facing a foreign trade deficit, and its gold reserves had shrunk to 70 million marks from 530 million marks in 1933. Germany had already suspended oil imports from the United States because of its highly adverse trade balance.[46]

Hence, it was imperative for both fascist countries to find sources of imported war materials that did not require the expenditure of foreign currency. However, the fascist regimes were hard pressed to obtain oil without foreign currency because the oil-producing countries were reluctant to engage in barter trade. Thus, Davis's Mexican barter deal was a fantastic coup for Germany and Italy.[47]

Davis's Mexican contract was a major business triumph. It was no small feat to snatch a Mexican oil monopoly out from under the noses of the major oil companies. Big Oil had to concede that Davis was a formidable opponent. To pull off his Mexican coup, he had played all the angles—the Roosevelt administration, the Mexican government, the Germans, and the labor movements in both Mexico and the United States. Despite the potential pitfalls, he had succeeded.[48]

This contract and other Mexican contracts that would follow were to make him very wealthy over the next one and one half years. From the first contract alone, he received a 5 percent commission for each barrel sold as well as a 10 percent commission on the material and equipment purchased by the Mexican government (or $1.5 million). In addition, he received profits from shipping the oil on his tankers and from refining the oil in his German refinery, but he took incredible risks to gain this wealth. He not only took on the powerful British and American oil companies but also risked destruction by the British and American governments. What motivated this mystery man to strive for the big score despite the enormous risks?[49]

Years later, Marquis Childs, an American newspaper reporter, wrote of interviewing Davis in Mexico City in the gaudy blue and gold presidential suite of the Hotel Reforma in 1938 where Davis stayed when in Mexico. Davis seemed the prototype of the oil tycoon with his iron-gray hair, expensive suits, and dynamic personality. Childs said of Davis:

> He talked mostly about his plan to further world trade. It was gigantic, tremendous, colossal . . . and while the man talked the whole thing seemed perfectly plausible. Thousands of tons of coffee that he had in Brazil, and on the other side of the world, rubber, and somewhere else cotton. This man had an American enthusiasm that was almost genuine. "Of course, I don't know, I'm just a boy from the country," he would say every now and then. Twice in the hour and a half I spent with him London called and once his secretary [Erna Wehrle] came in and announced . . . that the Mexican Supreme Court . . . chief justice wanted to talk to him.

Josephus Daniels described Davis by declaring, "Some people regarded Davis as a profiteer; others, as a man who would furnish needed markets for Mexican oil; and others as a . . . Nazi agent or as a crook. In reality, he was a composite of each of these descriptions."[50]

In essence, Davis's pro-fascist politics were secondary; Davis's real motivation in life was the big payoff. In this venture, as in all his schemes both before and after Mexico, Davis was after big money. Oklahoma oil wildcats, Peru, and Eurotank, all of these ventures had been high-stakes gambles. Mexico was just another big gamble for Davis.

Whether others shared in the profits on the first Mexican contract is unclear. Ernest Galarzo of the Pan-American Union stated that after this deal was consummated, Xavier Icaza visited him in December 1938 in Washington. Icaza told Galarzo that he had been sent by Toledano to follow up on the Davis deal.[51] He said it had been agreed

that Davis would pay "commissions" to Mexican and U.S. labor organizations on his Mexican oil deals and that the split would be fifty-
fifty. Icaza conferred with John L. Lewis, and then went to New York
for other meetings. Icaza, formerly a man of only moderate means,
had, since the Davis Mexican oil deals, acquired considerable property, including a farm, two homes, and an ice cream business.
Whether Icaza's newly acquired wealth was a payoff from Davis is unknown.[52]

Alejandro Carrillo also visited Washington in 1938. He, too, announced his intention to confer with Lewis. Carrillo said his mission
included the acquisition of a printing press with which to begin publication of the Toledano-backed labor newspaper, *El Popular*. Later it
was said that Davis purchased the press as part of a payoff for his oil
deal.[53]

The central question about Davis's Mexican-German oil contracts is
why Roosevelt did not stop the arrangement. The U.S. government
was fully aware that the oil was very valuable to Hitler's rearmament,
and by 1938, Roosevelt was worried about Hitler's military intentions.
One would think that thwarting Hitler's ability to wage war by stopping
the oil barter with Mexico would have been a central aim of Roosevelt.

Nor would the barter with Germany have been difficult for Roosevelt to stop. Given U.S. influence over the Mexican economy—let
alone American military might—Roosevelt would have had little trouble toppling the Cárdenas government, yet there is no record that Ambassador Daniels ever protested the Mexican government's selling oil
to Germany. In fact, in early April, Cárdenas sent Roosevelt a personal
message of thanks for the friendly attitude of the White House toward
the seizure of the oil properties.[54]

This acquiescence to Mexico's oil sale to Germany came directly
from the White House, because the U.S. State Department vigorously
opposed Cárdenas's policies. The State Department had been an active observer, and occasional participant, in the oil dispute for years.
Soon after Mexico's March 18 announcement of nationalization, the
State Department sent a strong verbal protest to Mexico, prodded the
U.S. Treasury Department to suspend monthly Mexican silver purchases, and instructed U.S. ambassador Daniels to return to Washington from Mexico for consultation. The suspension of the silver purchases on March 27, 1938, was of particular importance because
silver was as important as oil to the Mexican economy.[55]

Therefore, the State Department was displeased that Davis was
helping relieve Mexico from economic pressures at a time when
departmental officials were insisting that Mexico make prompt com-

pensation to the oil companies for the nationalized oil fields. Secretary of State Cordell Hull met with Davis in Washington on August 18, 1938, and told him that he expected him not to interfere with the State Department's attempts to obtain "just" compensation for the nationalization. Davis was warned that he was "fishing in troubled waters and might eventually find himself involved in difficulties as a result of it."[56]

Despite the State Department's actions, Daniels and U.S. secretary of treasury Henry Morgenthau Jr. blunted this pressure on Mexico with the direct cooperation of President Roosevelt.[57] Daniels softened the State Department's protest note and left no doubt that the United States opposed any right-wing uprising against Cárdenas. Morgenthau made vital ad hoc silver purchases that absorbed virtually the entire amount of silver exported from Mexico.[58] Thus, Roosevelt gave vital support to Cárdenas's nationalization policy even though Mexico was selling oil to Germany.[59]

Nor did the U.S. government attempt to block the entry of Mexican oil into the United States when the oil was to be reshipped to fascist Italy. From September 10, 1938, through January 4, 1939, eleven Italian ships sailed from Houston, Texas, to Italy with Mexican oil that had been refined at a Houston refinery. Also, large quantities of Mexican oil were transported through Davis's Meraux Terminal in Louisiana and then to Germany.[60]

Roosevelt's chief reason for not stopping the nationalization or subsequent sale of oil to the fascist states was his desire to maintain friendly relations throughout Latin America. He wished to develop closer military contacts with Latin America to prevent the fascist powers from establishing a foothold in the Western Hemisphere. Though recognizing that the United States might have to defend the hemisphere alone, Roosevelt was still eager to enlist the support of the Latin American states.

Roosevelt's principal advisers in this position were Ambassador Daniels and Secretary Morgenthau. Daniels viewed the Cárdenas government as the equivalent of the American New Deal and was a fervent advocate of inter-American alliances. Daniels argued that it was imperative to expand trade with Mexico to keep the door closed against Germany and Japan. As Daniels warned in June when Davis was negotiating with the Mexicans, "if the Mexican government should enter into arrangements to barter petroleum for goods made in Germany it will seriously affect the commerce of the United States manufacturers and turn the tide of Mexican purchases from American-made goods to German-made goods." Morgenthau was even more emphatic. He felt it was essential to prevent Mexico from turning to the fascist nations for economic assistance, as he said in December 1937, "We're going to wake up and find inside of a year that Italy, Germany, and Japan have taken over Mexico."[62]

Of lesser importance, but probably playing some role in Roosevelt's decision, were two other elements:

1. Roosevelt wanted to reward Davis for his substantial contributions to the 1936 Democratic electoral campaign. Davis claimed that Roosevelt gave him an unofficial commission to straighten out the Mexican oil situation.[63]
2. Roosevelt might have also been motivated by revenge. Standard Oil had been a major contributor to the Republican Party in 1936 and Roosevelt had little sympathy for its problems. In fact, Roosevelt made it clear in April 1938 that he thought that the oil companies were demanding more than they had invested in Mexico, and this was interpreted by some people as meaning that he condoned nationalization.[64]

However, Roosevelt did not totally approve of the nationalization or of Davis, since Roosevelt did support the oil companies in their claims for compensation. Roosevelt used the threat of suspending the ad hoc silver purchases as leverage to get the Mexican government to agree to compensate the oil companies. Roosevelt believed that if the government did not take steps to secure compensation for the American oil companies, that other South American countries might follow Mexico's lead in nationalizing their oil fields.[65]

Of course it can be asked why Latin American nationalization was necessarily bad for American foreign policy? If Roosevelt's primary interest in Latin America was preventing the fascist states from gaining allies in Latin America, how was this policy related to economic nationalization? It would seem that Roosevelt was confusing, as many American presidents have, American corporate interest with American national interest.

This confusion was reflected in the policy Roosevelt chose to follow in the Mexican crisis. His policy was a typical Roosevelt compromise between the demand by Hull that the government intervene on the side of the oil companies and the position of Daniels and Morgenthau that the government support Cárdenas. Roosevelt simultaneously refused to intervene directly on the side of the oil companies but allowed the oil companies to keep Mexican oil out of the United States. Roosevelt's policy envisioned the American government playing the role of a mediator between the oil companies and the Mexican government to resolve the crisis.

Unfortunately for Roosevelt, the oil companies were not willing to compromise. As Daniels complained to Secretary of State Hull in July, "The oil companies do not seem interested in their country and its commerce enough to concern themselves in the least about it." Big Oil's willingness to sacrifice the broad interests of the United States to protect its proprietary interests in Mexico completely undermined Roosevelt's policy and significantly benefited the Germans.[66]

In reality, Roosevelt had only one effective option: to support Cárdenas and help the Mexicans sell their oil in the United States. Roosevelt's intervention in support of Cárdenas would have destroyed the oil companies' boycott. No doubt, siding with Cárdenas would have taken courage on Roosevelt's part in facing down Big Oil, but the responsibilities of leadership often require resisting demands from powerful interests.[67]

Such an option would have strengthened the Good Neighbor Policy and kept the fascist nations out of Mexico. Of paramount importance, this realistic policy would have denied the fascist nations the oil resources of which they were in desperate need to sustain their armaments buildups. Instead, the policy Roosevelt chose met none of these goals. It was a major disaster because it directly assisted Germany and Italy in starting World War II.[68]

six

Mexico—Making War Possible

THE COMPLETION OF the Davis barter deal was a heavy blow to Big Oil because it was the first big breach in its blockade of Mexican oil. To the oil companies, Davis was an evil scoundrel; without markets the Mexican nationalization would fail. He breached the blockade just when Mexico most needed to export oil. The oil companies quickly set out to stop Davis and he soon saw the long arm of Big Oil thrust out to checkmate him in the courts, in the press, and in government foreign offices. As Wehrle later said, Big Oil made Davis "persona non grata."[1]

The Big Oil spokesmen claimed that Davis was a Nazi agent and that if Mexico had dealings with him it would demonstrate that it was a Nazi sympathizer.[2] To buttress their argument, they pointed to the appearance of Jean Schacht, brother of Hitler's former head of the Reichsbank, Hjalmar Schacht, in Mexico. He was seen frequently with Davis, though he asserted he was in Mexico on a pleasure trip.[3]

The Nazi charge was only a small part of the oil companies' massive campaign in the American media to smear the Mexican government and everyone connected to it. The overarching objective of this campaign was to demand that the American government change its policy and intervene on the side of the oil companies.[4]

Big Oil did not stop at words. In every port where they could impound it, the oil companies seized the "stolen" oil and brought suit against Davis.[5] Big Oil won a few of these cases, but it was often difficult to prove that a given cargo of oil came from nationalized properties because not all the foreign oil companies in Mexico had been nationalized. Eventually, these attempts to embargo Davis's ships through the courts failed.[6]

However, just filing legal suits was often enough to damage Davis. The prospect of possible legal battles scared away many customers from Mexican oil. Furthermore, Big Oil hoped that the legal fees Davis had to pay to fight suits in the courts would bankrupt him. Because of Big Oil's pressure tactics, relatively little Mexican oil entered the United States, Great Britain, France, or other countries in democratic Europe during the Mexican oil boycott.[7]

The oil companies also blocked Davis's financing from Swedish banks, which caused Davis to rush to Mexico City on August 1 from London to arrange the credits for the German machinery barter.[8] With Mexico reluctant to extend him credit, Davis was forced to seek help in American banking circles, which was difficult in view of the pressures exerted by Standard Oil. However, Davis found help from his former creditor, Bank of Boston.

Big Oil had approached Bank of Boston and offered to buy Davis's loans, the object being to call Davis's loans and bankrupt him. However, Bank of Boston refused to sell the loans and instead provided the credit Davis needed to continue his barter operations. Under the direction of Latimer Gray, who had also been instrumental in the bank's funding of Eurotank, the bank put up the money to buy the oil and fund Davis's Mexican operations. Gray had become a personal friend of Davis, and Mr. Mallet of the British Foreign Office said that "even if the First National [Bank of Boston] did not finance him [Davis] direct, I suspect that they will get around it by Latimer Gray's finding ways and means of Davis indirectly receiving such support." As Erna Wehrle said about Gray, "he was in charge of the whole thing."[9]

Even with the bank's help, Davis had difficulty obtaining the cash portion of the barter contract, and in September 1938 he began negotiating with Mexico for a new contract that required less cash. Although Davis's credit problem was eventually resolved, the Mexican government for the rest of the year insisted on being paid in full before allowing Davis's tankers to leave Mexico.[10]

Big Oil also tried to label Davis a traitor. On September 23, Standard

Oil officials asked Secretary of State Hull to prosecute Davis under the Trading with the Enemy Act of 1917 because Davis was shipping oil to Germany and Italy. This action by Standard Oil was hypocritical in that Standard Oil had been a major supplier of Germany through 1937. Big Oil had already sent a letter on June 21 to the War Department stating that Davis was involved in German espionage in the United States.[11] Although no action resulted from either of these claims, U.S. State Department agents followed Davis throughout his travels in Europe.[12]

Shell and Standard Oil also tried to get Germany to back out of its agreement with Davis. First, they reduced their oil prices in Scandinavia to dry up the market for Davis's Eurotank refinery products. Then, in September 1938, representatives of Shell and Standard Oil met with various high German officials at the Ministry of Economic Affairs in Berlin. Despite the oil companies' request, the Germans refused to cancel their agreement with Davis. However, to keep from completely alienating Big Oil, the Germans agreed not to increase its Mexican oil purchases beyond what was necessary to maintain Mexican oil exports at the 1937 level of 31 million barrels. This promise was meaningless to the Germans because they did not intend to import oil at that level for several years.[13]

After all their ploys to stop Davis failed, Big Oil tried to buy him off. Standard Oil and Sinclair Oil representatives approached him to find out what it would cost for Davis to withdraw from the Mexican market. Davis told these emissaries that Big Oil had waited too long and, furthermore, that he was from Alabama, where they did not trade in any such fashion. As usual, Davis was not satisfied with a small reward. He wanted the big score.[14]

Almost from the moment the oil contract was signed, Davis had difficulty refining the Mexican crude oil because neither Mexico nor Germany had sufficient refinery capacity to handle the quantities of crude oil being produced by Mexico. Davis exported 2.4 million barrels of Mexican oil between May 10 and August 1, 1938, but only 941,000 barrels of this went to his Hamburg refinery. In fact, the refinery had to operate at 100 percent of capacity to handle even that amount of crude oil. To overcome this problem, Davis slipped American refinery machinery[15] through the blockade. This machinery was used by the Mexican government in a $5 million expansion of the refineries at Tampico, Mexico City, and Minatitlán, the port for the southern Mexican oil fields.[16]

Because expanding the Mexican refineries would take several years, Davis developed another avenue to refine the oil in the meantime. The crude oil was sent to a refinery in Houston, Texas, owned by Eastern States Petroleum Company (Eastern). To avoid legal difficulties, Davis claimed that this oil was not from wells that had been nationalized. Rather, it was from wells that had always been owned by the Mexican government (never by Big Oil) and that Davis had signed an agreement to market that oil before nationalization.[17]

Eastern, a small oil company with big mortgages, was a wholesale dealer of petroleum products and depended on a large difference in price between crude oil and refined oil for its profits. In 1938, the margin between crude and refined oil was narrow and Eastern was in a difficult financial situation. Therefore, the Mexican contract offered a welcome escape from financial ruin.

In return for Eastern's assistance, the Mexican government took Eastern's mortgages in payment for the oil shipped, thus giving the Mexican government virtual control over Eastern. Its two-year contract was for 10 million barrels of oil, of which about 700,000 had been shipped by the end of October 1938. All of the oil was reexported, with the majority going to Italy.[18]

Standard Oil tried to block this outlet by using threats and coercion to (1) induce banks not to extend credit to Eastern, (2) persuade oil brokers not to sell Eastern's products, and (3) convince ship brokers to refuse to charter vessels to Eastern. Eastern filed suit in federal court on December 9, 1938, against various British and American oil companies charging that the oil companies were violating the antitrust law in a conspiracy to prevent Eastern from disposing of crude oil acquired from the Mexican government.[19] Eventually, a federal court in New York held that Eastern could not be prevented from purchasing Mexican oil and Eastern was able to continue its operations. By the summer of 1939, it was refining 10,000 to 15,000 barrels of Mexican oil per day and reshipping it on Davis's tankers to Germany and Italy.[20]

Another major problem for Davis during the summer of 1938 was unloading the bartered German goods. Mexico had only limited needs for the German barter goods and had an urgent need for cash. In particular, German oil industry machinery was not compatible with Mexican equipment, which was of British and American origin. Therefore, Mexico needed cash to buy the necessary replacement parts in the United States.[21]

To satisfy this need for cash, Davis, through Davecom, his Mexican subsidiary, began disposing of German goods as rapidly as possible. For a nice commission (in oil), the company sold the Mexican government's German merchandise. Some was sold to Mexican consumers, some was reexported to other Latin American nations, and some was sold to such firms as General Motors and British-American Tobacco by offering secret rebates as inducements. For example, General Motors's Mexican subsidiary purchased German Opel automobiles at a 3-percent rebate.[22]

The prime example of these trade deals was Davis's deal with Panhandle Producing and Refining Company (Panhandle), which agreed on August 23, 1938, to buy $600,000 of oil tubing, casing, and line pipe from Davis and Company for 235,000 shares of its stock. This deal was almost destroyed through the machinations of the major oil companies. Panhandle's application to list the additional shares of stock was filed with the stock exchange on September 6, 1938. Permission to issue the stock was given by the stock exchange on September 21, but this permission was suspended on October 20 when word of Davis's conviction for fraud in the Gica case in London on October 17 reached New York.[23]

Once again, Bank of Boston came to Davis's assistance. After investigation, the exchange allowed Panhandle to amend its application, which it did on December 21, 1938. This approval came only after Davis obtained backing from Bank of Boston. The stock was reissued in the name of Skelton and Company, as the nominee of Bank of Boston, and was pledged to secure Bank of Boston's loan to Davis to build and operate his German refinery. The complicated transaction was worked out by Bank of Boston's Latimer Gray with approval of the bank's board of directors.[24]

Despite the interference of the oil companies, by August 1938 Davis had exported more than 2.4 million barrels of Mexican oil. With this proven success behind him, Davis traveled to Mexico City in late August to open negotiations for the expansion of his oil contract with Mexico. John L. Lewis also arrived in Mexico City, to attend a Pan-American Labor Congress organized by Toledano. This conference established the Confederacion de Trabajadores de America Latina (Latin American Labor Confederation), which was to become a moving force behind the development of South American trade unions. At the founding convention, Lewis sat in the honored seat on Toledano's right.[25]

While Lewis was in Mexico City, he attended a mass meeting of the International Congress Against War and Fascism. Appearing before 50,000 Mexican workers, Lewis warned the audience that fascism threatened both Mexico and the United States. "Between us and fascism there can be no peace. . . . We know that . . . there are groups, agents of certain foreign countries and of our own super-patriots, which seek to consolidate . . . into the brutal system of fascism."[26]

Ironically, besides attending the conference, Lewis was also in Mexico City to reassure Mexican authorities of Davis's ability to provide enough tankers to deliver additional oil to the fascist states. To those who were aware of Lewis's activities, his pronouncements on the dangers of fascism must have sounded incredibly hypocritical.[27]

Two days before the start of the conference, Lewis had conferred privately with President Cárdenas, who asked the labor leader to deliver diplomatic messages to the American president. Because Cárdenas preferred to sell oil to the democracies, he secretly proposed to President Roosevelt the establishment of an inter-American economic boycott against the aggressor nations, even though such a move would cost Mexico the important German market for its oil.[28] However, Roosevelt was under too much pressure from the American oil companies to seriously consider Cárdenas's proposal.[29]

After Lewis returned to the United States, Davis told a member of the U.S. embassy staff that Lewis had really come to Mexico to confer about organizing a new confederation of labor that would displace Toledano's organization. "Lewis will furnish the advice and I will furnish the money," said Davis. Daniels thought there might have been some truth to this Davis boast. It is possible that this plan for a hemispheric labor organization with Lewis as leader was part of the reward that Lewis expected for his help for Mexico. However, nothing ever came of this plan.[30]

In Mexico City on December 8, 1938, Davis completed a huge all-barter transaction in which a variety of German products were to be exchanged for $17 million of Mexican oil. Germany agreed to ship typewriters, photographic materials, tons of sheet tin and steel, and miles of pipe for the petroleum industry and agriculture. More ominously, an additional part-cash arrangement was completed under which the German navy was to be supplied with $8 million of oil in 1939.[31]

These new agreements greatly expanded the already significant German oil trade with Mexico. By the end of 1938, Davis had moved approximately 60 percent of all Mexican oil exports.[32] In fact, Pemex, the Mexican government oil company, reported that it had almost oversold its export capacity and was increasing its oil drilling to expand production by 40,000 barrels per day to meet the new barter contracts.[33]

After Davis's large December contract and the resulting expansion of Mexican-German trade relations, the Roosevelt administration became alarmed at Davis's activities. Wall Street pundit Bernard Baruch had predicted back in March that if the Mexican government permanently took over the nationalized properties, it would be unable to operate them and would turn to others to do so. Those others might readily be Japan, Italy, and/or Germany, who needed the raw materials. He also contended that if the condition spread to Central and South American countries, America might find itself not only denuded of the investment represented but also shut off from the supply of those materials, except at prices that could be dictated by others.[34]

The Roosevelt administration realized that such a scenario was possible. Daniels warned Hull that if the trend continued, American interests in Mexico, both political and economic, were going to be seriously affected. He urged acceptance of the Mexican offer to stop selling oil to the fascist countries in exchange for an end to the oil boycott.[35]

Daniels met with President Cárdenas on December 9, 1938, the day after the second Davis contract was signed, and expressed concern about the extent of the new contract. Cárdenas replied that the contract was only short term and that he had instructed Minister of Finance Suárez to make no long-term contracts.[36] Cárdenas added that Mexico would greatly prefer to deal with the United States but that there were difficulties (i.e., the oil boycott).[37]

In response to the rapid growth of German influence in Mexico, the Roosevelt administration began to object to some of Mexico's trade deals with the fascist states. Representative of this new position was Daniels's response to Davis's next barter deal.

At a news conference in Mexico City on February 16, 1939, Dr. H. H. Hagemann, agent for the Junkers Aircraft Company, announced the start of negotiations for the barter of German airplanes in exchange for Mexican oil. Hagemann, who had arrived in Mexico City that week in company with Davis to negotiate the exchange, boasted that the agreement would be complete within a week. He proposed to trade seventeen German Junkers airplanes (which could be converted to bombers) for Mexican oil. The deal was promoted through pro-German Mexican military leaders, who had been attempting to obtain German airplanes for the past year. Davis and Company was to handle the oil part of the barter.[38]

However, the next day Ambassador Daniels complained about the Junkers negotiations to Gen. Jesus Augustin Castro, the new minister of defense. Given Roosevelt's goal of constructing a Western Hemisphere defense area, Daniels knew a German-Mexican military link could not be tolerated. Because the Mexican government was dependent on the Roosevelt administration's goodwill, it is not surprising that the Mexican government canceled the Junkers airplane deal, as Daniels announced on February 23, 1939. After learning that the airplane deal had been scuttled, an infuriated Davis and Dr. Hagemann departed for the United States on February 20.[39]

Although Daniels deplored the Mexican barter trade with the fascist countries because "it seriously affects the commerce of United States manufacturers and turns the tide of Mexican purchases from American-made goods to German-made goods . . . [and] from experiences in some South American countries, that trade influences other associations." The Junkers deal was one of the few Mexican-German trade deals Daniels was able to prevent because, as he reminded U.S. secretary of state Cordell Hull: "Mexico must barter oil for German, Japanese and Italian goods or be drowned in oil." As long as the oil boycott remained in force and the Roosevelt administration would not intervene to break the boycott, the German barter trade would continue.

Daniels's fears were magnified by figures showing that U.S. exports to Mexico had declined significantly. In 1937 Mexico had been the United States's preeminent client in Latin America, but by the end of 1938 Mexican purchases had decreased 35 percent. In the same period, Mexico's trade with Germany, Italy, and Japan had increased sharply.

This trade loss had a domestic U.S. political impact because it was grist to the Republican Party's anti-Cárdenas drumbeat in Congress. In February 1939, Republican congressman Hamilton Fish, ranking Republican member of the House Foreign Affairs Committee, singled out Davis's barter deals as the cause of the precipitous decline in American trade with Mexico. As Fish said, "This seized American oil is traded for German equipment, trucks and machinery, and is used to cripple American trade with Mexico." There were also calls for Senate hearings on Davis's activities in Mexico, but the Roosevelt administration squashed the hearings because Davis could tell the Senate too many things that were embarrassing to Roosevelt. It is little wonder that Daniels was concerned about the German barter trade, it was damaging both American foreign and domestic affairs.[40]

By the end of 1938 Davis was buying oil from Mexico at a rate of more than $1 million per month. Much as Davis had laid out in his three-cornered plan of 1936, Mexican oil was shipped to Germany for barter goods with Bank of Boston guaranteeing Davis's oil purchases. He expanded his Mexican office from Tampico to a major headquarters in Mexico City, which employed fifteen people. His Mexican operations were a tremendous success, but, as was typical of Davis, he was already planning to expand his contracts.[41]

Davis announced on February 16, 1939, that he was going to enlarge his contracts by another $8 million to be invested in equipment for modernizing Mexico's refineries and facilitating shipment of the refined oil. Further, Davis planned to double his volume of oil purchases in 1939 and increase it even more in 1940. He estimated that Mexico had the capacity to export as much as $70 million of oil per year.[42]

By April 1939, Davis's skill at providing oil so impressed Berlin that Davis was made the sole supplier of Mexican petroleum for Germany. Davis signed this exclusive agreement in Berlin with the German Finance Ministry. Handling the German side of this agreement was Helmuth Wohlthat, an American-educated economic adviser on Goering's staff.[43] Wohlthat was a ministerial director in the Finance Ministry and was indirectly in charge of the German navy's finances. He was the foremost oil specialist in the German government and was familiar with Mexico because he had made several trips there in the 1920s and 1930s. Wohlthat had recently taken over the Office of Trade Agreements, which negotiated and arranged oil shipments, and any matters pertaining to oil went through him. Although on Goering's staff, he worked as an almost independent official and often acted as a mediator between Goering and Foreign Minister Ribbentrop.[44]

Working with Wohlthat was Friederich Fetzer, Davis's longtime contact with the German navy, Dr. Joachim Adolf Gustav Hertslet of the Reich Foreign Economics Ministry, and Hans-Joachim Caesar, a subordinate of Emil Puhl, the vice president of Germany's central bank, the Reichsbank. In a series of meetings, these young economists arranged for Davis to fuel Germany through an Oil Import Board with offices in Berlin and Hamburg. The agreement emphasized providing fuel to the German navy.[45]

It was not surprising that the German navy wanted Davis to be in charge of providing the navy's oil. Davis had done much of his German business in the 1930s with Germany's navy and the German admirals were impressed with his talents for getting oil. Further, Admiral Erich Raeder, head of the German navy, was deeply concerned with stockpiling oil reserves for war. In a memorandum dated September 9, 1938 (just before the Munich crisis), to Hermann Goering, Raeder requested funds to develop an oil concession in Mexico. Raeder wrote that the oil was needed because "the [German] navy can only fulfill its tasks in war completely if . . . it . . . has . . . a stored reserve of approximately one war year's supply [of oil]." Davis, with his proven record of delivery, was the best man to supply the needed oil.[46]

As part of Davis's new exclusive oil contract, Wohlthat arranged a German credit of $50 million to Mexico to be used to build up Mexican industry. Using this new German credit, the Mexican government contracted on April 6, 1939, for Germany to supply harbor-dredging equipment, a hydroelectric plant, six diesel locomotives, twenty-eight diesel trucks, and other expensive products for government use. With this deal, the Germans had succeeded in pulling Mexico further into the German trade circuit.[47]

Thus, the intractable policy of Big Oil was pushing Mexico into the arms of the fascist states. By April 1939, the consequences of the nationalization had created an anomalous position in which Mexico's antifascist government had turned to fascist Germany and Italy as the principal markets for its oil. This bizarre anomaly would continue as long as Germany and Italy needed oil and as long as other countries continued to boycott Mexican oil.[48]

Not only was oil going to the fascist states, but American and British manufacturers were losing millions of dollars of business to German and Italian firms. Far more serious in the long term was that the Mexican-German barter trade would gear the Mexican refining industry to German machinery. Thus, orders for follow-up and replacement parts and equipment, totaling several times as much as the original purchases, would go to Germany. Only a major shift in U.S. foreign policy or a world war seemed likely to stop the German plans in Mexico.

By mid-1939 the rapid expansion of Davis's Mexican operations resulted in conflict with his Mexican workers. On May 31, his chief geologist, Otto Probst, was found dead in his hotel room in Mexico City. In an apparent suicide, a clothesline tied to the head of his bed had strangled Probst. Although the German embassy intervened and prevented an autopsy, investigators from the U.S. Federal Bureau of Investigation (FBI) determined that Probst had been poisoned. It turned out that he had bribed government officials and stirred up action against union organizers. It is possible that the labor unions had struck back.

Before his death, Probst had been countering union infiltration into Davis's growing oil empire. Strike movements among the oil workers in the Tampico area were expanding as the workers became more dissatisfied with low wages. The workers, believing that Cárdenas had not kept his promise to hand the management of the oil fields over to them, sent the Mexican government a strike ultimatum demanding that Davis be denied the right to dismiss workers and that his concession to drill ten oil wells be canceled. Given the importance of Davis's German connections, the government ignored the workers' demands and Davis used strikebreakers to crush the strike.[49]

At the same time Davis was encountering labor troubles, the Mexican government was exerting pressure on Davis's operations. The government sporadically refused to ship oil on Davis's contracts because the Germans were slow to ship contracted machinery to Mexico. The Mexican legation in Berlin began pressing for liquidation of the German debt as soon as possible.[50,51]

Despite these difficulties, the Mexican-German oil trade increased rapidly and Davis decided it was time to broaden his Mexican business. Davis proposed a plan to the Germans that would have made Germany the economic overlord of Mexico. His scheme involved construction of a railroad across Mexico from the Pacific Ocean to the Atlantic Ocean, purchase of ships for removal of guano fertilizer from Baja California, modernization of the Mexican oil-refining industry, and various other projects whose total cost would have been tens of millions of dollars. Although the Germans eventually rejected Davis's proposal as overambitious, his proposal stirred interest in Berlin to further expand the economic links between Germany and Mexico.[52]

Following up on this proposal, Wohlthat dispatched Joachim Hertslet, whom he knew well, and Eugen Brieschke, a member of the German Oil Import Board, to negotiate a comprehensive economic treaty with the Cárdenas government.[53] Hertslet was the leader of the German mission. He was slight and rather short, five feet, five inches tall, his balding head of blond hair cropped in the Prussian version of the crew cut, his pale blue eyes concealed behind the thick lenses of horn-rimmed glasses, fair complexion, bulging forehead, wide mouth, flat nose, and thin lips. He spoke English fluently and persuasively in a soft voice. Hertslet was a convinced Nazi. He had joined the Hitler Youth movement in 1929, risen rapidly in its hierarchy, and then worked for Dr. Goebbels in the Propaganda Ministry.

Now, at the age of twenty-five, he was a protégé of Marshal Goering and was recognized as "one of the three or four most skillful German officials" specializing in the economic penetration of Latin America. Davis had met Hertslet in Germany through Dr. Fetzer, and subsequently they had become friends and knew each other quite well.[54]

After meeting Davis in New York on July 15, Hertslet, Brieschke, Henry Wilson, Davis, and Davis's secretary, Erna Wehrle, flew to Mexico City on July 31. Davis usually flew because it took only one day to reach Mexico City by airplane. He also often stopped in Houston or Brownsville to attend to his Texas oil business.[55]

In Mexico City this group worked with the German embassy to reach a comprehensive trade agreement with Mexico. Davis and Hertslet held repeated conferences with Baron Rüdt, the German ambassador to Mexico, in the palatial presidential suite at the four-star Hotel Reforma, which Davis had reserved for all of 1939. The suave and dapper Hertslet also used the suite to host numerous social affairs and went out of his way to demonstrate that the Nazi Aryans did not consider the Mexicans inferior.[56]

In addition, Hertslet opened a German Import-Export Corporation in Mexico City, which was to aid Mexico in stabilizing its currency. The Germans' plan was to extend $150 million in credits for the development of Mexico's rich natural resources and pay themselves back out of profits from the exploitation of Mexico's resources and barter. Mexico would become Germany's Western Hemisphere trading post. It was Goering's plan to render Mexico a debtor nation to Germany so that it would be an ally in time of war. As part of the treaty negotiations, Davis, Hertslet, and Brieschke met with Finance Minister Eduardo Suárez on August 10 for discussions, and Hertslet had an audience with President Cárdenas.[57]

Knowing that the United States would oppose any widening of trade relations between Mexico and Germany, Davis devised a plan to placate the Americans. He revitalized his old three-cornered cotton deal on a more massive scale. The Germans would buy surplus cotton from the U.S. government to indirectly pay for Mexico's imports of German goods. The initial purchase of cotton would be financed by a loan from the American Reconstruction Finance Corporation (RFC). Thus, the United States would share in the Mexican-German trade deal. He broached his plan with Jesse Jones of the RFC, but the U.S. State Department quickly squelched this proposal.[58]

Whether the Germans' plans had any real chance for success is questionable. The Mexican government was never comfortable trading with the Germans, and it was also aware of Roosevelt's displeasure with the magnitude of the Mexican-German trade agreements. Thus, at the same time the German trade agreement was under discussion, the Mexican government was concealing from Ambassador Daniels the importance of Davis's German connection.

Two days before meeting with Hertslet, Suárez told Daniels that Davis was providing only about 25 percent of Mexico's export sales. Suárez said he would be happy to see an investigation of Davis's activities by the U.S. Senate because "the American people have been led to believe by newspapers that Mexico could not survive without him [Davis]." Suárez's statement was totally false because, in fact, Davis either directly or indirectly was providing almost all of Mexico's export sales. Suárez also told Daniels that Mexico would not sign a treaty agreement with Germany. Despite his distortion of Davis's role, Suárez's statements speak volumes about the Mexican government's anxiety about any widening of the German trade agreements.[59]

Mexico's trade talks with Germany were most likely a ploy. The Mexicans were using the threat of a German trade agreement to put pressure on Roosevelt to demand that Big Oil offer better terms in the ongoing negotiations to settle the oil dispute. It was unlikely that the Mexican government would sign the German contract so long as it could be used as a weapon to secure a settlement with Big Oil.

Standard Oil had been negotiating a settlement with Mexico since March 1939, but had made little headway because of an internal struggle within Standard Oil over the strategy to follow in the negotiations. Thomas R. Armstrong, a Standard Oil vice president, wanted to foment a revolution in Mexico and settle the oil question that way. On the other hand, Donald Richberg[60] and other Standard Oil officials were willing to consider a compromise with Cárdenas. This struggle within Standard Oil continued for several years.[61]

After a breakdown in negotiations between Big Oil and Mexico, the price of Texas petroleum was slashed on August 10, 1939, as the first step in a price war by Big Oil against Mexican petroleum. Big Oil also reduced its oil prices in Scandinavia, hoping to hurt Davis's sales of his Eurotank petroleum products. The Mexican government countered by agreeing to Germany's proposal for a comprehensive trade agreement.[62]

Thus, before he hurriedly left Mexico by flying boat as the war began on September 1, Hertslet had negotiated the outline of a comprehensive trade pact. Much like the short-term contracts of the previous eighteen months, the agreement stated that Germany was to furnish industrial products and Mexico was to furnish oil and raw materials. Although a great coup for Nazi Germany, the treaty was never ratified by Mexico because the start of World War II brought a British blockade of Germany.[63]

Whether the Mexicans would have ratified the German trade agreement if the war had not started is debatable. The most likely scenario is that the Mexicans would not have risked further antagonizing Roosevelt. However, they just might have been willing to gamble that a further escalation of the German trade link would have placed such pressure on Roosevelt that he would force the major oil companies to reach a settlement with Mexico.

The contemporary trade journals and newspapers reported that Davis had delivered 20 million barrels of oil to Germany and Italy before the war started. The total oil deliveries were actually much greater because Davis also consigned petroleum to the United States, Scandinavia, Venezuela, and Great Britain that eventually wound up in Germany and Italy. Many tankers left Mexico with papers recording that they were sailing to Land's End, England. These ships did not arrive in England; their cargoes instead went to Germany. Almost all of the Mexican oil exported to the United States was just refined there and then reexported, most of it to Germany and Italy.[64]

Taking into account Davis's shrewd actions, a recalculation shows that approximately 70 percent (24 million barrels) of all the petroleum exported from Mexico between the Mexican nationalization (March 18, 1938) and the British declaration of war against Germany (September 3, 1939) found its way into German-controlled refineries and storage tanks. This oil provided Germany with approximately a six-month supply of oil for its war machine at the start of the war. Including the oil shipped to Italy (12 million barrels), the two fascist states procured about 94 percent of the petroleum exported from Mexico during the oil boycott.[65]

Davis's Mexican oil, which accounted for about 30 percent of the German oil supply in 1938–39, played a critical role in providing Germany with the petroleum it required to invade Poland in 1939 and to strike France in the spring of 1940. Without this bartered oil, it is probable that Germany would have been incapable of defeating the French and British in 1940. Given the German shortage of foreign currency in the 1930s, Germany could not afford to pay with hard currency for all of the imported raw materials so vital for the production and operation of aircraft, tanks, guns, and ships. Even with the Mexican oil, the Germans had acute petroleum shortages in the winter of 1939–40. Therefore, without the Mexican oil, the German arms buildup would have proceeded at a much slower pace.

Such a slowdown in the German arms buildup could have had a profound impact on the character of World War II. By 1938, the British and French were beginning to respond to the German military buildup with their own arms buildups. In 1938, the French government began pouring money into the aircraft industry. The first modern French fighters equal to the German Messerschmitt 109 were just entering the French air force when the Germans invaded France in May

1940.[66] The British were also producing large stocks of munitions and actually out-built Germany in both aircraft and tanks in 1940. Thus, Germany's initial lead in modern armaments was quickly being eroded.[67]

If Germany's military buildup had been slower due to the lack of petroleum, it is conceivable that Hitler would have had to decide to either postpone starting the war for a full year or risk going to war with France and Great Britain on very unequal terms. In either case, the probability that the German attack on France would have succeeded would have been greatly diminished.[68] If the German attack on France had ended in a stalemate, the effect on both the duration and extent of World War II is indeterminant. Given their much larger resources, it is possible that France and Great Britain, much as in World War I, might have eventually defeated Germany. Thus, Davis's machinations significantly contributed to the success of Hitler's war and the Holocaust.

Davis, however, would not have succeeded with just his own cunning, despite his talents for seizing business opportunities. For Davis to succeed, he needed the political assistance of John L. Lewis, Senator Joseph Guffey, and Walter Jones. The financial support of Bank of Boston was also critical. Further, Davis required the avarice and intransigence of Big Oil and the complicity of the British government in Big Oil's blind greed. Finally, Davis's success was linked to Roosevelt's acquiescence to the oil boycott despite the negative impact of the Mexican-German oil trade on U.S. foreign policy. Thus, all of these participants were partially responsible for Davis's contribution to Hitler's victories.

seven

Peace Plan

THE IMPORTANCE OF Davis's peace plan has been slighted because of muddled facts and misunderstood motivations for the actors' behavior. This is not particularly surprising because everyone was trying to manipulate the events by lying to each other. As this chapter describes: Davis lied to Roosevelt, Berle, Lewis, Hertslet, and Goering. Hertslet lied to Davis and Roosevelt. Roosevelt lied to Davis. Berle lied to Davis, the FBI, and even to his boss, Roosevelt. The truth is hard to discern in this fog of lies.

It had become apparent by August 1939 that the Germans were preparing to invade Poland. The newspapers were full of foreboding bulletins on war preparations by the major European powers. As war clouds loomed, Davis and Hertslet were in Cuernavaca, Mexico, a wealthy resort town near Mexico City. Fearing that the coming war would destroy his Mexican business, Davis demanded that Hertslet find out what the Germans were planning. In response to Hertslet's inquiry to the German Foreign Office, Davis received assurance that the Germans were trying to keep the peace. This innocuous statement did not reassure Davis. He sought an appointment with

President Roosevelt hoping that the President would prevent the war from igniting, but Roosevelt declined to see him. A few days later, on September 1, the Germans invaded Poland.[1]

Hitler's attack on Poland and Great Britain's subsequent declaration of war threw Davis into a panic. He knew that the instant the British declared war (which they did on September 3), they would place a blockade on Germany, which would shut off the flow of oil between Mexico and Germany. Although Davis had heard ample war talk, the start of the war was still a great shock. He owned a major refinery in Hamburg and was afraid that British bombers would destroy it.[2]

Davis desperately needed to sell his Mexican oil because the Mexican government was holding Davis to his oil contracts, which required him to take a minimum amount of oil, war or no war. The Mexicans took the view that their contract was with Davis and what he did with the oil was his affair. Because Big Oil was maintaining its "stolen oil" boycott, Davis had few markets for his Mexican oil. Pressed for more and more oil in frenzied cables from Fetzer, but unable to deliver, Davis was facing a financial crisis. As Davis told Suárez before he left Mexico, "our bubble has burst."[3]

Davis was frantic to maintain his lucrative oil trade with Germany. Needing bold new strategies to overcome the blockade crisis, he hatched a risky plot to stop the shooting in Europe. Davis believed that his political connections in Washington would enable him to persuade President Roosevelt to arbitrate a cease-fire in Europe.[4]

Davis discussed his proposal with Joachim Hertslet, who agreed to take the proposal to Goering. Hertslet and Morris Geye, one of Davis's executives, flew to Berlin on the first day of the war.[5] Immediately after arriving in Berlin, Hertslet took Davis's proposal to Hermann Goering, who endorsed Davis's peace plan and asked the Abwehr to handle the arrangements. Goering, like most of the German leadership, was fearful of a war with France and Great Britain and wished to forestall large-scale hostilities. Therefore, Davis's proposal of American mediation was just what Goering wanted.[6]

In fact, even Hitler did not want war with Great Britain and France in the fall of 1939 because Germany in 1939 was unprepared for a general conflict extending over a number of years. In his long-range planning Hitler had reckoned on war with the French and British only in 1943 or 1944. His hope was that once Poland had been conquered and the solidarity of Germany and Russia was displayed (Germany and Russia had just signed a nonaggression pact) that the French and British would conclude that a long and disastrous war with Germany would be suicidal. From his experience in the Czechoslovakian crisis, Hitler was convinced that Great Britain and France did not really want to go to war with Germany over Poland.[7]

Hitler was not far wrong in his assumption that the British and French would quickly make a compromise peace. Unlike in 1914, no great outburst of joy by the British people met the declaration of war. The British prime minister's announcement was distinctly downbeat and regretful, referring more to his disappointment than to the necessity of defeating Germany. The British government found it hard to see how the war could be won, for the invasion and subjugation of Germany seemed a total impossibility in 1939. The British foreign minister Lord Halifax showed an interest in an early peace and a readiness to enter negotiations. He told U.S. ambassador Joseph Kennedy (President John F. Kennedy's father) that he would give any peace proposals from Germany careful consideration. He regarded trying to crush Germany as "not an end that has ever seemed to me to be practical politics."[8]

Like Great Britain, France had accepted the war with little more than resignation. It was common knowledge that certain government factions were opposed to the war. There was some reason to think that the French people, once they saw the German army arrayed on their border, would insist on an agreement that would spare the country another bloodbath.[9]

Hitler's strategy under these circumstances was to arrange a mediated settlement. He thought it best for a neutral country to take the first step toward peace discussions. Thus, Davis's plan to get Roosevelt to mediate fit neatly with Hitler's own designs for a victor's peace.[10] Needless to say, Hitler's peace terms would leave Germany in a more powerful position than before the Polish invasion. Hitler maintained that his condition for peace discussions was "an entirely free hand in Poland." Poland, however, was only Hitler's most recent demand, as had been Austria, Sudetenland (part of present day Czechoslovakia), and Bohemia (part of present day Czechoslovakia) before Poland.[11]

While Hertslet was in Berlin promoting Davis's peace proposal, Davis had left Mexico for New York to prepare his plan to stop the war. As the first step in stopping the war, Davis tried to arrange an interview with Roosevelt through Walter Jones via the State Department. Davis told the State Department that Goering had told him of a peace plan and he wanted to go to Berlin with semi-official status and bring the peace plan back to Washington. To bolster his case, Davis implied that the peace plan was coming from Goering rather than from Davis. The State Department thought Davis's proposal was a hoax and turned him down.[12]

Davis went home to New York but refused to give up. His determination was based not only on his desire to save his business but also on his deep hatred of U.S. involvement in a European war. His experiences during World War I had convinced him that this kind of war was hell. He would do anything to stop the war before it became a catastrophe. Wehrle said, "he just thought war was so crazy and we should never get into it if we possibly could." He believed that the war could still be stopped because Germany and France had yet to strike serious blows. As Wehrle told the author, "he thought with his contacts in Germany that if he talked with the American government that somehow he could stop the war before it became serious." His staff thought he was crazy, but as Wehrle said, "What can you say to a man who thinks he can stop a war."[13]

Davis exchanged a series of telegrams with Hertslet in Berlin, who told him the Germans would welcome intervention by the U.S. government to prevent the war from spreading. Davis returned to Washington and met with Walter Jones, John L. Lewis, and Senator Guffey. In a meeting on September 5, he outlined his views to them and showed them his cables from Hertslet. The three Washington insiders agreed to help him get a White House audience. Anticipating events, Davis notified Hertslet that the White House was with him and that he would soon be on his way to Europe. On September 11, Hertslet cabled back that Davis should come to Rome on September 26 and meet a group of German officials (including Goering). In the same cable, Hertslet told Davis that Goering was ready to seize power in Germany. It looked as if Davis's plan had a chance of success; all Davis needed was to convince Roosevelt.[14]

At the request of Davis, John L. Lewis, who had far more political clout than Davis, telephoned Roosevelt on September 14. He had no difficulty getting through and said, "Mr. President, there's a man here I think you ought to see. He's got some important ideas on the war." He told Roosevelt that Davis had information "on a matter that might be of the highest importance to the country and humanity." He asked that the meeting be kept secret. Roosevelt declined to guarantee secrecy but did agree to meet with Davis the next day.[15,16]

Lewis had agreed to help Davis because Lewis adamantly opposed U.S. intervention in the European war, and knew that Washington was preparing contingency plans for possible U.S. involvement. In his traditional Labor Day radio address on September 1, Lewis had warned interventionist American politicians of his opposition to their policies:

> It [war] kills off the vigorous males who, if permitted to live,
> might question the financial and political exploitation of the race.
> . . . Labor in America wants no war nor any part of war. Labor
> wants the right to work and live—not the privilege of dying by
> gunshot or poison gas to sustain the mental errors of current
> statesmen.

Clearly anxious about possible U.S. involvement in the European
conflict, Lewis, the labor statesman, was ready to consider peace with
the antilabor Nazis. Was this the result of his growing animosity toward Roosevelt? Whatever the origin and the rationale of his isolationism, it was intense. The Germans were thrilled with Lewis's attitude
and asked Davis on September 13 to have Lewis send Goering a letter
endorsing Davis's peace plan.[17]

Davis's peace overtures came at a time when Roosevelt was trying
hard to restore peace in Europe. Davis's story was plausible, and nobody knew for sure whether it was a hoax, a Nazi trick, or a sincere effort. Roosevelt's fears of war and hopes of compromise with the Germans were still strong, but there was a split within the Roosevelt
administration over whether it was still feasible to arrange an accommodation with Hitler. Some advisers argued that the Germans could
be coerced into an acceptable settlement by using economic sanc-
tions and the threat of military force, while others argued that the
Germans must be crushed through the United States declaring war
on Germany.[18]

Important State Department officials, such as Under Secretary of
State Sumner Welles and European Division Chief J. Pierrepont Moffat, believed that appeasement of German economic demands would
placate Hitler. They rejected a collective security system directed
against Germany, fearing that destruction of Hitler would lead to the
spread of communism. They argued that the United States should
seek an accommodation with the fascist states, regardless of their internal policies, in order to restore stability to Europe and avoid a disastrous war.

In opposition to this perspective were the anti-appeasers, such as
Assistant Secretaries of State George Messersmith and Adolf Augustus Berle, who argued that German expansion was the central problem in Europe and must be met with collective security arrangements
and economic pressure. Their aim was an overthrow of the Nazi government.

Roosevelt's position was somewhere in the middle. Although he did
not adamantly oppose appeasement policies, he feared that what he

saw as irresponsible appeasement that submitted to extravagant German demands would not prevent conflict but help bring it about. Although Roosevelt wanted the United States to play a major part in arranging a stable peace, he believed this was probably not compatible with the continuation of Hitler's regime. On September 11, Roosevelt had told U.S. ambassador to Great Britain Joseph Kennedy, who was urging negotiations, that "the people of the United States would not support any move for peace initiated by this Government that would consolidate or make possible the survival of a regime of force and of aggression."[19]

On the morning of September 15, Roosevelt met with Davis in the Oval Office of the White House for one and one-half hours.[20] Assistant Secretary of State Adolf Berle, Roosevelt's adviser on espionage and security matters, was also present. Davis asked that what he was about to tell the president be kept private and complained when Berle began busily taking notes of Davis's conversation. Davis declared to the president, "I thought this was to be a confidential conversation between you and me." Roosevelt brushed off Davis's protest with "Oh, Adolf's [Berle] all right."[21]

Davis told Roosevelt and Berle the following story. He described how he had been exchanging telegrams for the past several weeks with Hermann Goering. Just before the outbreak of the war, Davis said he had received a series of cables from Germany through Joachim Hertslet in Mexico City, who Davis identified as Goering's aide and a friend of Davis. These cables stated that Goering was rapidly assuming substantial command of the German government, displacing Goebbels and Ribbentrop in influence. Goering had requested that Davis investigate whether Roosevelt would arbitrate the Polish conflict to avert the outbreak of a full-scale European war.[22]

Just three days before this meeting with Roosevelt, Davis explained, he had received another urgent cable that came from Goering through Hertslet. Goering said that he and the German army staff had been convinced that France and Great Britain would not go to war over Poland and that he was eager to prevent an all-out European war. Goering asked Davis to determine if Roosevelt would either act as a peace arbitrator himself or assist in securing the leader of another neutral nation to act in that role. Goering said that Germany would accept arbitration of the Polish conflict if assured that control of Danzig (present-day Gdańsk, Poland), the Polish corridor, and Silesia (made up of parts of present-day Poland, Czechoslovakia, and Germany) would be submitted to a plebiscite. If Roosevelt agreed to the plan, Hertslet would come to Washington as ambassador to negotiate for the Germans.[23]

Davis told Roosevelt that, based on these cables, he had arranged the current meeting with the president to present Goering's proposal. Davis added that he and his friends[24] were in close touch with the German army as well as with Goering and that the military also wanted the war to stop. Davis concluded his presentation by asking for the president's reaction to the German proposal.[25]

The president, knowing Davis's reputation as a boaster, was cautious. Although not rejecting the plan outright, he remained noncommittal. Like any shrewd politician, Roosevelt kept his options open. Roosevelt pointed out that various Americans had already made unofficial suggestions that he should intervene in the European crisis. He declared that he was ready to consider the possibility of negotiations and suggested three principal ways of solution: arbitration, mediation, or conciliation. However, he said he could not deal with the crisis through private individuals; his intervention would require that he be officially asked by the interested governments. This position no doubt disappointed Davis because Hertslet had asked him to get official recognition from Roosevelt for Davis's peace scheme. Roosevelt went on to point out that he did not think it likely that the British and French would consider making peace on the basis of the status quo (i.e., German control of Poland) unless they could be assured there would be no future interruptions of the peace (i.e., no further German territorial expansion).[26]

Davis said that the German government had asked him to meet secretly with high German officials in Rome on September 26. He also expected to confer with Benito Mussolini, who was sympathetic to the German peace proposal. Davis asked Roosevelt if he would like for him to report to the president on what took place at the Italian meetings. Roosevelt said that naturally any information on the European situation would be interesting, but reiterated that until an official proposal from the German government reached him that he could not take a position. This response was important because Roosevelt could maintain that he had not authorized Davis to be his peace emissary to Hitler but neither had he entirely closed the door on Davis's effort.[27]

After Davis left, the president and Adolf Berle discussed the amazing tale they had just heard. Berle pointed out that it was quite possible that Goering and his friends were at odds with other Nazi leaders over the course to follow. It was just possible that Goering had in fact so isolated Hitler that he was now able to dominate German policy. Roosevelt was intrigued by Davis's story primarily because of the possibility of overturning Hitler. He considered it unlikely that the British government could survive if it called for peace talks with Germany while Hitler remained in power.[28]

In fact, Davis, believing Hertslet's cables, had exaggerated Goering's power and intentions. Hitler remained supreme in the Nazi leadership. Goering remained completely loyal to Hitler, and he kept Hitler informed of his peace overtures. Knowing from experience that Davis often fabricated events, Roosevelt thought the peace plan was very likely a complete figment of Davis's imagination. In particular, he had doubts about Davis's story because Davis had not provided any telegrams to substantiate it. Nevertheless, there was a possibility the story was true, and Roosevelt's interest was piqued.[29]

Roosevelt decided to play along with Davis for the time being. Immediately after seeing Davis, Roosevelt met with Secretary of Agriculture Henry A. Wallace. Wallace asked Roosevelt about Davis, with whom Wallace had struck up a conversation while they both waited to see the president. Roosevelt excitedly told Wallace that Davis had just told him "the most amazing story about the possibility for peace that you ever heard. Probably nothing will ever come of it but I am going to follow it up just the same." Despite his excitement, Roosevelt, always the clever politician, told Berle to keep the White House's involvement secret and to proceed cautiously. Roosevelt wanted to avoid being the subject of ridicule and embarrassment should Davis's account turn out to be a hoax.[30]

For the third time in three years, Davis had succeeded in getting Roosevelt to go along with one of his schemes that served Nazi Germany. This scheme would end like the three-cornered trade deal of 1936, with Roosevelt persuaded to drop American participation, rather than like the Mexican oil barter trade of 1938, in which Roosevelt's acquiescence greatly benefited Germany.

On September 19, in a speech at Danzig, East Prussia, Hitler made his first offer of peace to Great Britain and France. On the same day, through Lewis, Davis continued to press his peace plan. Lewis forwarded to Roosevelt a cable that Davis had received from Hertslet. The message contained a request that the Roosevelt administration hold off on making any changes in existing neutrality legislation until after Davis returned from his upcoming trip to Europe. In return for Roosevelt's help, the United States would have a free hand in the Orient with German backing.

Roosevelt was amused by the naïveté of the offer and asked Berle for his opinion. Berle said he was appalled by the immorality of this German offer, which so casually toyed with the lives of millions of people. What Berle did like was that it provided an opportunity for Berle to decipher Davis's commercial code and thereby read his international cables. Berle immediately directed the New York office of the FBI to obtain copies of all of Davis's recent overseas cables.[31]

At the same meeting, Berle and Roosevelt discussed a telephone call by Walter Jones to the White House that same day to protest the decision of the U.S. Passport Office to deny Erna Wehrle a passport to accompany Davis to Europe. On the previous day, Lewis had also telephoned the president asking for assistance in obtaining Wehrle's passport. Davis had asked for passports for himself, his wife, and Wehrle to go to Italy on September 21. When the Passport Office denied passports for his wife and secretary, Davis got Lewis and Jones to protest the denial of Wehrle's passport.[32] The president asked Berle for his recommendation on the matter.[33]

Berle was a bitter foe of Nazi Germany and considered any accommodation with Nazi Germany a mistake. To Berle it seemed probable that one of the results of Davis's proposal would be to strengthen the Nazi hold on Germany. Therefore, in the first of a series of moves by Berle to sabotage Davis's peace plan, Berle advised Roosevelt to deny Wehrle a passport because he considered her a possible German espionage agent. Berle suspected that Wehrle might actually be the representative of the German government through whom the negotiations would be carried on. Ironically, it was probably Berle who held up Wehrle's passport in the first place. Berle had close links with the FBI, and Ruth Shipley, director of the Passport Office, was a close ally of the head of the FBI, J. Edgar Hoover.[34]

Berle also observed that it was possible that Lewis and Davis were in violation of the Logan Act[35] and he recommended that the FBI investigate Davis and Lewis. Based on this recommendation and Goering's telegram confirming that Davis's story was not a hoax, Roosevelt directed Berle to place Davis and Wehrle under FBI surveillance. Monitoring Davis also provided an indirect means for watching Lewis through any contact that Lewis might have with Davis. Roosevelt knew that it was politically too dangerous to monitor Lewis directly. Therefore, he wanted the surveillance kept secret and instructed that the FBI report directly to Berle without informing either the State or Justice Departments.[36]

Berle's recommendations at this meeting were a normal part of his duties for Roosevelt. Among Berle's many responsibilities were coordination of information from the FBI and diplomats abroad for

Roosevelt. Berle had been in the intelligence arena in 1917–19 and he enjoyed the clandestine game. In fact, Roosevelt had placed Berle over J. Edgar Hoover, preferring to have all of the FBI's reports siphoned through Berle and analyzed by him before they reached the president's desk.[37]

Although not legally authorized to operate overseas until 1940, the FBI, with State Department encouragement and in violation of the law, kept tabs on German agents in the United States and elsewhere in the Western Hemisphere during the 1930s. The FBI's Edward Tamm kept Berle informed of Nazi agents' activities. Unlike many State Department employees, who considered the FBI's domestic activities to be violations of American civil liberties and often leaked the FBI's activities to the press, Berle had a good relationship with Hoover and encouraged FBI counterintelligence.[38]

On the same day as Hitler's peace offer, Davis cabled Hertslet that he would be leaving for Europe soon and that Roosevelt was ready to mediate a peace agreement. This was a gross exaggeration of Roosevelt's position, but as usual, Davis was not letting the truth get in the way of his plans. The next day, Davis departed for Europe by Pan-American flying boat bound for Lisbon, Portugal,[39] and Wehrle cabled Hertslet that Davis would be coming alone because she could not get a passport. Note that if Roosevelt had not wanted Davis to go to Europe, he could have, like he had with Wehrle, canceled Davis's passport for travel to Europe.[40]

Having been tipped off to Davis's trip by Adolf Berle, the British secret service shadowed Davis in Bermuda and Portugal on his way to Berlin, and the FBI kept Berle informed of Davis's movements through their contacts at Pan-American Airways. Davis became aware of the surveillance almost immediately because, when the plane was grounded in Bermuda for almost two days due to poor flying conditions, a British intelligence agent came to the airport and questioned Davis closely. The agent seemed to know all about Davis's peace trip and told Davis that he should return to the United States or his passport would be lifted. Only after Davis insisted on his rights as a U.S. citizen did the British agent back off.[41,42]

After arriving in Lisbon on September 22, Davis was delayed. The unexpected layover in Bermuda had caused him to miss the flight to Rome that Hertslet had arranged for him on an Italian airline. Pan-American Airways told him that he would not be able to depart for Italy until October 12. As this delay would be a serious setback for Davis, he desperately sought other transportation to Rome. After three days, he finally caught a flight to Morocco and from there a flight to Italy.[43]

He arrived in Rome on September 26, where he was met by his German friends: Brieschke from the Import Board, Wohlthat from the German navy, Hertslet from the Economic Ministry, and representatives from the army and the SS. Although Davis had expected to meet Goering in Rome, he was not there (probably due to Davis's delay in reaching Rome), and the Germans seemed to be in Rome merely to greet Davis before he proceeded to Berlin. Davis could not have been too surprised about this state of affairs because he had known for several weeks that he would be going to Berlin and the Germans had arranged flights for Davis to Berlin on September 9. Of course, Davis had not told Roosevelt that he would be going to Berlin, and, although his passport specified that he could visit only Italy, Davis believed that the importance of the trip justified his overlooking that technicality.[44] The next day Davis and Hertslet went to Berlin to meet with Goering.

Davis left that night by train and arrived in Munich on September 28. Unlike the British in Portugal and Bermuda, the Germans gave Davis the VIP treatment and placed an airplane at his disposal. As he often said, he had "no trouble when I am among the Germans." Before proceeding to Berlin, the Germans took him on a twenty-four-hour inspection tour of the war fronts. First, he flew along the German fortifications of the Siegfried line on the French border. From the air, it was evident that neither side was serious about fighting, with only single guns heard at about thirty-minute intervals. At one point the plane landed just behind the German lines at Saarbrücken and his party drove along the frontier. During this excursion, Davis said he caught sight of a soccer game in progress between French and German soldiers.[45,46]

After spending the night in an underground bunker in the Siegfried line, he flew to Danzig in East Prussia. From there, with an escort of two German officers, his plane flew over occupied Poland and zigzagged from Warsaw to Vilna (present-day Vilnius, Lithuania) and from there to Łódź. The purpose of this trip was to counteract Allied propaganda about the grievous destruction in Poland, which Davis, after this excursion, thought was greatly exaggerated.[47] Arriving in Berlin late that night, Davis lodged in Hertslet's residence.[48]

While Davis was traveling, German and Russian forces had completed the conquest of Poland, and Hitler had decided he should seek peace. On the 28th, he and Soviet leader Joseph Stalin issued a joint proclamation calling for an end to hostilities because neither of them had any "further territorial claims." Hitler had already told the British through informal channels that if they agreed to his mastery of Central Europe, then he would not challenge Great Britain's massive maritime empire.[49]

There was a strong impetus within the Anglo-French leadership to accept this proposal. Lloyd George, British prime minister during World War I, was "frankly terrified" and "did not see how we could win this war." He was arguing with his friends for a secret session of Parliament to discuss how and under what terms they might sue for peace.[50]

British prime minister Neville Chamberlain was ripe for peace overtures. Chamberlain and his close friends in the British cabinet were hoping Goering would join in one of the anti-Hitler plots that were simmering in Germany, and seemed convinced that Goering would be ready to betray the führer. This wishful thinking was a complete misreading of Goering's character, who remained loyal to Hitler. In Paris there were quite a few French leaders who also were willing to stop the war on Hitler's terms. The French justice minister Georges Bonnet was trying to reach an understanding through contacts with Mussolini.[51]

After resting on September 30, Davis met with Goering on October 1 and for the next three days for lengthy discussions on the Mexican oil situation, the Roosevelt peace intrigue, and the 1940 presidential election. Also present at the meetings were Hertslet and Wohlthat, who wined and dined Davis during his stay in Berlin.[52]

The entire set of Davis-Goering discussions were recorded by a series of stenographers and Davis would return to America with a copy of these notes. Goering told him the discussions would be kept secret from the Foreign Ministry (i.e., Ribbentrop) but that Hitler and Alfred Rosenberg knew of them. The Berlin discussions ranged over a wide range of topics, which affected subsequent events in Davis's life, but this part of the story concerns only the conversations on the peace plan. The most crucial of the discussions on the peace proposal took place on the first day, October 1, in Goering's sumptuous Gothic office in the German Air Ministry.[53]

As their conversation began, Davis explained to Goering that he was "not in [a] position officially or unofficially to guarantee any results whatsoever in this matter"; that is, on Roosevelt's possible role of mediation. Nevertheless, Davis's presentation was a mix of Roosevelt's and Davis's own opinions, with much more of the latter than the former. His tone in the conversation was sympathetic with Germany and critical of the British and French.[54]

He condemned the U.S. ambassadors to Germany and France, Biddle and Bullitt, respectively, as warmongers, but had words of praise for Joseph Kennedy, U.S. ambassador to Great Britain. He said Roosevelt thought Germany should regain all of its former provinces ceded under the Treaty of Versailles, regain its overseas colonies, and receive a large financial loan. Roosevelt would support Germany in efforts to gain a just and lasting peace and the president was prepared to conclude an agreement with Germany under which the United States would supply war materials. The only point on which Davis suggested a possible departure from Germany's position was when he indicated that Poland and a Czech state should be reconstituted.[55]

As was his style, he told the Germans what they wanted to hear just as he had told the Americans what they wanted to hear. By weaving truth and fiction, he hoped to get both to agree to a peace conference. If the Americans agreed to mediate the conference, the British and French would be forced to attend the conference or be branded warmongers. Once all the parties were at the conference table, he calculated they would come to some sort of agreement that would stop the fighting.

Goering expressed surprise at Davis's rendition of Roosevelt's position, inasmuch as "the impression in Germany is that Mr. Roosevelt's feelings are now against Germany and that he is sympathetic to England and France." Goering said he could now see that Roosevelt's views corresponded

> substantially to the views of Mr. Hitler and his government. A world conference appears under the circumstances to be the only practical medium through which these mutual hopes can be achieved. Germany will welcome the aid of Mr. Roosevelt in bringing about such a conference. . . . The fundamental and motivating purpose of such a conference must be to establish a new order in the world designed to assure an enduring peace.[56]

The one-and-one-half-hour October 1 discussion then turned to the present and future role of John L. Lewis in American foreign and domestic policy. Davis told Goering that Lewis was a very good friend and that the Germans could reach an agreement with Lewis through Davis. Lewis was not tied to either of the two major American political parties but was a freelancer as far as political decisions were concerned.[57]

Davis said that Lewis feared that prolonged war "would have the greatest social and economic repercussions in the United States" and, therefore, Lewis favored a speedy end to the European hostilities. Davis told Goering that Lewis had dropped his opposition to the Nazis since the Nazi-Soviet nonaggression pact and was willing to pressure Roosevelt into stopping the war. Lewis was "prepared to mobilize the resources of his entire organization behind the move for peace" and, if necessary, would "create a situation in which American working men would simply refuse to produce war materials for England and France." Davis took some of the credit for Lewis's change in attitude, saying that he had shown Lewis how the Nazis had substantially raised the German workers' standard of living. Lewis agreed that the economic and social problems of the United States could be resolved through the work-community and common-good concepts of the New Germany.[58]

The Germans listened with rapt attention as Davis emphasized the commanding political influence that Lewis exercised over Roosevelt. In addition to the 9 million organized members of the trade unions, there were large groups of unorganized workers who looked to Lewis for leadership, so that Lewis controlled a bloc of approximately 14 million votes. Davis said that Roosevelt could attain his goal of a third term in the White House only with Lewis's active support. Therefore, the president would accede to Lewis's demand for a negotiated peace settlement favorable to Germany. To support his claim of influence with Lewis, Davis telephoned Lewis in the United States during the conference and reported to him on the course of the discussions.[59]

Goering believed Davis's description that the American president was at the mercy of Lewis and that Davis had the ear of Lewis. After consulting with Hitler, Goering, at his third and final meeting with Davis on October 3, urged Davis to follow up on the White House peace initiative. Goering gave Davis an advance copy of a speech that Hitler would make on October 6 to the Reichstag. Goering said that in this speech Hitler would make suggestions for peace that would "embody some of the points" that Goering and Davis had discussed. If Roosevelt believed "the suggestions of Mr. Hitler afforded a reasonable basis for a peace conference, he will have the opportunity which we have provided to take the initiative in bringing about a settlement."[60]

Goering remarked that "you may assure Mr. Roosevelt that if he will undertake mediation, Germany will agree to an adjustment whereby a new Polish state and a new Czechoslovakian independent government would come into being." What Goering did not say was that Hitler would never agree to return to the prewar frontiers, but rather would insist on incorporating the ethnic German regions of Czechoslovakia and Poland into the Reich and leaving only the remainder for the Czechs and Poles.[61]

Goering added that these proposals were to be submitted to Roosevelt only, that they were to be treated as highly confidential, and that they were to be used by the president only if they were necessary to bring about a peace conference. He suggested the conference be held in Washington with Roosevelt presiding and said he (Goering) would be willing to attend.[62]

Goering detailed Hertslet to accompany Davis back to Washington as Goering's personal representative. Goering promised Hertslet appointment as German ambassador to Washington if he succeeded in his primary mission of getting Roosevelt to serve as a peace mediator. This was a huge incentive for the twenty-five-year-old Hertslet. Hertslet was also given a secondary assignment by the Abwehr—to set up commercial links in South America if the peace mission failed.[63]

Davis was back in Rome on October 4 with peace terms approved by Goering in his pocket. In his private code, he cabled Walter Jones to contact Roosevelt and tell the president that he was returning with confidential messages for the president from Goering. In Rome with Davis were the Hertslets (husband and wife), who were traveling under forged Swedish passports.[64]

The next day, when he was ready to fly to the United States, Davis told the personnel in his Rome hotel that he was flying back to Berlin. He hoped this subterfuge would throw off the intelligence agents who he believed were following him and thus prevent the flight problems he had encountered coming to Europe. The conspirators then flew from Rome to Lisbon, bound for the United States.[65]

On the 6th, while Davis was in Lisbon, Hitler, after reviewing his troops in Warsaw, made from the Reichstag's podium his only comprehensive peace appeal to the Anglo-French alliance. Hitler advocated the holding of a European conference on the problems arising from the collapse of Poland, including Germany's colonial claims and the limitation of armaments. Hitler said the conference should be held "before millions of men are . . . uselessly sent to their death and billions of dollars worth of property destroyed."[66]

His words were shrewdly calculated to appeal not only to the German people, who after the easy conquest of Poland desired an end to the war, but also to the peoples of Great Britain and France. "Why should war in the West be fought? For restoration of Poland? . . . It would be senseless to annihilate millions of men . . . in order to reconstruct [this] state. What other reason exists? War in the West cannot settle any problems."[67]

To the surprise of the Germans, the terms of peace were widely reported in the British newspapers. Lloyd George, the famous author George Bernard Shaw, senior church figures, the substantial pacifist movement, and a number of prominent financiers declared their desire for an early negotiated peace, nor was it only among the British upper classes that there was opposition to the war. In the three days after Hitler's peace offer, more than three-quarters of the 2,450 letters received on the subject by the British prime minister were in favor of stopping the war.[68]

The terms of Hitler's peace proposal were publicly rejected by the anti-Nazi French premier Edouard Daladier on the day after Hitler's speech. British prime minister Neville Chamberlain, however, did not respond until October 12 because of a split in the British cabinet over how to respond to Hitler's peace overture. Chamberlain and the other appeasers were willing to let Germany keep part of Poland in return for a lasting peace. Another cabinet faction, led by Winston Churchill, was determined that Poland must be restored in toto.[69]

The entire British cabinet did agree on one thing, however; if the government directly accepted Hitler's proposal, it risked a vote of no confidence in Parliament. On the other hand, mediation by a neutral party might make negotiations with Hitler a political possibility. As Ambassador Kennedy had told Roosevelt two weeks earlier, "the British government as such certainly cannot accept any agreement with Hitler, but there may be a point when the President himself may work out plans for world peace."[70]

Hitler was aware of such a possibility. On the day after Hitler's speech, Alexander Kirk, the U.S. chargé d'affaires in Berlin, relayed to Secretary of State Hull an unofficial message from Hitler suggesting that Roosevelt respond to Hitler's speech by sending a message encouraging him in his peace offer. Therefore, in this week of British indecision, an offer of mediation from Roosevelt just might tip the balance in favor of the British appeasement faction. If the British agreed to negotiate peace terms with the Germans, the French would no doubt be forced to follow. It appeared that Davis's peace plan was about to succeed.[71]

William Rhodes Davis.

Adolf Augustus Berle, Roosevelt's assistant secretary of state and advisor on espionage and security matters. He ordered surveillance of Davis by the FBI.

Werner C. Clemm, son-in-law of the vice president of Citibank, employee of Davis, and Nazi spy.

Josephus Daniels, U.S. ambassador to Mexico, 1933–40, and close friend of President Franklin D. Roosevelt. He was a key participant in stopping Davis's oil smuggling to Nazi Germany.

Library of Congress

Hermann Goering, head of the Luftwaffe and number-two man in Nazi Germany. In 1939 he used Davis to convey Nazi peace overtures to Roosevelt, who Goering hoped would mediate a settlement.

Library of Congress

U.S. Senator Joseph Francis Guffey, a Pittsburgh oil man who worked extensively for Roosevelt in 1932 and was a major player in Davis's Mexican oil deals with Nazi Germany.

Library of Congress

John Lewellyn Lewis, head of the Congress of Industrial Organizations from 1937 to 1940, as well as head of the United Mine Workers. He interceded for Davis during his Mexico oil purchases for Germany and worked with him on the 1939 German peace plan and on Wendell Willkie's presidential campaign.

Library of Congress

PhotoAssist Inc./Library of Congress

Aviator Charles Lindbergh was a major isolationist leader who worked with Davis.

Library of Congress

Sam Pryor (right) was Wendell Willkie's campaign manager in the 1940 presidential campaign. He brought Davis into the campaign.

O. John Rogge was a U.S. assistant attorney general who was fired from his job for exposing Senator Burton Kendall Wheeler's role in Davis's espionage.

Corbis/UPI

Axel Wenner-Gren, Swedish industrialist and wealthiest man in the world in 1940, was an intermediary for peace negotiations between the British and German governments. He was also a friend of the Duke of Windsor and a business associate of Davis.

AP/Wide World Photos

U.S. Senator Burton
Kendall Wheeler, a major
isolationist leader backed
by Lewis and Davis for the
1940 Democratic
presidential nomination.

Wendell Willkie, the
Republican presidential
candidate in 1940,
unknowingly received secret
financial backing from Nazi
Germany.

eight

Peace Plan Collapses

ROOSEVELT WAS ALWAYS less interested in the peace talks than in overturning Hitler. When it became apparent that Hitler was not going to be overthrown, Roosevelt began having second thoughts about the plan. He knew that the British and French were considering abandoning the war, which would leave the Germans in a highly favorable position. Because an even more powerful Nazi Germany was not in the best interests of the United States, Roosevelt did not want to do anything that would encourage the British and French governments to leave Hitler in control of Poland.[1]

In a conversation with Treasury Secretary Henry Morgenthau on October 3, Roosevelt said, "If Germany or Italy made a good peace offer tomorrow, Joe [Ambassador Kennedy] would start working . . . to get everybody [the British leadership] to accept it." Roosevelt's implication was that he had no interest in any peace offer from Hitler—even a good one. When Morgenthau speculated that the peace or war question would likely be settled that week, Roosevelt replied that "the trouble nowadays is that the thing you expect to happen does not happen and it does not follow necessarily that it will this week." A few days later, Roosevelt decided to make sure it did not happen.[2]

As Davis was arriving in Lisbon, Walter Jones delivered a cable from Davis to the White House indicating that Davis was returning and bringing a peace proposal from the German government. In the cable Davis cautioned the president against making any comment that would commit the United States until Davis had an opportunity to talk with him. Davis also requested that the president discourage the British government from making statements from which it would be difficult to back down. Finally, he congratulated Roosevelt because "Roosevelt's view" had been entirely accepted by the Germans.[3]

Roosevelt discussed the message with Berle, who convinced him that the Germans were playing him for a fool. After Berle presented two massive dossiers showing Davis's Nazi connections, Roosevelt concluded that the entire Davis peace plan was just a German scheme to dupe him into ending the war on Hitler's terms. At this point, Roosevelt decided to abandon the whole business and turned the matter over to Berle to wrap up the loose ends.[4]

Berle's assignment required careful handling. An outright rejection by Roosevelt of a German peace proposal would infuriate Davis, and Davis would then publicize the negotiations, which would bring charges from the powerful American isolationist movement that the president was a warmonger. A Davis announcement could be particularly damaging at that moment because Roosevelt had just asked Congress to amend the Neutrality Act so that the British and French could buy arms from America.

The president's request to revise the act had touched off an explosion of isolationist propaganda. Hundreds of thousands of letters were sent to Congress imploring that the act not be amended. American public opinion was sharply divided on whether to amend the act, with only 57 percent in favor of the amendment in a mid-September Gallup opinion poll. Behind the scenes, Roosevelt took personal command of the amendment battle and kept close tabs on the voting inclinations of noncommitted congressmen. Only by pursuing cautious tactics and deliberately cultivating conservative Democratic senators did Roosevelt hope to get the amendment passed.[5]

The situation was delicate, and Roosevelt could not afford anything that might hamper his efforts. Rejection of Davis's peace proposal, if made public, might be enough to stop the proposed amendment. Berle had the complicated assignment of both keeping the peace negotiations secret by discouraging Davis from publicizing his peace effort and at the same time actually abandoning the plan.[6]

Although Berle's task was daunting, he relished such complex assignments. He was extremely intelligent, energetic, and had wide experience in both foreign and domestic politics. At forty-four years of age, the short, but suave and good-looking Berle was already well known as a member of Roosevelt's original "brain trust," which had formulated Roosevelt's New Deal policies. The quintessential liberal of the 1930s, Berle favored government regulation of capitalist enterprise. He had played a major role in New York City liberal politics and in early 1938 was appointed assistant secretary of state. Since arriving at the State Department, he had forged a strong link with Roosevelt and often wrote speeches for Roosevelt on both foreign and domestic issues.[7]

If he had a political fault, it was his inability to compromise, which was normally required in State Department dealings. He was a maverick whose sense of self-esteem irritated many of the government officials with whom he worked. However, as a fierce opponent of Nazi Germany, Berle was trusted completely by Roosevelt. With his intelligence, political experience, and Roosevelt's mandate, the cocky Berle was exactly the right man to destroy Davis's plan.[8]

He decided that the best way to destroy Davis's plan was to keep Hertslet out of the United States, which would allow Roosevelt to legitimately argue that the peace plan was not officially from the German government. Roosevelt would then have grounds to refuse considering the plan. Berle, by decoding the cables that Davis sent to his New York office, learned that Hertslet was using a forged Swedish passport, in the name of Carl Clemens Buecker, to avoid being seized by the British at the Bermuda stopover of the Pan American clipper. Berle advised Pan American Airways to be on the lookout for a false passport in Lisbon.[9,10]

When Hertslet came to pick up his ticket at the Pan American Airways office in Lisbon on October 6, two local employees recognized him. The local traffic manager had dealt with Hertslet only a month before when Hertslet went through Lisbon on his way to Berlin. The employee remembered Hertslet because Hertslet would not let the employee help him with his satchels on his previous stop in Lisbon, insisting that no one touch them but himself. The employee also remembered that the German legation had sent a car to the Lisbon airport to pick up Hertslet. In fact, the employee said, "I even recognized Hertslet's same hat."[11]

Because Hertslet was not Buecker, the Pan-American employee refused to give him a ticket. Davis intervened vigorously, berating the ticket agent and insisting that Hertslet was Buecker, an official of his

German subsidiary. When it became apparent the ticket agent would not be swayed, Davis decided to get the U.S. consulate to intercede.[12]

When Davis and Hertslet appeared at the consulate on October 7 to obtain a visa for Hertslet, U.S. consulate general James Barclay Young easily determined that Hertslet's Swedish passport was false. The most obvious problem was Hertslet's age. Buecker was supposed to be forty-four years old, which the twenty-five-year-old Hertslet clearly was not. To get Young to acquiesce to the Hertslet subterfuge, Davis told the American diplomat with a wink that Berle was aware that Davis would be returning from Europe with one of his European directors (i.e., Hertslet [alias Buecker]).[13]

However, when Young cabled Berle for instructions on how to proceed, Berle instructed Young to deny Hertslet a visa. Berle's message to Young implied that Davis was something of a crackpot "as he [Davis] often attempted to get access to the White House, usually without success." This statement was not an outright lie but it certainly stretched the truth about Davis. Davis had seen the president only three weeks before and Roosevelt had asked for a report when Davis returned from his trip to Europe.[14]

With these instructions from Berle, Young denied Hertslet a visa. Indignantly, Davis cabled the State Department and Roosevelt, protesting to both. Despite this protest, when the Pan American clipper left on October 8 for the United States, Hertslet was not on the plane. Berle had effectively scuttled Davis's peace mission before it had ever begun by excluding the German representative. Berle kept Roosevelt fully informed and Roosevelt approved of Berle's actions.[15]

For Hertslet, the visa denial was a major disaster because he would not be in Washington to represent Germany at Davis's meeting.[16] Davis tried to charter a Pan American clipper to fly Hertslet to the United States without passing through Bermuda but Pan American refused to charter a plane to Davis. With his passage to America blocked, Hertslet sailed for Brazil a day or two later and much later entered the United States on his own German diplomatic passport.[17]

Having notified the White House on October 7 of his imminent arrival, Davis returned on October 9 with papers that outlined the terms on which the Nazis would make peace with Great Britain. As he left the airport, newspaper reporters confronted him. Warned by his secretary, Erna Wehrle, that his trip to Berlin had been leaked by the State Department to the press, Davis was circumspect with reporters about the reasons for his trip to Europe, saying only that he had been in Rome for two weeks on business. The State Department confiscated his passport as he came through customs to prevent him from returning to Europe without its permission. When Roosevelt was asked the next day at a press conference if he knew what Davis was doing in Europe, he replied evasively that he had read about the trip in the newspaper.[18]

The day after his return, Davis, through John L. Lewis, tried to make an appointment with Roosevelt. Despite a telephone request from Lewis, Roosevelt (following the advice of Berle) declined to see Davis. The closest the insistent caller could get to the president was Brig. Gen. Edwin M. "Pa" Watson, the chief executive's genial appointments secretary. Roosevelt was far too busy to see the oil tycoon, Watson said over the telephone. Not giving up, Davis, Erna Wehrle, and another of Davis's secretaries, Viola Anderson, took the train to Washington and ensconced themselves in Walter Jones's offices at the Mayflower Hotel. Davis tried to reach Roosevelt again and telephoned the White House receptionist, Miss LeHand. After a brief pause she informed him that "the chief" was "in conference" and could not be disturbed.[19]

With Roosevelt refusing to see him, the White House told Davis to give his documents to the State Department. After first refusing, he had Walter Jones meet with Adolf Berle on October 11 and ask Berle to meet with Davis. Although he agreed to meet with Davis, Berle, in his meeting with Jones, set the tone for all future discussions by the Roosevelt administration with the Davis group. He declared that he "hoped that both Mr. Jones and Mr. Davis understood that the only position this government could take was that it was glad to receive information. Mr. Davis's activities in Germany were primarily his own business." In the meantime, Davis wrote two long letters to Roosevelt (dated October 11 and 12, 1939) in which he described his travels in Europe, and he had Erna Wehrle record an English version of the German stenographer's notes of his conversations with German officials in Berlin.[20]

Davis's one-and-one-half-hour October 12 meeting with Berle and Pierrepont Moffat of the State Department was not a happy experience. Accompanied by Walter Jones, Davis described his travels in Europe to Berle and asked that this information remain confidential. He also gave Berle the two letters he had written to Roosevelt. The meeting took a hostile turn after Berle read the letters. Berle implied that Davis had misrepresented the facts and indicated several places in the letters where Davis's summation of events could be misconstrued. Berle pointed out the following:

1. Davis's Rome meeting was not arranged at the behest of the president.
2. Davis had not been an unofficial representative of Roosevelt.
3. Davis's statements to the Germans about Roosevelt's positions were purely Davis's conception.[21]

Davis agreed that the letters could be misinterpreted on these points, but insisted that when the letters were read as a whole these interpretation problems vanished. Berle's intent in this content review of the letters was to make it clear that Roosevelt had not sent Davis to Europe as his representative and that Roosevelt had not yet accepted a mediator's role. Nor would he until the German government officially approached the U.S. government.

Berle also tested Davis's truthfulness by asking him about Hertslet. He asked Davis if Hertslet had stayed in Berlin. Davis hesitated a moment (he probably was deciding what Berle was likely to know about Hertslet's movements) and then said that he had left Hertslet in Rome. This was a lie and Berle knew it was a lie. Davis then compounded the first lie by saying that Hertslet was going to remain in Rome to work on German oil interests. Berle also knew this was a lie, because by this time Hertslet had left Lisbon by ship for South America.[22]

The meeting then turned to the possibilities of American negotiation of European peace. First, Berle asked if Davis still thought that Goering was going to take over the German government. Davis admitted that he had found no indication in Berlin that this was going to occur. In fact, Goering had told him that Hitler incarnated the German will and his removal would spell disaster for Germany. Berle then stated that he did not think that mediation was likely after Hitler's speech of October 6, which had set out conditions much harsher than those conveyed by Davis in his meeting with the president on September 15. Mr. Moffat reinforced this view by saying that after having seen the three speeches of Hitler, Chamberlain, and Daladier, it would seem that the two sides were very far apart in their conditions for a peace settlement.[23]

Davis answered that he still believed there was a possibility that mediation by Roosevelt could bring the two sides to the peace table. Davis stated that something had to be done to stop the war. Berle replied that Roosevelt would not mediate, except on the request of a government, and would not mediate even then unless both sides of the conflict indicated their willingness for Roosevelt to mediate. Berle then said that although he appreciated the information that Davis had provided, the American government would not initiate any peace proposal.[24]

It should have been immediately apparent to Davis that Berle had just expanded the conditions under which Roosevelt would mediate. Roosevelt now required a formal request to mediate from both the Allies and the Germans, not just from the Germans, before he would agree to a peace conference. This expansion of his preconditions indicated that Roosevelt was unlikely to ever agree to the German peace proposal.

Davis could tell the meeting was not going well. Irritated by Berle's tone, Davis asked curtly if he knew whether the FBI was following him. Davis told him that Walter Jones had seen agents in their hotel near Davis's room. Berle said he was unaware of any surveillance, which was a lie. Possibly because of Berle's hostile attitude, Davis decided not to give Berle the original documents initialed by the German government officials who had attended the Berlin conference. This probably upset Berle because as long as Davis had the originals he would have evidence to support any claims he might make to the newspapers.[25]

On this negative note, the meeting concluded. David left wondering why Berle was so hostile. The FBI followed Davis to the Washington airport on his way to catch a flight to New York. Wehrle and Henry Wilson noticed that "someone came over and looked at the tags of our baggage to see where we were going." Later the same day, reporters called Davis and queried him about his secret peace proposal from Germany, which further infuriated Davis. Clearly, Berle had leaked the subject of their meeting to the newspapers despite Davis's request for secrecy. It was now clear to Davis that he was persona non grata at the State Department. As Davis said a few weeks later to Bruce Lockett, the American commercial attaché in Mexico City, "Just who is Mr. Adolf Berle? I believe he hates me."[26]

On the basis of the Davis meeting, Berle told Roosevelt in a meeting on October 16 a damning story about the Davis peace mission, which Berle hoped would destroy any lingering desires by Roosevelt to continue his association with Davis:

1. The supposed plot to overthrow Hitler was a fake. The Davis mission was just an extremely clumsy intrigue by the Germans to get the president committed to something that would serve the Germans' desire to end the European war on their terms.

2. Hertslet was probably a Himmler spy within Goering's organization.
3. Davis had lied about his attempt to bring Hertslet to the United States.
4. Davis was likely in touch with German espionage agents in the United States.
5. Davis had used his interview with the president as a springboard and had misrepresented himself to Goering as Roosevelt's unofficial emissary.
6. Davis had passed off his own views to Goering as those of the president and had conveyed the impression that Roosevelt agreed with the German position.

Some of this report was true, some an exaggeration, and some just speculation by Berle, but it had its intended effect.

After listening to this blistering report, Berle said that Roosevelt "squarely hit the roof." Further infuriating Roosevelt was a report from Sam E. Woods, the American commercial attaché in Berlin, that while in Germany Davis had described the president as being under the control of John L. Lewis, who "in turn controls a block of fourteen million votes." If Roosevelt had known all the facts of what Davis had told Goering, Roosevelt would have no doubt been even more furious. Roosevelt decided that he wanted no further part of Davis.[27]

Roosevelt needed to avoid giving the isolationists political ammunition, however, and thus decided to string Davis along for a week or so. He would have Watson, his appointments secretary, advise Davis that Watson had turned over Davis's letters to the State Department for review. A response from the White House would be forthcoming only after the letters came back from the State Department. At the end of this period, Roosevelt instructed Berle to tell Davis that the White House would not consider his proposal because it did not come through official government channels.[28]

On the same day as Davis's meeting with Berle, Neville Chamberlain publicly rejected Hitler's peace offer. The British cabinet had come to an agreement that Hitler must be ousted because he could not be trusted to keep his word. Because there seemed little likelihood that Hitler would fall and there was nothing (such as a mediation offer by Roosevelt) to convince him otherwise, Chamberlain reluctantly rejected Hitler's peace proposal. Davis's plan was effectively dead. All that remained was for Davis to recognize the futility of his actions.[29]

Davis, anxious because the president had not responded to his letters, sent a letter to Roosevelt on the 14th that informed him that

Hertslet had called Davis from Rome asking for word on the president's mediation decision. Hertslet wanted to know the terms under which the president would offer to mediate so that an unofficial statement of the German government's attitude could be given.[30]

About the same time, Goering sent a message urging the president to abandon his fight to revise the American neutrality laws and to support the German peace drive. The Germans were pressing Davis for a response from Roosevelt, and Helmuth Wohlthat called Davis from Berlin on October 18 asking what Roosevelt had decided. Davis could tell him only that Roosevelt had still not responded to the German proposal. Unfortunately for Davis, Roosevelt had decided to oppose mediation by the American government.[31]

Lewis had no better luck than Davis with Roosevelt and the tough-minded Berle. Lewis met confidentially with Berle on October 20 at Berle's private residence, both to avoid newspaper reporters and because Berle thought the State Department was secretly recording his conversations. Obviously nettled over Roosevelt's refusal to see Davis, the labor leader warned Berle that the political support of the CIO for Roosevelt could no longer be taken for granted. He noted that at his request resolutions supporting the president had been passed at the recent CIO convention. He could just as easily have passed resolutions opposing the president. Lewis said he represented a large number of people who thought the best way to keep out of the European conflict was to make a general peace. He understood that Davis had a message from high German officials that made peace a possibility. Lewis wanted to know the administration's position on this German peace offer.[32]

Berle replied that the British and French were not interested in the German peace proposal. Any move by the American government to assist the Germans would be interpreted by the Allies as an unfriendly act. Therefore, attempts at mediation by Roosevelt at this time were not only futile but also counterproductive. Berle then reiterated the administration policy that Roosevelt would consider only a proposal that came through recognized government channels. Lewis then asked if the administration would like to have the German government say what Davis was saying unofficially. Berle refused to answer the question.

Exasperated, Lewis asked if anything could be done at all. Berle responded that he could not think of anything practicable at the moment nor did he know of anything that would indicate any immediate hopeful opportunity. Lewis asked if Davis's communication did not indicate some basis for action, leaving aside the fact that it did not come from a government. Berle responded that there was nothing in Davis's message that Hitler had not said in his speech on October 6, which had already been rejected by the French and British.[33]

The meeting then took on a threatening note when Berle observed, with a meaningful look at Lewis, that international intrigue led one into very deep water. Lewis promptly replied that he had no desire to get mixed up in international intrigue, but that he did have a real desire for peace. Berle wrote in his diary that Lewis was simply out of his depth and had no clear understanding that he was part of German intrigue. The meeting between the two ended in discord and threats.[34]

Having failed with Berle, Lewis met with Roosevelt several times on the peace plan in late October. Lewis's daughter, Kathryn, later told friends that he returned from one of these meetings heaping furious profanities on the president, who had again refused to take up the peace proposal.[35]

With pressing business requiring his presence in Mexico, Davis sent Edwin Watson a letter on October 21 asking him to give the president his telephone number in Mexico City. He also included in this letter a cable he had received from Hertslet that day. In the cable, Hertslet told Davis, "if you deem advisable we will send representative of our government who will have official power to reiterate contents of your memorandum to Roosevelt." Thus, Roosevelt's requirement of an official request by the German government would be met if Roosevelt gave the word. But Roosevelt did not give the word because he was not interested in peace with a strong Nazi Germany.[36]

By this time, Berle and Roosevelt did not need to hide behind clouds of bureaucratic delay because the amendment to the Neutrality Act was about to pass. The need to keep Davis from telling his story had become less pressing. The U.S. Senate passed the amendment on October 27, the House on November 2. Berle's tactics of keeping Hertslet out of the country and putting off Davis had worked brilliantly.

Ironically, unknown to Berle, Davis, too, had decided that it was best not to publicize his peace negotiations because it would put him in the public spotlight. Davis, always a realist, saw that Roosevelt was not welcoming his efforts. Wehrle had already told Hertslet that Washington was not interested in Germany's peace plans. As usual with Davis, he had another scheme under way.[37]

Davis knew all along that the peace plan was a long shot, so, in parallel with his peace maneuvers, he had been developing an alternative method to save his Mexican oil trade by breaking the British blockade. Because he was getting heavily involved in smuggling Mexican oil to Germany through the British blockade, he decided it was best to keep a low profile.

While Davis's peace plan was proceeding, Goering was instigating other German peace schemes. One of these was an unofficial peace negotiation attempt by old friends of Davis—Lord Inverforth, Francis W. Rickett, and Bernard Smith—through their connection to Hertslet. Like Davis, Smith and Rickett went to Europe to get firsthand information on the war situation.

To bolster the image of their trip, Rickett, who never let the truth get in his way, fabricated an impressive background for their mission. According to Rickett, President Roosevelt personally sent them on this fact-finding mission. He said that the president wanted an unbiased opinion because he felt that Ambassadors Kennedy (a well-known isolationist) and Bullitt were too pro-Allies to be reliable supporters. There was not one word of truth to this story.

Rickett and Smith stopped in Rome for an audience with Mussolini, and Ben Smith went on alone to Berlin. Rickett, a British citizen, was not allowed to travel to Germany. Although Smith did not see Hitler while he was in Germany, he met with leading Nazi officials. After rejoining Rickett in London in mid-October, the two self-appointed diplomats returned to America. Before leaving London, Rickett told his friends he would be back in ten days and that the war would be over in the near future.

Like political contributors today, Smith was granted an appointment at the White House because of his large gifts to the Democratic Party. He met with Roosevelt on the morning of November 1 and later with Steve Early, Jesse Jones, and Adolf Berle. The Germans had completely won over Smith and he informed Roosevelt that the war was only the usual sort of imperialist conflict, which the United States should avoid. He did not see any reason why the war should continue. He said that there was a substantial element of English big business working for an early peace with Hitler and mentioned that Lord Inverforth was in this circle of business leaders.[38]

After meeting with Smith, Berle discussed Smith's trip with the president, who suggested that they place Smith under surveillance. However, Berle decided this was not necessary and did not follow up on Smith's overtures. On the orders of President Roosevelt, Berle met with the British ambassador, Lord Lothian, at the White House on November 9 and told him about Bernard Smith and the Inverforth group and their attempts at negotiating a peace. The British were surprised that Smith had access to the president and that Lord Inverforth was involved in Smith's peace talks. Like the Davis scheme, nothing further came of the Inverforth peace plan, except Berle's communication to the British, which would have unfortunate consequences for both Inverforth and Davis.[39]

Berle had successfully sabotaged Davis's peace plan and ended any possibility of a negotiated peace to World War II in 1939. Then and later, many isolationists accused Roosevelt of encouraging war in Europe. Roosevelt and Berle's actions in the Davis peace plan would only have confirmed these isolationists' suspicions; they had both lied and manipulated events to ensure the failure of Davis's peace plan. No doubt a confirmed isolationist would argue that Roosevelt's actions had condemned the world to a catastrophic war that killed at least 60 million people during the next six years. The isolationists are no doubt right that Roosevelt could probably have initiated a peace settlement in the fall of 1939.

Roosevelt, however, was profoundly opposed to Hitler and came to believe that Nazi Germany was a long-run threat to democracy, world peace, and, ultimately, world civilization. By 1939, he doubted that there was any possibility of compromise with Hitler. With forceful prodding by Adolf Berle, he recognized that Davis's plan would result only in a more powerful Nazi Germany. Despite the real possibility that a peace settlement might be brokered if he intervened, Roosevelt decided that such a settlement would be a mistake.

The major result of a peace settlement in 1939 would have been a lifting of the British economic blockade of Germany. Germany could then have renewed its barter trade with Mexico and other countries for oil and other war materials, accelerating the development of Hitler's war machine. With the blockade lifted, Hitler's lead over the French, British, and Soviet military would have increased.

In the end, Hitler would not have upheld such a peace agreement. His writings and speeches made it clear that he meant to dominate Europe and would never tolerate another continental power that would rival the Third Reich. No doubt he would have struck again, maybe as soon as the spring of 1940. His most likely targets would have been France or the Soviet Union. In either case, with the blockade lifted the probability of a German victory and eventual domination of Europe could only have increased. Despite the horrors of war, the British and French governments' best strategy in 1939 was to remain on the defensive and maintain the blockade of Germany while their own armament industries had a chance to catch up with Germany's.

Roosevelt saw this difficult choice as the best option to restore democracy in Europe. He knew that this strategy was being forcefully advocated by Churchill, who argued in a September 25 memorandum that "it would seem our duty and policy to agree to nothing that will help him [Hitler] out of his troubles and to leave him to stew in his own juice during the winter while speeding forward our armaments." Roosevelt also knew that many British and French leaders were tempted by Hitler's offer. Therefore, he decided it was best if he did nothing to encourage German peace offers. Abandoning the Davis plan was the best way he could avoid another "Munich surrender."[40]

Although at first confused and tantalized by Davis's proposal, Roosevelt should be applauded for ignoring it. In the author's opinion, the hero of the Davis peace scheme is Adolf Berle, who convinced Roosevelt that the plan was a threat and who systematically unveiled and unraveled Davis's intrigue. Despite Berle's ruthlessness, it is fortunate that Roosevelt had such an able adviser at this critical moment.

Smarting from Roosevelt's refusal to mediate a European peace agreement, both Davis and Lewis swore to destroy Roosevelt. Up until 1939, Davis had been on relatively good terms with Roosevelt and only one and one-half years before had hoped to gain a cabinet post in the Roosevelt administration. Even in the fall of 1939, Davis still had mixed feelings about Roosevelt. He considered Roosevelt too pro-British, but still believed he might be willing to consider the Germans' position.

With Berle's destruction of the peace plan, Davis felt betrayed by the president. Roosevelt had accepted Davis's campaign contributions, but had turned his back on Davis when he needed help. As Davis saw it, just when he had successfully negotiated a peace agreement with Germany that would restore peace in Europe and also restore his oil business, the president had refused even to see Davis to discuss the peace plan. Wehrle said, "Davis had some confidence in Roosevelt because he thought Roosevelt would keep us out of the war. . . . He felt that Roosevelt had encouraged him and Davis was very disappointed."[41]

Both Davis and Lewis would in the following year go to great lengths to bring down Roosevelt. They would both become integral players in the plans of isolationists to stop Roosevelt from being reelected in 1940 and thereby prevent the United States from entering the war against the fascist states. Davis and Lewis's actions in the peace plan effort had resulted in FBI surveillance, and the U.S. government would closely follow their machinations in the coming year. Although both men were to be bitter enemies of Roosevelt, Davis, unlike Lewis, was willing to take great risks to bring the president down. These provocative pro-German activities would ultimately spell his end.

nine

Breaking the
Blockade

DAVIS KNEW THAT his peace plan was a long shot, so he had
other schemes in the works to keep his Mexican oil business
alive. During the next two years (1939–1941), he tried three
strategies to keep his oil business going: smuggling oil through the
British blockade to Germany, breaking Big Oil's boycott of Mexico,
and opening a new oil field in Texas. He succeeded at all three ventures and by the middle of 1941 he had not only kept his business
alive but also increased his wealth. In the process of building his new
oil empire, he became deeply involved in German espionage and
became a marked man in the eyes of the American and British intelligence agencies. These powerful enemies would eventually strike
heavy blows and destroy all that he built during these two years.

With the start of the war, Davis immediately called his New York
office to find out how many of his ships were on the high seas. Learning that a number of ships were sailing to Germany, he shifted the
destination of his tankers to neutral ports. Under international rules
of war any oil shipped directly to Germany could be seized by British
or French warships, without any payment to the owner. To prevent

this, Davis redirected all of his tankers bound for Hamburg to his Swedish subsidiary in Malmö. The British government, however, was determined to keep Davis from breaking the blockade.[1]

Davis had eight tankers at sea bound for Europe when the war started. The British navy stopped five on the high seas in late September and early October. Davis thought that these five neutral Norwegian tankers would be safe from British seizure because their destination was Malmö in neutral Sweden and they had sailed from neutral Mexico before the British declared war against Germany.[2]

Davis was wrong about the safety of his ships because the British demanded that every shipment to a neutral European country be within an annual quota set by the British and that the cargo not be for use by a British foe. To enforce these rules the British navy was forcing neutral ships bound for Europe with suspicious cargoes into British ports for searches. Two of Davis's tankers, the SS *Charles Racine* and the SS *Pedder*, were taken to England where, after inspection, their cargoes were confiscated and the ships were impounded. The British government declared that Davis's oil, in reality, was destined for Germany because Sweden's supply of oil with reserves on hand was more than all the Scandinavian countries would normally require.[3]

With the seizure of the tankers, Davis's business in Mexico was paralyzed and his Mexican operations manager, E. S. Walne, began preparing to close the company's offices. Davis was in desperate financial straits because most of his funds, about 10 million marks, were in German banks, and could not be used outside Germany. He frantically cabled Hertslet to transfer funds from his other European accounts to meet his Mexican expenses. Hertslet responded by helping Davis sell off part of Davis and Company's Scandinavian assets.[4]

Hoping for additional financial assistance from the Germans, Davis cabled Hertslet on September 13 with the enticing information that he had three oil cargoes for immediate delivery, and that he could send three to seven tankers from Mexico every month. With the start of the war, the Mexicans began demanding cash to pay for all cargoes and Bank of Boston was balking at advancing the funds. Because Davis did not have the cash, he could not send the oil. He asked Hertslet if the Germans would provide the needed funds. The next day, Hertslet replied in the affirmative and said that the funds would be waiting at the neutral European ports when the tankers arrived. Thus, the Germans were willing to pay in cash, but only if Davis could get the oil through the British blockade.[5]

With a solution to his money crisis in sight, Davis was faced with another crisis, this one in Mexico. He learned from his contacts in the Mexican government that Cárdenas was considering canceling his oil contract and turning the oil trade over to a Mexican company. After his successful meeting on September 15 with Roosevelt on the pease plan, Davis immediately flew to Mexico City to stabilize the situation. He told his Mexican clients that he (as Roosevelt's representative to Germany) was about to stop the war, which would allow the oil trade to resume.

He also had the German government assure his Mexican clients that it would soon be possible to do business as usual because a way had been found to circumvent the British blockade. The Mexicans were told that Germany would send trade goods through neutral Holland where the Mexican consul would take title to the merchandise. The Germans would use neutral Danish, Swedish, Norwegian, and Italian ships to transfer the goods to Mexico. Germany would purchase Mexican oil through the same route. Having momentarily calmed the Mexicans' fears, Davis flew back to New York on September 17 to catch the Pan-American clipper to Europe.[6]

In another move to bypass the British blockade of Germany, Davis increased oil shipments to Italy with the intention of sending the oil on to Germany. To expedite this evasion, Davis sent Nils Hansell to Italy a few weeks after the war started to arrange for an Italian company to store Davis's oil shipments from Mexico and Texas. Hansell, at Davis's request, also proposed formation of an Italian-Mexican company to transport Mexican oil to Italy and to build a joint Italian-Mexican refinery to process and store the oil.[7]

The cover story for the Italian trade was that the oil would be sold to neutral European countries such as Italy, Switzerland, and Yugoslavia. In fact, it was to be shipped to Germany. In early October, Goering had told Davis he wanted all the Mexican oil that Davis could get through the British blockade. When Davis traveled back through Rome after his Berlin conference, he and Hansell, with Hertslet's assistance, got the Italians' acquiescence to the smuggling of oil to Germany through Italy. Until the refinery was completed, the Mexican oil for Italy would be refined at the Italians' favorite American refinery, Eastern States Petroleum, in Houston.[8]

Hansell also arranged with the Swedish government to construct a large refinery, which would be operated by Davis's Swedish subsidiary. No doubt Davis had gotten his Swedish friend and oilman, Axel Johnson, to open the doors for this new refinery. Davis was calculating that he could use Sweden as another conduit to Germany for his Mexican oil.[9,10]

Although Davis publicly denied sending oil to Germany through Italy and said that the Italians were not helping the Germans obtain oil, these statements were just camouflage to hide the Italians' complicity in smuggling oil to Germany. Immediately on Davis's return to America, five Italian tankers went into service between Mexico and the Italian naval base of La Spezia. Also, a third oil barter deal with Italy, signed on October 6, 1939, provided that Mexico would get 2.2 million pounds of rayon for petroleum. Previously, Italy and Mexico had concluded deals for $5.5 million of oil in exchange for three Italian tanker ships and 7.9 million pounds of rayon.[11]

While he was in Berlin, Davis also tidied up his German business affairs. He sent the last American employee left at Eurotank back to the United States and closed the company's Berlin office. Unfortunately, when he closed the Berlin office, Davis had to lay off Karl Von Clemm, who became angry and accused Davis of disloyalty in a cable he sent from Berlin. He told Davis that the Gestapo had gone through the company books and were making unspecified charges against him. To placate Von Clemm, Davis asked Hertslet to use his influence with Goering to get Von Clemm a diplomatic posting to Rome.[12]

To maintain his control of Eurotank, Davis got his friend, Dr. Friederich Fetzer, appointed custodian of the Hamburg refinery, and turned operation of the plant over to him. Since the outbreak of the war, the Germans had been pressing Davis to turn over operation of the refinery to the German government because the oil industry as a whole, and the refinery, in particular, were so critical to the German war machine. Davis, tipped off by Dr. Bockelmann, the Eurotank plant manager, that the German government was considering confiscating the refinery, prevented the confiscation by turning operations over to Fetzer.[13]

Even with Davis out of the picture, Eurotank continued to refine petroleum and make profits for Davis and Company. Bockelmann remained manager of the refinery and it remained under Davis and Company control. Despite the Royal Air Force's repeated attempts to destroy the Hamburg refinery in 1940–41, Eurotank continued to operate at full capacity with petroleum from German and Romanian sources, as well as some smuggled Mexican oil. The Eurotank refinery never was destroyed and functioned throughout the war.[14]

Before he left Berlin, Davis made a fateful decision. He allowed the Abwehr to enroll him as a *Vertrauensleute* (confidential agent), code number C-80. Very little is known about these intelligence agents because the Germans destroyed most of their files. Usually citizens of the United States, some resided in the United States and some overseas. Their roles varied, some were involved in propaganda and political influence, while others provided intelligence to the Abwehr. Davis was to play both roles.[15]

On the surface, Davis's formal recruitment as a German intelligence agent did not significantly affect his activities. He continued with his normal business, and the Abwehr exercised only very limited and tenuous control over his affairs. Unlike a typical spy, Davis was assigned activities for the Germans that did not focus on tactical information of direct use to the German military. His important contributions were in other areas.[16] Despite his independence, his German espionage activities would attract the attention of British intelligence.

Why Davis enlisted formally in the German intelligence network rather than continuing his fellow traveler role is not known. It possibly had to do with the German's rigid bureaucratic rules. One of the decisions made at the Goering "peace plan" meetings was to finance a "defeat Roosevelt" campaign in America, which would require large sums of money. For Davis to be given responsibility for the money, the pedantic German bureaucracy would require his formal enrollment in the intelligence network. The Germans may also have put pressure on Davis to become a formal agent by threatening to seize the Eurotank refinery, but his subsequent actions do not suggest that he was working for the Germans under duress.

While Davis was in Berlin, the Abwehr made another interesting decision, registering John L. Lewis in German military files as a subagent of Davis (agent C-80/L). Lewis's listing as a German agent does not mean that he was necessarily a conscious agent of the Germans. Given Davis's exaggeration of his influence over Lewis, it is quite possible that the Germans assumed Lewis would do Davis's bidding. Although there is no hard evidence that Lewis was ever an intentional German agent, some of his actions in 1940 certainly raise suspicions.[17]

After returning to America, Davis placed his international business organization at the disposal of his German friends. The German Abwehr spy network meshed with Davis's offices in Europe and Latin America and his trusted subordinates began acting as couriers for German intelligence. In particular, Davis had excellent contacts inside England, which the Abwehr used to its advantage to collect information from influential British businessmen and financiers. Davis could do this with impunity under the cover of American neutrality, which gave him entry into countries from which the Germans were barred. Several times, Davis's vice president, Henry Wilson, carried information from London and Paris to Abwehr operatives in neutral Spain, Italy, and Mexico.[18]

London proved an especially fertile field for Davis's intelligence collection efforts, thanks to Davis's close friend, Lord Inverforth, whom Wilson met a number of times from 1939 to 1940. Inverforth, whose knowledge of the British munitions industry was extensive, gave Wilson supposedly secret information on British military technical advances. In addition, as a former cabinet minister, Inverforth was well informed about economic conditions in Great Britain and the strategic plans of the government. Further, his daughter's fiancé, Royal Navy officer Ronald Langton-Jones, was a source of information about naval matters for Wilson. After each visit to London, Wilson stopped in Madrid on his return to the United States to deliver his newly acquired information to the Abwehr through a German coal dealer, Jennsen, who was posing as Davis's representative in Spain.[19]

However, this secret information turned out to be phony. Since 1938, Davis's international organization had been under intense scrutiny by British intelligence. Davis's activities were considered so detrimental to Great Britain that even the British prime minister was kept informed of Davis's activities. In November 1939, the British had been informed by Berle of Inverforth's contact with the German government to stop the war. It is not surprising that soon after Wilson contacted Inverforth, British intelligence used its power to force Lord Inverforth to become one of their own agents. Following the directives of his British intelligence handlers, Inverforth provided Wilson with "false information."[20,21]

To Davis's consternation, soon after his oil shipments through Italy began, the British started inspecting every ship that passed Gibraltar. This British response to Davis's Italian oil shipments had come surprisingly quickly thanks to Josephus Daniels, who learned in early September that Germany and Mexico had reached an understanding to continue shipments of oil to Germany via Italy and in return Mexico would receive German or Italian goods via Italy. Daniels passed this information on to the State Department, which in turn passed the information on to the British. To further discredit Davis and provide cover for its leak to the British, the State Department passed on to the newspapers a report that much of Davis's oil to Italy was actually being sold to Germany.[22]

Despite Davis's denial and the lack of hard evidence that any of the oil shipped by his company to Italy was being transshipped to Germany, the Italian government severely limited the amount of oil that Davis could transship to Germany because this activity jeopardized an Anglo-Italian trade agreement. Italy wished to remain on good terms with Great Britain in 1939 because the Italians were receiving desperately needed British currency in exchange for Italian products. Moreover, due to the lack of cargo ships, the Italians were unable even to keep up with their own goods payments for Mexican oil. Italian shipments of rayon to pay for the Mexican oil were so slow that Mexican textile mills had to curtail their operations.[23]

Despite all of his clandestine efforts, the establishment of the British blockade was severely damaging Davis's Mexican oil business. Mexican exports to Latin America remained limited because the British and American oil companies had lowered their prices to meet the Mexican competition, thus shutting out the Mexicans. The oil companies were willing to lower their prices for the short term because they were convinced that Great Britain's blockade of German ports would bring Mexico to its knees by depriving it of its best oil customer. In mid-September, the British government asked the Roosevelt administration to change its position on the Mexican nationalization of oil and to support Big Oil's demand for the return of its Mexican properties. The British argued that if the Americans would support the British it would be impossible for the Mexicans to refuse British demands because of the blockade of Germany. Fortunately for the Mexicans, Roosevelt did not change his policy because he did not want to ruin his good relations with Latin American countries.[24]

Also damaging Davis's Mexican oil trade was a tightening of the British blockade. The British began asserting their right to seize German products even if they were shipped from neutral ports and began requiring all neutral ships to receive a certificate (called a navicert) from British authorities to certify the innocent character of the cargoes before the neutral ship left port. Davis's scheme of passing German goods through neutral Holland was destroyed by the navicert system. In addition, the navicert system was particularly damaging to Davis because the British used the system as a concealed method of blacklisting companies that they did not like, such as Davis and Company, by refusing to grant them navicerts. Thus, Davis's sale of oil directly to Germany became impossible,[25] and the sale of oil through European neutrals very risky.[26]

The war profoundly changed Mexico's oil situation. Just before the war started, Pemex had proudly announced that all oil available for export had been sold and that it did not have any more to sell. With the start of the war, suddenly, there was no market for Mexico's oil. Oil exports from Mexico dropped dramatically, by more than 50 percent in the fall of 1939.[27]

Monthly Exports of Mexican Oil, 1939 (Millions of Pesos)[28]

August	11
September	4
October	6
November	4
December	5

Much of Davis's contracted oil could not be immediately sold elsewhere, and within a short time Mexico's storage tanks were full.[29]

Having serious trouble selling Mexican oil, Davis closed his Mexican subsidiary, Davecom, on September 30 and opened a new Mexican subsidiary, Damex Engineering Company, which used the same officers and staff as the old company. This curious reorganization may have been the first step (in a repeat of his actions with his Danish problems) toward ending any legal obligations he had to buy the Mexican oil. As his cash flow dried up, his checks started bouncing at Bank of Boston. All signs pointed to Davis pulling another of his financial shenanigans to avoid his creditors.[30]

Despite his preparations for bamboozling the Mexicans, when Davis returned to Mexico in late October after his German peace mission, he announced that the war would be brief and he was prepared to resume his barter deals when the war ended. For this reason, he said, he intended to maintain a small office in Mexico City even though his operations there had been concluded.[31]

His renewed optimism was the result of the firm German support he had received in Berlin. The Germans had promised to continue making payments to Davis for his oil and did so as late as the spring of 1940, with total payments of at least $440,000 since the start of the war. The money was indirectly siphoned to him through the Bank for International Settlements in Zurich, Switzerland, via Lisbon and Buenos Aires. These payments came in a year in which the Germans were desperately trying to create a dollar fund in the United States and were refusing to pay debts owed to scores of other American businessmen. Obviously, the Germans valued Davis's services highly (both in the economic and espionage arenas) or they would never have made these payments.[32]

This generous compensation may have been in part for Davis's services in arranging the payment of $7 million to the Mexican government, which Germany still owed Mexico for oil shipped in 1939. Because Germany could not spare the foreign currency and the British blockade prevented the shipment of merchandise, the Mexican government had not been paid. To ensure Mexican cooperation in German oil smuggling operations, the Germans needed to pay the debt. At Davis's suggestion, the German government agreed to transfer the titles of six German tankers trapped in Mexican ports by the British navy to the Mexican government and the value of the tankers would be applied against the money that Germany owed Mexico. The Mexicans could use these ships to supply oil to the Mexican Pacific Coast, which until then had purchased its oil from the United States. After a long series of negotiations, Davis arranged for the sale of these tankers to Mexico in March 1940.[33]

With a cloud over his European holdings and desperate for new sources of income, Davis began spending a lot of time in Texas. On the advice of the company's geologist, Paul Fly, Davis purchased 12,000 acres of supposedly useless snake-infested land in the Rincon oil field in Starr County in mid-September. After preliminary drilling showed promising results, Davis convinced Bank of Boston to back his development of this potential oil property by lending him $500,000. The bank agreed because Davis owed the bank millions and this venture seemed the bank's one chance of retrieving its loans.[34]

Luck was with Davis, his third well struck a large pool of oil and Rincon became the largest oil field in South Texas. Control of this huge field enabled Davis to pay off a great share of his debt to Bank of Boston. After Davis got forty producing wells in operation, he negotiated a series of new loans in early 1940 for about $1.5 million from Bank of Boston. Davis used these funds to build an ocean terminal and storage tanks in Brownsville, Texas, on the Mexican border. He also established a gas recycling plant with a capacity of 60 million cubic feet per day in nearby Alice, Texas. By early 1940, the Rincon oil strike had saved Davis from the financial crisis caused by the British blockade of Europe and his company's cash position was strong enough to meet all his obligations. He was back in good graces with Bank of Boston and the bank was ready to extend new credit for his projects.

Despite his new oil fields in Texas, Davis still had large investments in Mexican oil reserves, from which he was getting only meager profits. Because smuggling oil to Germany was absorbing only modest amounts of Mexican oil, Davis sought ways to break Big Oil's boycott and sell Mexican oil in the United States. Using his connections at Eastern States Petroleum, he got the Houston company to agree in early November 1939 to try to sell Mexican oil in the American market. But Eastern was a small company with few customers; Davis needed a much larger company to break Big Oil's boycott of Mexican oil.[35]

In late 1939 Davis entered the negotiations that would lead to the end of Big Oil's blockade of Mexican oil from the American market. A foolish mistake by Big Oil provided Davis with his opportunity. The previous spring Standard Oil had sent Donald Richberg to Mexico City to discuss an oil settlement with Cárdenas, who in turn had proposed that the two sides enter negotiations to set the form and amount of payment by Mexico for Big Oil's Mexican properties. However, Richberg would discuss only the conditions under which the oil fields were to be returned to Big Oil. Because no agreement about who would have final authority over the oil fields could be reached, the negotiations died. Richberg resigned soon after in disgust when he learned that Standard Oil officials in Mexico were working against his efforts to reach a compromise with Cárdenas.[36]

With the failure of these negotiations, some of the smaller oil companies became restive under the rigid no-compromise policy imposed by Big Oil. One of these companies, Sinclair Oil, decided to break away from Big Oil's boycott stance. Although a relatively small company, Sinclair Oil had, before the expropriation, accounted for about 25 percent of the American production in Mexico and the boycott was a significant financial burden for the company. It was later said that Sinclair Oil broke Big Oil's boycott because it learned that Standard Oil had informed the Mexicans that Sinclair Oil's interests were meager and that, if the Cárdenas government settled with Standard Oil and the other large companies, Sinclair Oil would be forced to settle. Sinclair Oil construed this statement as a breach of faith by Standard Oil and decided to act alone. Soon after Richberg's March 1939 negotiations, Sinclair Oil asked Francisco Nájera, the Mexican ambassador in Washington, if Mexico would consider settling Sinclair Oil's claims separately from the other companies. Nájera turned Sinclair Oil down in this June proposition, but the Mexicans reconsidered the proposal after the war started.[37]

In late 1939, Sinclair Oil began secret discussions with Mexico to settle the company's claims. In December, the Mexican finance minister, Eduardo Suárez, went to the United States to confer with State Department officials in Washington about the oil dispute. Before these meetings, Suárez, Ambassador Nájera, and Mexican treasurer Jesus Herzog secretly spent two days in New York in discussions with Harry Sinclair, his attorney and former U.S. secretary of war under President Hoover; Patrick J. Hurley; John L. Lewis; and, at the specific request of Lewis, William Rhodes Davis. At a subsequent meeting in Washington, D.C., Lewis was again present. The presence of Lewis (let alone Davis) was, to say the least, a mystery at the time.[38]

The story later told by oilmen about these secret meetings was that Hurley, knowing that Davis and Lewis had cooperated in Mexico and were on good terms with the Cárdenas government, asked them to intercede on behalf of Sinclair Oil. Davis claimed that he was brought into the negotiations by Lewis after Hurley[39] had asked Lewis for his assistance. Lewis, in turn, asked Davis to assist him. Davis agreed as a favor to his friend, John L. Lewis, who later said he agreed to help Hurley because Sinclair Oil had agreed to a union contract with the CIO.[40]

Lewis said he was attending the meetings for patriotic reasons, to further good relations between the United States and Mexico; to keep the United States from adopting too harsh a posture toward Mexico; and to ensure that the United States did not push arbitration of the dispute, as he considered it premature. Lewis asserted that by protesting to President Roosevelt he had prevented the American government from sending a stiff note to Mexico in 1938 after the oil expropriation. In the same way, he said, he had kept the American government from proposing arbitration of the expropriation controversy in 1939. However, Hurley privately informed the Mexican ambassador that Lewis's explanation for his presence was a lie and that Lewis had a close "business interest" in Mexican oil. Whether Lewis was actually a silent partner in Davis's oil bartering is not known. If it is true it would certainly explain Lewis's odd behavior toward Davis and his Nazi oil deals.[41]

In any event, Sinclair Oil began secret discussions with Mexico. Hurley served as chief negotiator for Sinclair Oil, and he and Ambassador Nájera dickered through the spring of 1940 over the price of compensation for the Sinclair Oil property. By April, an agreement satisfactory to both sides had been worked out. Eduardo Suárez announced the agreement with great fanfare on May 7, 1940, in Mexico City.[42]

Davis later claimed that it was his influence with the Cárdenas regime that allowed Sinclair Oil to get such a generous agreement. Big Oil was furious about the agreement and stepped up its propaganda war against Mexico and Davis. In the long run, the agreement with Sinclair Oil significantly weakened Big Oil's boycott and by the end of the year American buyers had purchased almost 16 million barrels of oil, or more than 75 percent of total Mexican exports. Thus, the Rincon field and the breaking of Big Oil's boycott significantly improved Davis's financial health and, with Joachim Hertslet's return to Mexico, Davis's losses in Mexico were about to be over.[43]

Having slipped through the British blockade from Lisbon in the fall of 1939, Hertslet had spent the winter in Argentina and Brazil. On the orders of Goering, he left for Mexico in February 1940, where he arrived on March 5 from Rio de Janeiro. He was back in Mexico to help Davis slip oil out of Mexico to fuel German warships.[44]

When Hertslet arrived in Mexico, he posed as a German embassy economic counselor. In reality, he ran an oil smuggling operation from Davis's Mexican subsidiary, Damex. Like Davis, Hertslet had become an agent for the Abwehr, apparently because the acquisition of oil was too critical a matter to be left solely under the purview of the German Economics Ministry.[45,46]

The Abwehr, at the outbreak of the war, had set up a major intelligence outpost in Mexico to gather information, influence the Mexican government, and smuggle war materials to Germany. The German operation employed several hundred agents throughout Mexico. Hertslet was in charge of all nonmilitary espionage and supervised the gathering and sifting of strategic financial and economic information. The existence of such an operation depended on the Mexican authorities maintaining a decidedly lax attitude about legalities. Hertslet counted on such benevolence for his smuggling operation because he was sure the Mexicans would not want to anger Germany, one of their best petroleum customers.[47]

Correct in his evaluation, Hertslet had few problems with the Mexican government because in 1940 both the Mexican political left and right had pro-German positions. Hertslet's magnetic personality charmed everyone; he spoke many languages (including Spanish) and radiated confidence. His son described Hertslet as a young Napóleon in character. With these talents, he developed a wide circle of influential Mexican friends whom he and his pretty young wife entertained lavishly at their residence in the fashionable Monte Blanco section of Mexico City. He worked closely with Davis, who was frequently in Mexico after the war started. Davis and Wehrle would visit Mexico City for a week or so and stay in the Reforma Hotel.[48]

With the assistance of Mexican finance minister Eduardo Suárez, Hertslet and Davis were able to ship large amounts of oil to Germany. Hertslet made frequent trips to Mexico's Pacific Coast to oversee these operations. The oil and the bartered German goods slipped through the British blockade under the cover of false manifestos as consignments to Mexican consuls in neutral countries. Most of the petroleum was shipped on Japanese tankers across the Pacific to Vladivostok in Soviet Siberia.[49]

Joseph Stalin, who was eager to keep on good terms with Hitler, hoped that helping the German dictator would keep Hitler's attention focused on Western Europe. Thus, the Soviets were willing to transport Mexican oil across the Soviet Union to Germany on the Trans-Siberian Railway. How much oil reached Germany by this means is unknown, but during 1940 Mexico "officially" exported to Japan more than 1 million barrels of oil. Certainly thousands of tons of oil reached Germany by this circuitous route. Through the smuggling operations, Hertslet and Davis succeeded, by the fall of 1940, in sending another $2.5 million of German goods to Mexico in exchange for oil and other war materials.[50]

Their smuggling did not remain a secret for long. When asked by American newspaper reporters in April if he was shipping oil to Germany, Davis said:

> it is a little difficult to see what (is) wrong for an American or, for that matter, any other neutral in selling oil to Germany. . . . It is quite true that we bought substantial quantities of petroleum from Mexico which were sold to German importers, including our own German company (Eurotank).[51]

Despite Davis's acknowledgment of his activities, the British navy never tried to intercept Davis's chartered Japanese ships. Great Britain was too weak in 1940 and Japan was too powerful for the British to enforce their unilateral navicert system on Japanese shipping and risk antagonizing the Japanese government.[52]

Hertslet also tried to establish secret bases in the Gulf of Mexico and the Caribbean where long-range U-boats could refuel. Goering, who had proposed setting up these bases in October 1939 when Davis was in Berlin, later told American interrogators "there was discussion to make oil available at certain locations in the ocean." An elaborate attempt was made to establish hidden oil depots on secluded islands where German submarines could refuel. Davis planned to charter several cargo vessels in Mexico, buy hundreds of drums of oil, and ship them to these out-of-the-way islands. However, British and American authorities found out about the project and stopped the scheme by preventing Davis from chartering ships.[53]

In May 1940, Davis sent three of his employees, Henry Wilson, Fritz Flanley, and Charles E. MacDonald, to Europe from Mexico City to accelerate the flow of oil to Italy. Davis had signed a contract with the Italian government in April to supply 150,000 barrels of oil from his Texas oil fields. While Wilson flew on to London for another rendezvous with Lord Inverforth, Flanley and MacDonald went to Rome carrying a coded secret intelligence report on Davis's Mexican smuggling operation. They delivered the report to the German consul general in Genoa, Italy, who forwarded it to the Abwehr in Berlin.[54]

Davis's Italian efforts soon collapsed when Italy declared war on Great Britain on June 10. MacDonald returned to the United States, but Davis refused to give up on shipping oil to Germany through neutral European countries. He had Flanley stay in Portugal to arrange oil shipments to Spain and Portugal. Not long after, Davis and Company started making oil shipments from Texas to Spain, which were sent on to Germany.[55]

General Francisco Franco and the fascist Falange Party controlled Spain, and the Spanish government was friendly with Nazi Germany, which had given substantial military aid to Franco during the Spanish Civil War. Spain's neutrality provided an avenue to bypass the British blockade that the Germans were quick to exploit. Since the start of the war, oil tankers had been carrying oil and gasoline from Latin America to Spain, where much of the fuel was then sent on to Germany. Franco also made an agreement with the Germans to allow the Germans to secretly use Spanish ports to refuel and provision their submarines.[56]

Fuel for the first German submarine, U-25, was provided in January 1940 and the Germans rapidly extended their refueling operations. At Las Palmas in the Spanish Canary Islands, oil from the Americas was transferred to the storage tanks of a Spanish submarine base that the German navy had helped construct. Much of this fuel was used for German submarines operating in the North Atlantic. Tankers at the Spanish mainland ports of Vigo, Cádiz, and Cartagena also serviced German submarines. Unfortunately for Davis, he had only a small portion of this immoral trade; Texaco and Standard Oil had the majority. They had been supplying Spain with large quantities of oil since the war began even though they were aware that much of this oil was probably being sent to Germany.[57]

Soon after Davis set up his Spanish connection, the British put a stop to the trade when the American government warned it about the smuggling operations. American secretary of the treasury Henry Morgenthau's staff had compiled statistics in June that revealed Spain was importing oil at a rate 50 percent higher in 1940 than in 1939. Morgenthau believed the excess oil was being sent to Germany. To stop this smuggling, Morgenthau denied permits to ships under American

registry to take oil to Spain, pressured American oil companies to reduce shipments of oil to Spain, and notified the British in July of his
suspicions about the final destination of the oil. The British increased
their naval monitoring of tankers bound for Spain and through diplomatic channels quietly protested to the Spanish government about
the magnitude of the oil shipments. By July 1941, this hole in the
British blockade had been sealed shut.[58]

Having reached agreement with Sinclair Oil, the Mexican government hoped that the other oil companies would be willing to negotiate. However, Big Oil still refused to negotiate and instead tried to replace Cárdenas with a Mexican president more to its liking. The oil
interests placed their hopes on conservative general Juan Andreu Almazán. Almazán had refused to go along with the nomination of Cárdenas's candidate for president, Gen. Manuel Avila Camacho, and
had launched his own campaign as the candidate of the Revolutionary
Party of National Unification (PRUN).[59]

Almazán, from a family of wealthy landowners, was one of the richest men in Mexico. He had amassed his vast personal fortune through
bribes and other graft related to public works contracts, mining concessions, and fishing rights that he had controlled during his years as
minister of communications and as an army general. Almazán, a sub-
tle and dangerous enemy of Cárdenas, had built a broad base of support as he slowly and deliberately campaigned across Mexico. He
knew better than to attack the oil nationalization outright, but in his
public declarations he pointed out that Mexico needed foreign capital
in order to develop, making it clear that he was ready to scrupulously
respect Big Oil's legitimate rights. Through this clever campaign, Almazán succeeded in getting the backing of many important elements
in Mexican society. His campaign also created a split within the ruling
Party of the Mexican Revolution (PRM) and laid the groundwork for a
reversal of Cárdenas's policies.[60]

Northern Mexican industrialists were solidly behind Almazán, and,
of course, he had the backing of the foreign oil companies. He had
the support of Catholic organizations because of his promise to allow
church-operated schools. The major newspapers that regularly printed
Standard Oil handouts and the middle classes were largely on his
side, and even some of Mexico's powerful army generals supported
him. Further, Almazán had good political connections in the United
States through outgoing American vice president John Garner, a good
friend. Most important, he had the solid support of the Mexican right,
and many of the men backing Almazán were ardent supporters of
General Franco. The Spanish fascist government was a major booster

of Almazán and in August 1940 described Almazán as "the future Mexican President, friend of Franco."[61]

The Mexican fascist organizations were very active in the Almazán organization, with German, Italian, and Spanish agents playing prominent roles in his campaign. The fascists had learned that Cárdenas's chosen candidate for president of Mexico, Avila Camacho, was preparing to strengthen Mexico's links with the United States. As part of this change in policy, Camacho planned to shut down the German smuggling and espionage operations. Because Camacho's plans were a threat to Davis's operations, Davis became involved with Big Oil's Almazán intrigue. On learning of the connection between Davis and Almazán, Roosevelt asked the FBI to place Davis under surveillance again and to keep the president informed of Davis's activities.[62]

On February 12, 1940, Ambassador Daniels reported that Davis, working in collusion with other oil companies, was smuggling arms to Mexico. The arms were to support a coup attempt by Almazán if he were defeated at the polls. Daniels's report said that the arms smuggling operation was using "Pacific Fruit Express refrigerator railway cars . . . each loaded with arms . . . under the floor of these cars . . . [and] large sums of oil money are being paid out on the border for protection" of the arms smuggling. Moreover, there were disturbing reports that German businessmen in Mexico were contributing large amounts to the Almazán campaign. This money supposedly was not for the campaign but for a revolt planned to follow Almazán's defeat in the election. In the spring, as election day approached, there were rumors of heavy arms smuggling across the U.S. border and of a coming march against Mexico City or the establishment of an independent government in northern Mexico by Almazán followers. The British Foreign Office was speculating that Cárdenas's successor might never take office because "events may occur during the period of uncertainty from July to December (most Mexican revolutions start at the beginning of the dry season in November)."[63]

Ironically, Almazán's opponent, Camacho, was neither a fire-breathing leftist nor a charismatic populist. Cárdenas had been expected to support his longtime political ally, Francisco Múgica, champion of the left wing of the ruling PRM. However, Cárdenas was under intense foreign and domestic pressure because the Mexican economy was in a grave crisis due to the war in Europe, which blocked oil exports and caused rampant inflation. Faced with the possibility of a united big-business and foreign Big Oil front, and with part of his own army against him, Cárdenas had decided in early 1939 to slow the pace of reform. He, therefore, supported his secretary of defense, Camacho, a moderate and traditionalist Roman Catholic.[64]

Camacho had resigned from his post as secretary of national defense in the Mexican government in early 1939 to focus on his campaign. He had the blessing of some of the more conservative elements in the PRM, but despite this conservative support, he also received the endorsement of the leftist Lombardo Toledano, who believed Camacho would carry on the progressive program of Cárdenas. Cárdenas and Toledano's support for Camacho over other moderate candidates was not surprising because Camacho had been a close friend of Cárdenas since 1920 and was a childhood friend of Toledano. Other endorsements followed and on November 3, 1939, Camacho won the nomination of the PRM.[65]

Camacho went on to defeat Almazán in the presidential election on July 7. Following his defeat, Almazán claimed that there had been widespread fraud and that force had been used to prevent his supporters from voting. Almazán also claimed to have polled 90 percent of the total votes and that he intended to take office on December 1, 1940. Although the elections may have been rigged, it is unlikely that he would have received 90 percent of the vote.

Having left the country not long after the election, Almazán sought the support of American financiers and political leaders for his cause and used San Antonio, Texas, as his base of operations. The U.S. consul in Monterrey, Mexico, began hearing rumors that Almazán was plotting a "Franco-type" coup and he reported that a rebellion was probable. Almazán claimed that the oil companies promised him $200,000 to buy arms and that Elliot Roosevelt, the president's conservative son, who was a heavy investor in the oil industry, had agreed to use his Texas radio stations to support an Almazán revolt. Meanwhile, Almazán's followers set up a "rump congress" in Mexico City.[66]

On Mexican Independence Day, September 16, 1940, crowds in front of the presidential palace in Mexico City began shouting for General Almazán. The police violently dispersed the crowd, leaving five men dead and seventy-two people wounded. On the same day, in northern Chihuahua, Lt. Col. Cruz Villalba led 700 men into the hills, but his revolt fizzled. Two weeks later on October 1, 1940, a widespread plot in the name of General Almazán was foiled when police burst into a building in Monterrey from which about 200 conspirators were about to set out. In an exchange of shots, the reputed inspirer of the plot, Brig. Gen. Andreas Zazosa was shot dead. A close friend of General Almazán, he was said to have entered Mexico from Texas clandestinely a few days before the revolt began. He planned to seize the town hall, police station, power station, and principal federal buildings. The outbreak in Monterrey coincided with various movements by small rebel bands in several parts of northern Mexico, but the military authorities quickly had the situation in hand and restored calm.[67]

Although Almazán's initial moves to overthrow Cárdenas had failed, the Mexican government was worried that Almazán's movement would grow in strength. In response to this insurgent activity, President Cárdenas's government began more conciliatory policies toward the expropriated oil companies. President-elect Avila Camacho appropriated much of Almazán's program in an attempt to win over his supporters. Camacho pledged not to introduce further reforms and promised to encourage foreign investment. Consequently, a number of Almazánistas, including Gen. Emilio Madero, president of the Almazánista political party, came over to Camacho's side.[68]

The Mexican congress on September 23, 1940, announced a 16-to-1 majority vote for Camacho as president. In November, President Roosevelt announced that vice president elect Wallace would be his representative to Camacho's inauguration, which signaled to the Mexican right that the United States would not support an insurrection against Camacho. The Roosevelt administration was not willing to encourage Almazán because of his known fascist sympathizers. On November 27, with prospects for a revolution unlikely given the government's recognition of Camacho's election, Almazán, who had returned to Mexico, renounced his claim to the presidency, thus ending the rightist challenge to Cárdenas.[69]

In 1940, as the British and American blockade began to tighten around Mexico, Davis traveled to and from Mexico purchasing mercury (fulminate of mercury was used to make bomb detonators) and other strategic minerals and sending them on Japanese ships to Germany. Because mercury was much more valuable, pound for pound, than oil, it would take fewer ships to transport and would be easier to get through the British blockade to Germany. In the fall, two Davis agents, Alberto Cuevas and Frederico Franco Arch, made inquiries in Mexico about buying or leasing mines that produced war metals: mica, sulfur, mercury, tungsten, antimony, and molybdenum. According to the manager of his Mexican subsidiary, Davis wanted to buy one ton of mercury per week.[70]

In the summer of 1940, in an expansion of his efforts to bust the blockade, Davis chartered five ships, which he operated between

Mexico and Vladivostok for the transshipment of mercury and other minerals to Germany by the Trans-Siberian Railway. Financing for the purchase of these ships came from Davis's new banking connection with Harris Trust Bank of Chicago, Illinois. Over several months, these ships transported considerable quantities of war metals to Germany from Manzanillo on Mexico's Pacific Coast. The traffic was especially heavy in mercury, which was at a premium price on the world market.[71]

In the meantime, Hertslet prepared to leave Mexico, but before doing so he organized the transfer of German funds from the United States to South America to prevent the U.S. government from freezing the bank accounts. With the assistance of the head of Bank of Mexico, Montes de Oca (who had been Almazán's campaign treasurer), Hertslet completed this final task. Soon after, he left Mexico for Japan on September 24, 1940.[72]

Despite Hertslet's move to Tokyo, he continued to play a role in Mexico. With the success of Davis's mercury venture, Hertslet formulated a plan for the Japanese to act as a major conduit for German barter trade with Mexico. The German's plan was to trade Mexican mica, tungsten, mercury, and antimony for Japanese rayon. Hertslet sent K. Von Walfeld, German commercial attaché in Tokyo, to Mexico in December 1940 with a Japanese trade commission to present Hertslet's plan to the Mexican government.[73]

With a new smuggling scheme in the works, Davis decided to go to Europe to put in place the German end of the business. On January 10, 1941, he asked the U.S. State Department for a passport for himself and Erna Wehrle to visit various European countries, including Germany. However, by 1941 the Roosevelt administration's attitude toward Davis was cold and suspicious and the State Department denied the request. The State Department also leaked information to the press on Davis's Mexican activities. In typical fashion, Davis emphatically denied the story. He said that he was "not dealing in war materials, or foreign business of any kind whatsoever. Moreover, I have no intention of going anywhere outside of the United States."[74]

Despite the seeming success of the Hertslet-Davis smuggling operation, its days were numbered, as the Mexican government began to put pressure on the undercover traffic. U.S.-Japanese relations were deteriorating markedly and Washington informed the Mexicans that it was not pleased with the Japanese oil shipments. Wanting to discourage American support for Almazán's insurgent activities, the Mexican government offered in the summer of 1940 to embargo the shipment of strategic minerals to the Axis powers.[75]

As a quid pro quo, the United States agreed, "in view of circumstances presently impending," to go along with the Mexican proposal to settle the oil conflict by appointing a joint commission to work out a compromise. The diplomatic phrase about the circumstances obviously referred to the accelerating pace of the German and Japanese threat to the world balance of power. The Axis threat was the paramount consideration in the American decision to negotiate with the Mexicans.

Responding to the American overture, the Mexican government canceled its export contracts with Japan on October 24 and rescinded the Japanese concessions to drill for oil in Mexico. By the end of the year the Hertslet-Davis-Japanese smuggling route was drying up. On December 20, just after Camacho took office as Mexico's president, the German ambassador, Baron Von Rüdt, cabled Berlin that the Mexicans had just told him that the oil traffic via Vladivostok would no longer be permitted.[76]

With the Mexican government actively opposing his operations, Davis's oil smuggling adventure ended, although he slipped out a few more cargoes during the next six months. When Hitler invaded Russia in June 1941, Davis's shipments of oil to Germany via Vladivostok came to a stop. Bulk cargoes such as oil and strategic minerals were just too difficult to slip by the now-vigilant British and American eyes, and Davis's blockade-running days were over.[77]

Hertslet's connection to Mexico also came to an end when his wife left Acapulco, Mexico, in April 1941 to join him in Japan. Soon after she arrived, he was ordered to return to Germany. War was imminent with Russia, and the German Economics Ministry did not want a person who they considered "indispensable for the providing of material of military importance" stranded on the other side of the globe. Hertslet made his way to Manchuria and from there returned to Berlin via the Trans-Siberian Railway.[78]

Davis had spent one and one-half years trying to slip oil and other strategic minerals through the British blockade to Germany. Sweden, Holland, Italy, Spain, Japan, and the Soviet Union had all been conduits for his smuggling. Despite this activity, most of these affairs did not amount to much. Only the circuitous route through Russia resulted in large amounts of oil reaching Germany, and even this route was good for only slightly more than a year. Nor were the smuggling operations critical to the survival of his oil enterprise. His Rincon oil field was the true savior of his business. Without this new source of wealth, Davis's company would no doubt have collapsed. The most that can be said for the smuggling operations is that they may have sustained Davis through early 1940 until he began to acquire money from the Rincon field. The smuggling was only marginally profitable and was clearly risky to the long-term viability of his company because the activities attracted the notice and active displeasure of both the American and British governments. Why did a man who was always most concerned with his own profits take on this smuggling?

Although the smuggling itself was only marginally useful to sustaining his business, it had other financial benefits. Through the spring of 1940, the Germans continued to make substantial cash payments to Davis when he most needed those payments to keep his business alive. However, the Germans expected Davis to reciprocate for their assistance by helping them smuggle oil out of Mexico to Germany. They also expected his participation in their espionage activities. Therefore, Davis at first had strong monetary incentives to aid the Germans in their smuggling operations.

When the Rincon field began operating, these financial imperatives disappeared and the importance of the Mexican operations declined. But Davis continued his assistance to the Germans, probably because he had become intoxicated by visions of a victorious Nazi hegemony where he would become master of the world oil trade. In 1940–41, Germany was at the peak of its power and it seemed on the verge of conquering Europe. Davis was always a man with big plans and large ambitions. Given his attraction to the Nazi idea of a world dominated by a master race and his gambler's personality, he was willing to carry out risky and unprofitable smuggling and espionage operations because he believed that the Germans were on the brink of winning the war. In the process he was making powerful enemies.[79]

By 1940 British intelligence knew not only that Davis was behind numerous attempts to smuggle oil into Germany but also that he was carrying out espionage assignments for the Abwehr. He had gone from just being a Nazi fellow traveler to a full-fledged German agent. His entire international business network was at the service of German espionage and he had drawn many of his top employees into the web of German intelligence. He was no longer just an irritating nuisance to British foreign policy; Davis had become a mortal enemy of the British war effort. Although the British could not get their hands on Davis and could not prove he was engaged in illegal activities, they most certainly were looking for ways to restrain this adversary.

Davis might have survived if he had gone no further with his pro-German efforts. The British were no doubt hesitant to destroy Davis because he was a well-known and powerful American businessman with important political connections, but his hubris provided the

British with their opportunity. He did not stop his pro-German operations; his newfound wealth and his belief in ultimate German victory
gave him both the means and the motivation to continue with this
dangerous behavior. Finally, he undermined his political protection by
attacking the most powerful politician in the United States: Franklin
D. Roosevelt.[80]

ten

Defeat Roosevelt

GERMANY'S MOST IMPORTANT objective with regard to the United States from 1939 to 1941 was to encourage American isolationism.[1] Officials in Berlin reasoned correctly that they should not take on the United States while trying to consolidate Germany's hold over Europe.

The main obstacle to their plans was President Roosevelt. They saw him as a dangerous enemy whose declared neutrality was merely a political maneuver. The Nazis believed that Roosevelt's sole reason for remaining neutral was his inability to turn a majority of the American people against Germany. They believed that once Roosevelt had the backing of Congress he would declare war on Germany.[2]

Thus, the chief goal of the Germans in America in 1939–40 was to defeat President Roosevelt in the 1940 election. German foreign minister Ribbentrop said that it was "essential to defeat Roosevelt because he, more than any other American, was capable of making sweeping political decisions" that could be damaging to Nazi Germany.[3]

The Nazis organized a multifaceted effort to prevent President Roosevelt's reelection. Two major players in this effort were William Rhodes Davis and John L. Lewis. As Ribbentrop said, "in attempting to influence the 1940 election against Roosevelt, we made use of (the) oil man Davis. In the 1940 elections we placed our faith in Lewis, that he would oppose the re-election of Roosevelt. Davis and Hertslet worked with Lewis."[4]

Before the destruction of his peace plan, Davis had been satisfied with the continuance of a New Deal administration in Washington. He had significant political influence in the liberal establishment through Guffey, Walter Jones, and Lewis. His close associate, Walter Jones, told Harold Ickes over a long lunch on August 9, 1939, that he (Jones) wanted a liberal for president. Jones said that although he opposed a third term for Roosevelt, he would support Roosevelt if the president ran for a third term. In the summer of 1939, Jones was still on good terms with the Roosevelt administration. In fact, James Farley, who chaired the national Democratic Party, asked Jones if he would consider running for the presidency if Roosevelt decided not to seek reelection. Jones said he did not believe he could be elected.[5]

Despite Jones's blandishments about Roosevelt, Davis was already considering how to defeat Roosevelt before the president rejected his "peace plan." Davis had first broached the subject of destroying Roosevelt at his conference with Goering in early October 1939. Davis described to Goering his plans to defeat Roosevelt in 1940 by exploiting Lewis's influence to split the labor vote. Davis said that Lewis single-handedly could determine the outcome of the 1940 presidential election by his sway over the unions. Moreover, the Democratic Party was incapable of conducting a successful national political campaign without substantial backing from Lewis.[6]

According to Davis, if Roosevelt persisted in supporting the British in their war against Germany, Lewis intended to bring about Roosevelt's downfall by opposing his reelection. Davis guaranteed that Lewis would openly oppose Roosevelt if the president deviated from strict neutrality. Goering said that Davis "presented himself as a very good friend of John L. Lewis. . . . Davis told me that by use of his influence on Lewis, he could influence the elections in such a manner so the re-election of Roosevelt, which, in his opinion, would mean war, would be prevented." Goering's response to Davis's plan was very clear. He wanted President Roosevelt defeated in 1940.[7]

Goering said that Davis suggested that he could obtain

strong political influence by way of Lewis by letting him have
certain sums for that purpose. He was willing to put millions of
his own money into the scheme to have Lewis help him defeat
Roosevelt, but added that he would need additional support from
the Germans. He further stated that in the event he was successful in having Roosevelt defeated, he [Davis] wanted to become
Secretary of State.

After consulting with Hitler, Goering gave Davis the go-ahead and
promised that if Roosevelt did not agree to end the war, Germany
would provide millions of dollars for the "defeat Roosevelt" project.[8]

However, despite Davis's plans to destroy Roosevelt, he had not
quite given up on the president. After the peace plan debacle, Jones,
acting as a go-between for Lewis and Davis, had lunch with Ickes on
November 19. He told Ickes that Lewis would still support the administration if he was handled in the right way. Jones said that he was
also prepared to go along with a third term for Roosevelt. Ickes considered Jones an important supporter and later discussed Jones's comments with the president. However, nothing came of these overtures
because Roosevelt had no use for the Davis-Lewis peace plan, which
was central to gaining their support for his reelection.[9]

When the president refused to participate in Davis's peace plan,
the "defeat Roosevelt" drive was launched. Erna Wehrle said that
Davis was convinced "that Roosevelt was driving America to war and
it was time to get him out of office." Incensed by Roosevelt's refusal to
get personally involved with Davis's peace plan, Lewis agreed to work
closely with Davis to defeat Roosevelt. Davis and Lewis would meet
many times during the next year to carry out their plan and they developed a sense of mutual confidence.[10]

Lewis, in October 1939, seized an early opportunity to lash out at
the president. The occasion was a proposal, conceived by Roosevelt
administration officials, for a conference of progressives from eleven
western states to consider future political action. In a sharply worded
letter to California governor Culbert Olson, Lewis denounced "secret
plans to use the conference to launch a third-term boom" and ordered
a CIO boycott of the gathering.[11]

Many union leaders believed that what really angered Lewis about
the conference was the omission of Senator Burton Kendall Wheeler
from the list of dignitaries invited to the conference. Lewis had
already decided to back the isolationist Democratic senator from

Montana as a candidate for president in the 1940 elections to replace his enemy, Roosevelt.[12]

Wheeler, an attractive candidate, was in the forefront of the isolationists in the Senate, was popular throughout the western states, and had friends in both labor and business. By November, Wheeler-for-President clubs were operating in several states and Wheeler let it be known that he was considering a run for the presidency.[13]

Soon after, Lewis tried to boost Wheeler's candidacy by inviting him to be the featured speaker at the UMW's Fiftieth Anniversary Convention in late January. Lewis's intention was to get the union to adopt a resolution endorsing Wheeler as its presidential candidate. To set the stage for Wheeler's endorsement, Lewis went public with his quarrel with Roosevelt on January 24, recommended that the UMW refrain from endorsing Roosevelt for a third term, and predicted "ignominious defeat" for Roosevelt if the Democrats renominated him.[14,15]

Despite Lewis's blast at Roosevelt, his plans went awry; the UMW convention refused to endorse Wheeler. The best Lewis could get from his own union membership was the withholding of an endorsement of Roosevelt. This incident indicated that Lewis's control over the labor movement was limited and that Davis's plan to defeat Roosevelt through Lewis might not succeed.

The next move in Davis's political campaign was to destroy Senator Joseph Guffey, who had backed away from Davis in the late fall of 1939 when Davis and Lewis began efforts to block Roosevelt's reelection. Guffey had been increasingly nervous through the summer of 1939 because of the public exposure of his involvement with Davis in the Mexican-German oil trade.

Early in the summer, Marquis Childs, an investigative reporter for the *St. Louis Post-Dispatch*, had been leaked information by the State Department[16] on the activities of Guffey, Lewis, and Davis in Mexico. Childs had then published an embarrassing exposé of Guffey's activities that June in the *St. Louis Post-Dispatch*. At the end of July, Republican U.S. senator H. Styles Bridges of New Hampshire announced that he intended to seek a Senate investigation of Guffey's role in the Mexican oil affair. Bridges charged on the Senate floor that if Childs's newspaper story was true, then Guffey was in violation of the Logan Act because Guffey had negotiated an oil deal with Mexico while Mexico was in a dispute with the U.S. government over the oil nationalization.[17]

Guffey, his voice straining with anger, termed the newspaper story "100 per cent false, malicious, character-destroying lie. I have dealt with reporters for 25 years and this is the first time I have had one send such a character-destroying lie." Guffey charged that the author of the newspaper story had "received compensation for sending that story out (other) than that which he receives from his regular employer. He was paid for writing that article." Saying that "I have nothing to conceal," Guffey demanded "to have all the facts brought out."[18]

Despite his angry denial, Guffey was worried by the newspaper report because the story was true. Moreover, all the major newspapers picked up the denunciation of Senator Bridges and the entire country became aware of Guffey's Mexican intrigue. His anxiety only increased when a few days later Marquis Childs filed a $50,000 slander suit against Guffey, charging that Guffey had injured his professional reputation when he accused Childs of taking a bribe to write the story. Guffey knew that he would have to retract his charges against Childs at some point or risk a trial where his behind-the-scenes machinations would come out. Either way, Guffey knew the story would be powerful ammunition for potential opponents in his upcoming 1940 reelection campaign.[19]

In late October, Guffey's anxiety was turned into near hysteria when Davis told him that an FBI man had been to his office in New York and told him that the FBI was going to get Davis, Lewis, and Guffey. Guffey immediately went to see Frank Murphy, the U.S. attorney general, on October 26, and asked him if the Justice Department was having the FBI investigate him. Murphy told him there was no FBI investigation of the senator but perhaps his name had come up as part of an investigation of Walter Jones.[20]

Not satisfied with this answer, Guffey met with Adolf Berle on October 28 and demanded to know why Berle had the FBI investigating him. Berle told Guffey that he had nothing to do with any FBI investigation of the senator. Berle added that he understood there was some interest in Davis and suggested that perhaps Davis had used the senator's name. Guffey lied and claimed that he barely knew Davis and had had nothing to do with him for many years.[21]

Guffey followed up his meeting with Berle by calling J. Edgar Hoover, who repeated what Berle and Murphy had said. He suggested that Davis was jittery and was trying to solicit Guffey's aid by making it appear that Guffey was also under investigation. Berle, Hoover, and Murphy were all probably telling the truth, that there was no direct investigation of Guffey. It would have been too politically dangerous for the FBI to directly inquire about a U.S. senator. As in the case of John L. Lewis, the FBI could monitor Guffey through its surveillance of Davis.[22]

With the FBI trailing him around Washington, Guffey began to have serious reservations about his connection to Davis. When Davis and Lewis started maneuvering to stop Roosevelt's reelection, Berle saw his chance to put an end to Guffey's cooperation with Davis. With Guffey in a state of panic, Berle arranged a secret meeting with him to show him information that the FBI had collected on his activities with Davis. Threatened with exposure, Guffey, despite his close ties to Lewis, broke off contact with both Davis and Lewis and agreed to work for Roosevelt's reelection.[23]

Retribution from Davis soon followed. All the support Guffey had previously received from Lewis vanished and Davis decided to unseat Guffey in the upcoming April Democratic primary. In February 1940, Davis, acting through Walter Jones, paid about $60,000 to a representative of a Pennsylvania Democratic faction. The purpose of the payment was to promote a candidate for U.S. Senate in opposition to Senator Guffey. Then, in a bizarre political maneuver, Walter Jones on March 4 filed for the Senate seat of his longtime friend, Joseph Guffey. Davis's money had been put to good use because in the week after filing for the Senate seat, Jones learned that he had the support of at least thirty of the sixty-seven county chairmen in the April 23 Democratic Party primary election.[24]

A few days later, on March 12, Guffey opened his campaign for renomination and took the opportunity to retract his charge that Marquis Childs had been paid to write his story on Guffey. Guffey said that the facts in the story "were substantially correct, but the interpretation placed on it was entirely wrong." He apologized to Childs and said that he deeply regretted his charge: "It was an injustice to him and I ask permission to withdraw it."[25]

Despite Davis and Lewis backing Jones's campaign, their attack on Guffey ended in failure. Two weeks before the primary election, all of the major Pennsylvania newspapers printed a story by Marquis Childs on Walter Jones's close links to Davis and the Mexican-German oil trade. Quoting liberally from a letter written by Davis to Ben Smith, Childs made a strong case that Jones was a puppet of the Nazi-tainted Davis. Reached by reporters on the campaign trail, Jones declined to either confirm or deny Childs's allegations. Jones knew that he could not talk about his connections to Davis because anything he said would only makes matters worse.

The story was devastating to Jones's election campaign because it showed him succoring the Nazi war machine just as the Germans invaded Norway and Denmark. Hounded by these allegations, Jones's campaign collapsed. Guffey won the Democratic nomination and went on to be reelected in the fall. This was a double disaster for Davis because not only had he lost the political influence of a powerful senator but also he had made Guffey an implacable enemy as well.[26]

It is not known for certain how Childs obtained a copy of a private letter from Davis to Ben Smith. He did not get the letter from Davis and there is no reason to believe that Smith would give him a copy. The most likely source of the letter was Adolf Berle. Childs was a conduit for Berle's leaks of information that were aimed at discrediting Davis. Berle also had close links to the FBI, and it is known that the FBI was reporting to Berle on all of Davis's activities and was opening Davis's mail. It is likely that the FBI intercepted this letter from Davis to Smith and sent a copy to Berle. Berle in turn passed a copy on to Childs as part of Berle's efforts to discredit Davis.

If this conjecture is valid, then several other questions arise. Was Berle repaying Guffey because Guffey had abandoned the Davis cabal? Was Berle the originator of the plan to destroy Jones or was President Roosevelt involved? It is known that Berle kept Roosevelt informed about Davis's activities and that Roosevelt took a personal interest in Davis's schemes. It is possible that Roosevelt personally okayed the Jones ambush.

As long as it seemed that Roosevelt would not seek a third term, the Germans concentrated on encouraging Lewis to promote Senator Wheeler, an isolationist, for the presidency. However, in February 1940, Hans Thomsen, the German chargé d'affaires in Washington, informed the German Foreign Ministry that the odds in favor of a third-term bid by Roosevelt "have greatly increased" and "it is necessary to reckon with his re-election next fall." Responding to this information, Goering told Joachim Hertslet to go to the United States and assist Davis in stopping Roosevelt's reelection. From his new post in Mexico City, Hertslet contacted Davis and other isolationists and told them he was coming to the United States.

Hertslet was spotted leaving Mexico City by airplane for the United States on March 17 by U.S. naval intelligence, who immediately notified the State Department and Adolf Berle. Berle, in turn, asked the FBI to follow Hertslet everywhere he went in the United States. Curiously, Hertslet gained entry to America using an old visa (valid until July 11, 1940), which allowed short visits to the United States. Hertslet had obtained this visa with the aid of Lewis, who provided the State Department with an affidavit guaranteeing the "maintenance" of Hertslet in the United States. Why did the American government not revoke Hertslet's visa? It could be that Berle and the FBI wanted him to enter the United States so that they could follow him and find out who he contacted.[27]

On his way to Washington, Hertslet stayed overnight in Houston, Texas. Davis, who was in Houston developing his new Rincon oil field, met him at the airport. Hertslet stayed in a hotel room reserved by Davis, and the following day Davis, his wife, and Erna Wehrle accompanied Hertslet to Washington.[28]

Significantly, Hertslet's first stop in Washington was not the German embassy, but John L. Lewis's office in the UMW building where Davis introduced him to the famous labor leader. Only after visiting Lewis did he call at his embassy. Hertslet's priorities speak volumes about the importance of Lewis to German plans.[29]

The German embassy knew nothing about Hertslet's mission, and embassy officials were at first dubious about his claim that he was on official government business. Only after the German Foreign Office in Berlin vouched for Hertslet did Thomsen, the head of the German mission, agree to meet with him. Hertslet told Thomsen that he was in the United States to implement a plan of Goering's to support John L. Lewis's opposition to Roosevelt. Thomsen said that Hertslet told him that "he knew John L. Lewis personally very well, and that he could exercise a lot of influence on the trend of American politics. . . . He said that his influence with Mr. Lewis was strong enough to make the election run against Roosevelt. He said through Lewis he could swing the election against Roosevelt." Hertslet told Thomsen that he had at his disposal $5 million to implement this plan.[30]

Hoping to broaden the extent of his operations and tap Thomsen's widespread contacts with American isolationists, Hertslet suggested that "it would be a practical political idea" if the embassy would join him and Davis "to boost Mr. Lewis." However, Thomsen, envious of Hertslet's control of this enormous $5 million fund, which was many times the funds under Thomsen's control, tried to persuade Goering to recall Hertslet and turn the Lewis operation over to him. When Goering rebuffed Thomsen, he refused to work with Hertslet. The two Germans soon went their separate ways, unwilling to coordinate their efforts to defeat Roosevelt.[31]

Hertslet left Washington for New York on March 23 and stayed at Davis's home in Scarsdale. At an evening conference at Davis's home, Hertslet had a long discussion with John L. Lewis about the upcoming elections. Through the evening and part of the following day, they talked about Davis's Berlin discussions with Goering. Davis informed Lewis that he had told Goering that Lewis had the support of 10 million workers and could use this support against Roosevelt. Lewis agreed with this assessment of his power. After their discussions, Lewis announced that he would come out against the reelection of Roosevelt.[32]

Lewis's meeting with Hertslet is the most damning piece of evidence that he was in league with the Germans. He most certainly knew that he was meeting with a representative of the Nazi government and that they were jointly plotting to determine the outcome of an American election. Whether he also knew of the German funds for his anti-Roosevelt campaign is not known. Even if he did not know about the money, such a meeting with a Nazi official was clearly a traitorous act by Lewis, both to his country and in the long run to the workers he claimed to represent.[33]

With the conclusion of this successful meeting with Lewis, Davis asked Hertslet to arrange to get the funds Goering had guaranteed for the "defeat Roosevelt" campaign. This request was not easy to fulfill. To pay for Davis's scheme, Hertslet needed U.S. currency, and wartime restrictions on currency transfers made it difficult to get funds from Europe.[34] Fortunately for Hertslet, the Italians had money in New York that had been sent from Rome to finance fascist espionage and propaganda in the United States. Goering persuaded the Italians to let Hertslet have part of this money in exchange for favors in Europe. An Italian courier, Luigi Podestá,[35] took $5 million to the German consulate in New York. After receiving the funds, the German consulate general in New York, Hans Borchers, with two bodyguards, took the money to the German embassy in Washington.[36]

Returning to Washington on March 26, Hertslet's first stop was the German embassy, where he told Thomsen that Lewis would oppose Roosevelt's reelection. Thomsen observed that Lewis's opposition could be of critical importance, controlling perhaps 8–10 million votes. Thomsen also calculated that Lewis was acting "not . . . because of any pro-German sentiments, but because he fears that America's involvement in a war would mean the establishment of an American dictatorship and the placing of his organization under emergency laws."[37]

Hertslet also asked Thomsen to send a telegram to Berlin requesting that active sabotage campaigns not be conducted in the United States and that all secret agents engaged in such activities be withdrawn from the United States. Hertslet was concerned that these activities would severely damage his plans for keeping the United States out of the war through political means. It is doubtful that the Abwehr paid any attention to Hertslet's request.[38]

In the meantime Davis and Wehrle had arrived in Washington to take charge of the German funds that had been transferred from New York. After checking into the Mayflower Hotel on March 28, Davis received part of the money from Hertslet. Davis opened accounts for the funds in Bank of Boston, Irving Trust of New York, Bank of America, and Banco Germany of Mexico City. Davis immediately left Washington for New York on the evening train, with Hertslet seeing him off at the train station. As a token of his esteem, Davis furnished Hertslet with a Cadillac limousine for the duration of the German's stay in Washington.[39]

After a few more days of business in Washington, Hertslet flew back to New York on April 5 and stayed in Erna Wehrle's apartment on 68th Street in Manhattan. He frequented the German consulate in New York, and met with Davis and Wehrle at the Davis and Company New York headquarters in Rockefeller Plaza. What Hertslet was doing in New York is unknown, but most likely it involved his Mexican smuggling operations.[40]

The FBI followed Hertslet everywhere he went in New York and placed both Wehrle's and Davis's residences, as well as the Davis and Company offices, under surveillance. Hertslet eventually spotted the FBI agents and, in typical spy novel fashion, the FBI agents were in turn followed by German agents as Hertslet traveled around New York. Hertslet left New York on April 9 for Washington. Having completed his mission for Goering, he returned to Mexico on April 12 on a ticket paid for by Davis and Company.[41]

As Hertslet returned to Mexico, the "phony war" in Europe ended with successive Nazi victories in Denmark, Norway, Holland, Belgium, and France in April, May, and June 1940. These rapid conquests stepped up the tempo of the great debate over foreign policy in the United States. Suddenly, the Atlantic Ocean did not look so broad to many Americans. Where six months before most Americans were opposed to taking sides in the war, public opinion polls now showed a majority favoring active aid to Great Britain.[42]

However, many Americans still opposed Roosevelt's antifascist support for Great Britain. These isolationists argued that the war in Europe was not an apocalyptic struggle between democracy and fascism, but just another bloody page in European power politics. Because the United States had no stake in such a conflict, the isolationists thought it better to do business with Hitler. Charles Lindbergh, the famous aviator and a leading isolationist, maintained that an accommodation with Germany "could maintain peace and civilization throughout the world as far into the future as we can see."

This quarrel over foreign policy was exacerbated by the presidential campaign. The isolationists were vitally interested in keeping the country out of the war and hoped that the presidential campaign of 1940 would give the electorate an opportunity for a clear-cut decision on U.S. foreign policy. In the spring of 1940, when it looked as if Roosevelt might not seek a third term, John L. Lewis promoted Senator Wheeler as a progressive and isolationist alternative.[43]

On May 1, Senator Wheeler announced his willingness to become a candidate for president "if Roosevelt did not seek another term." Wheeler had a prominent reputation as a progressive leader and had been nominated vice president on the Independent Progressive Party slate with Robert LaFollette in 1924. Influential Senator Norris had already announced that if Roosevelt did not run Wheeler would be his choice for the nomination. In addition, the railroad unions and the teamsters were on the verge of declaring for him. Lewis gave his public endorsement to Senator Wheeler for the Democratic nomination and did what he could to assist the Montana senator. Lewis's support included more than $1 million that he pledged to give Wheeler when the time was right. With this backing, Wheeler appeared to stand a good chance of gaining the nomination.[44]

But the time was not right for Wheeler's Democratic candidacy. By the end of May, Roosevelt had decided to run for an unprecedented third term. With the collapse of France and the threatened German invasion of England, Roosevelt felt he must stay in office in this time of crisis. With Roosevelt in complete control of the Democratic party apparatus, Wheeler had no chance of gaining the Democratic Party's nomination.[45]

In response to Roosevelt's decision, Lewis considered forming a third "Peace" party of anti-Roosevelt Democrats and running Wheeler for president. He had the backing of various liberal groups, including the National Association for the Advancement of Colored People, the Townsend Old-Age Pension groups, and the American Youth Congress. Wheeler was amenable to the proposal and announced, "I do not want to have to break with the Democratic Party, I shall break with it if it is going to be a war party."[46]

White House officials regarded Wheeler's growing importance as the isolationist spokesman, evidenced by his appearance on the cover of *Time* magazine in April, as genuinely dangerous to the president's chances of reelection. There was deep concern over the possibility of a Wheeler third-party candidacy throughout the spring and summer. With Wheeler's declaration that a "new and great antiwar party" would be formed unless the Democrats pledged not to send American soldiers "to a foreign shore" and with Lewis's full support of a "peace party," the White House envisioned Roosevelt coming in second in a three-way race.[47]

However, nothing came of Lewis's scheme because most other union leaders refused to support his proposal. They argued that despite Roosevelt's shortcomings, a third party would give the election to the Republican candidate, who would be much worse than Roosevelt. Without labor's critical support, Lewis's scheme never got off the ground.[48]

Despite Lewis's failure to stop Roosevelt from seeking a third term, Goering did not refrain from trying to cultivate Lewis. He instructed Hertslet to return to the United States and raise with Lewis the possibility of organizing a general strike in the United States if American intervention in the war appeared likely. Although this request must have seemed farfetched to Hertslet, with the additional urging of Davis to assist in his efforts to influence the Republican convention, Hertslet agreed. Hertslet flew from Mexico City on June 25 (just before the start of the Republican convention in Philadelphia) and arrived in Washington the next day. The FBI closely monitored his trip.[49]

The Germans had many plans for influencing the American political party conventions. On the eve of the Republican national convention, they mounted "a well camouflaged lightning propaganda campaign" in the major newspapers to support the isolationists. They also paid a Republican congressman $3,000 for rounding up a contingent of fifty isolationist Republican congressmen to go to the Republican convention in Philadelphia in June and vote for a isolationist plank in the party's platform.[50]

At the conclusion of the Republican convention on June 30, the foreign policy plank of the party was firmly opposed to U.S. involvement in the war. The Germans were pleased with this position, especially because it was taken almost verbatim from the German-instigated full-page advertisements placed in the *New York Times* and other major American newspapers just before the start of the convention.[51]

Lewis and Wheeler also appeared at the Republican convention. Lewis, without advance notice, spoke to the convention's Resolution Committee. The Republicans sat in silence when Lewis demanded to know what they intended to do about unemployment, but then cheered when Lewis denounced Roosevelt's proposal to introduce military conscription. He was followed by Wheeler, who described Roosevelt's plans for introducing a military draft as "a fantastic suggestion from a mind in full retreat."[52]

Despite the Germans' success with the foreign policy plank and

Lewis and Wheeler's appearances, the Republican convention did not end well for the Germans. The convention blew up in the faces of the isolationist old guard. The party's convention delegates nominated an internationalist who represented eastern big business, Wendell Willkie, for president. Willkie overwhelmed the convention with a slick operation that lined up delegates with a media blitz and used his Wall Street connections behind the scenes to garner votes.[53]

With the FBI following him and the Republican convention over, Hertslet decided it was best to return to Mexico. His visa would expire on July 11, so he would have to leave soon anyway. As he reported to Berlin, "continued presence here inadvisable due to strictest surveillance." Accompanied by Davis's friend, Nils Hansell, Hertslet flew to Mexico on July 1.[54]

Their partial success during the Republican convention encouraged the Germans to attempt a similar effort at the Democratic convention in Chicago the following month. Again, the principal goal was the incorporation of at least a formal pledge of nonintervention in the Democratic Party platform. Seeking to build up delegate strength, Davis had distributed $100,000 to buy approximately forty Pennsylvania delegates to vote against Roosevelt at the convention. The Nazi press adviser, Kurt Sell, arranged for several other Democratic congressmen to attend the convention on German embassy funds. Sell also financed a number of prominent antiwar advertisements, notably one in the *Chicago Tribune* on July 15, the opening day of the convention.[55]

It is difficult to estimate the impact of the Nazi strategy, but isolationist views certainly evoked wide sympathy among the delegates, and the Democratic Party platform announced: "We will not participate in foreign wars, and we will not send our army, naval or air forces to fight in foreign lands outside of the Americas." Up to this point, the platform could hardly have been better for the Germans than if it had been composed in Berlin. However, attached to the end of this statement were the words "except in case of attack." This phrase would have a mighty impact in December 1941.[56]

A little-known figure a few months before, Willkie was an enigma to the isolationists. He was the former president of a large southern utility company and had fought the creation of the Tennessee Valley Authority, one of the key components of the New Deal. He appealed to business by presenting himself as a businessman who had been victimized by the New Deal; he was not an old guard Republican. Although he was a magnate of one of the big utility companies whose office was just off Wall Street, he had grown up on an Indiana farm and actually still farmed his own land. He had been a lifelong Democrat who voted for Roosevelt in 1932 and had only recently changed his party affiliation. He accused Roosevelt of wanting to push America into the war. At the same time, Willkie backed aid to Great Britain. With a country-style haircut, his eloquent candor, and disheveled charm, he was the first Republican candidate since Teddy Roosevelt who appealed to the common man. Overall, he was a very atypical Republican leader.[57]

During the summer following Willkie's nomination, the isolationists tried to determine the character of this charismatic Republican nominee. Both Senator Wheeler and Colonel McCormick, owner of the rabidly isolationist *Chicago Tribune*, met with Willkie to try to draw from him a commitment against military conscription. Although Willkie did not unequivocally endorse the isolationist cause, he soon found that an antiwar message evoked a positive response from his audiences. The temptation to exploit this sentiment was difficult for Willkie to resist.[58]

Once he began campaigning across the country, Willkie quickly elicited an enthusiastic endorsement from millions of middle-class Americans tired of the New Deal and vexed that the depression was not over. Willkie's message of liberating business and reducing government regulation scored a hit with many independents and received the backing of such important newspapers as the *Cleveland Plain Dealer* and the *New York Times*. It was to be a long, noisy, sometimes nasty, campaign. Willkie was a good campaigner and isolationist sentiment was strong in the country. For all his continued popularity with the people, Roosevelt was by no means assured of victory.[59]

Although the Nazis knew that Willkie was not a friend of Germany, they also knew he would not be as zealously opposed to the German Reich as Roosevelt. Paul K. Schmidt, head of the press department of the German Foreign Office, said, "Both Ribbentrop and Hitler were of the opinion that any President would be better than Roosevelt." They believed "that Willkie would not be friendly to Germany but would not be as energetically opposed" as Roosevelt.[60]

The Germans decided to surreptitiously help Willkie through secret contributions to the various pro-Willkie political clubs. To avoid the political ruin of their American friends should the Americans seize the German embassy, Thomsen had all receipts and statements that described who received payments from the Germans destroyed. How much the Germans spent on the 1940 presidential campaign and who received the money will never be known for sure.

Whether Davis and Hertslet spent all $5 million of their funds on

Willkie's campaign is unclear. Supposedly, $3 million of the money that Podestá delivered to the Germans was found in the German embassy when the FBI seized it in December 1941. Whether the other $2 million was spent on the Republicans is not known. Some of this money may have been spent on Democratic Party candidates that the Germans favored. The Germans also had other sources of money. Where this other money went and how much there was is also unknown. The entire flow of German money to the presidential election campaigns is murky. What is known is that total Republican presidential expenditures in 1940 were almost $15 million. Regardless of whether the Germans spent only $2 million or the entire $5 million or possibly even more, a large percentage of the Republican Party's funds in 1940 came from Adolf Hitler.[61]

Not surprisingly, following the Germans' lead, Davis aided Willkie's campaign by contributing large amounts of money. He directly gave at least $48,000. To sidestep the federal limit of $5,000 in campaign donations, Davis used several methods. He gave each of his family members $3,000 or $4,000 to donate to the Willkie campaign. He made contributions to individual Republican Party state committees. He also persuaded several of his longtime business associates, including Ben Smith, to become financial supporters of Willkie.[62]

Davis decided that it would be best for Lewis to support the Republican candidate. In return for Lewis's endorsement, Davis wanted Lewis appointed U.S. labor secretary if Willkie were elected. In early July, Lewis predicted that Willkie would defeat Roosevelt in the fall. Despite efforts to reconcile Lewis with the Roosevelt administration, Lewis remained staunchly opposed to the president's reelection. Knowing of Lewis's implacable hostility to Roosevelt's candidacy, Davis opened negotiations with the Willkie camp.[63]

In early September, Davis telephoned Sam Pryor, a Republican national committeeman from Connecticut and an early Willkie booster. Pryor had been previously introduced to Davis through Arthur Hobson, a Davis and Company employee who knew Pryor from Hobson's connections with Bank of Boston. Davis asked Pryor to secretly meet with him at Davis's first wife's home in Bronxville, New York, to discuss the possibility of a Lewis endorsement of Willkie. Readily agreeing, Pryor met with Davis a few days later. At this meeting, Davis told Pryor that he was out to defeat Roosevelt and was ready to contribute up to $1 million to that cause. Davis informed Pryor that he would pay for a nationwide radio broadcast in which Lewis would declare for Willkie. Although no definite assurances had yet come from Lewis, Davis was confident that Lewis would do his bidding.[64]

Pryor telephoned Willkie from Davis's home and told him of the oilman's willingness to pay for the Lewis broadcast. Willkie wanted to immediately meet this mysterious man who would make an offer of such dimensions. Pryor used his private plane to fly Davis to meet with Willkie, who was then at his home in Rushville, Indiana. After Davis repeated his offer to Willkie in person, the Republican nominee pointed to the contribution limits of the federal election law and suggested that the money be given to various Willkie clubs to maintain the legalities. Davis concluded the meeting by reiterating to Willkie his offer to carry the cost of a nationwide radio speech by his friend John L. Lewis, who would publicly endorse Willkie.[65]

Willkie later said that he had never heard of Davis before being informed that Davis would sponsor the Lewis broadcast, and that he would have rejected the offer if he had known who Davis was. Willkie's profession of ignorance seems implausible, because by this time Davis's Nazi connections had been widely publicized in the newspapers. Soon after the Lewis broadcast, Willkie wrote Davis a letter asking Davis not to publicly endorse him because of the allegations that Davis had German connections.[66]

Willkie's willingness to take Davis's money puts a tarnish on Willkie's incorruptible image both because of Davis's known Nazi connections and Willkie's early public insistence that the federal campaign finance laws be adhered to in the spirit as well as the letter of the law. When Willkie was later asked if he was aware of Davis's contributions to the Republican Party, Willkie lied and said he never knew about these funds. These questionable actions show that Willkie, like many politicians, was more interested in winning than in the morality of what he had to do to win.[67]

At the conclusion of the Davis-Willkie meeting, an arrangement was made for Willkie to meet Lewis in New York on the night of September 28. To prepare for this meeting, Davis and Wehrle met with Pryor and several other Willkie supporters, including Gene Tunney, the famous boxer,[68] to discuss his support for Willkie at New York's Waldorf Astoria Hotel. Pryor wanted assurance that Lewis would endorse Willkie. Davis said, "I'll call Lewis and I think he is ready to make a pro-Willkie statement." Davis telephoned Lewis and Lewis agreed to endorse Willkie. Davis returned to the meeting and told Pryor of Lewis's answer, and the Willkie supporters left the meeting excited about the boost that a Lewis endorsement would give Willkie's campaign.[69]

Soon after, Lewis called Willkie from Davis's home in Scarsdale to confirm their upcoming meeting. Willkie met with Lewis at the Manhattan apartment of Sam Pryor. Joe Martin, the national chairman of the Republican Party, was also present. Late into the night, Lewis and Willkie engaged in a brisk conversation about their politics.[70]

Willkie's highly personalized campaign needed a shot in the arm. He was trailing in the polls and a personal endorsement by Lewis just might provide the margin of victory that Willkie needed. Willkie wooed Lewis by declaring that when he was elected, he would honor the gains labor had won through the New Deal. He did not promise Lewis a post in his cabinet, but Willkie did say that his secretary of labor would come from the ranks of labor. In return, Lewis offered his support if Willkie agreed to repeat these promises publicly in Willkie's upcoming labor speech, which was scheduled for Pittsburgh on October 3. Willkie agreed and their meeting concluded.[71]

Willkie kept his part of the bargain. In a Pittsburgh speech before an audience of 30,000, he promised to uphold the gains made by labor and to appoint someone from the ranks of labor as his secretary of labor. Now it was Lewis's turn to keep his part of the bargain. Before endorsing Willkie, Lewis had one last meeting with President Roosevelt.[72]

Roosevelt's staff had been worried for some time that Lewis would abandon his silence and strike hard at the administration by coming out for Willkie at an opportune moment. They were aware that Willkie's agents had been cultivating Lewis and made one last effort to keep Lewis from endorsing Willkie. Using a close friend of Lewis, Saul Alinsky, as an intermediary, Roosevelt persuaded Lewis to see him. Lewis agreed to meet Roosevelt only after the president promised to discuss giving labor a larger voice in the growing armament industries.[73]

Lewis came to the White House on October 17 and was ushered into the president's bedroom. Trying to create a measure of intimacy with Lewis, the president said to Lewis, "John, sit down here by my side." Lewis said later that Roosevelt looked nervous and ill and spoke longingly of retirement.[74]

After assuring Lewis that the labor laws would be enforced in the burgeoning defense industry, Roosevelt asked Lewis directly for his support in the coming election. Lewis responded by asking, "What assurances can you give the CIO?" Roosevelt answered, "Haven't I always been a friend of labor, John?" Lewis responded that if he was such a friend of labor, "Why is the FBI tapping all my phones?" "That's a damn lie," snapped Roosevelt. Lewis, who had actually seen FBI agents trailing him, burst out an angry retort: "Nobody calls John L. Lewis a liar and least of all Franklin Delano Roosevelt." The labor leader got up and started out the door. Contritely, the president called out, "Come back."[75]

Walking back to Roosevelt, Lewis asserted that former U.S. attorney general Frank Murphy had admitted to him that he had seen an order to the FBI for surveillance of Lewis. Roosevelt continued to deny that any such order existed. After some more small talk, with the meeting having ground to a halt over Lewis's accusation, Lewis left, with no agreement reached between the two men.[76]

Despite Roosevelt's denial, the FBI was tapping Lewis's telephones and was following him. A few days later J. Edgar Hoover was asked by a newspaper reporter if Lewis was under investigation. Hoover's reply was only technically correct when he said, "This Bureau never has and is not now making any investigation of John L. Lewis." Although Lewis was not the subject of an investigation, he was under surveillance as part of the investigation of Davis.[77]

This last meeting between Lewis and Roosevelt has a curious feel. The actions of both men make it questionable whether either was interested in settling their differences. For example, the fact that the FBI was following Lewis does not explain why he brought it up at this critical meeting with the president. Since Davis, through Walter Jones, had already told Lewis of the surveillance activities, Lewis's accusation was a provocation. It is probable that Lewis had already made up his mind to support Willkie. The meeting simply offered Lewis an excuse to feign anger and outrage at the FBI surveillance, stalk out of the president's bedroom, and break off all further discussions aimed at rapprochement. Likewise, it seems Roosevelt expected little from his meeting with Lewis. Later that day Roosevelt made a joke for Berle out of his meeting with Lewis by doing an imitation of Lewis coming to call on him. With the failure of these last-minute negotiations, Lewis went ahead with his endorsement of Willkie.[78]

Lewis sent a telegram to Willkie asking him to send his press aide, Paul C. Smith, to Washington to discuss with Lewis the terms on which the labor leader would deliver a speech in support of Willkie. After working out the details with Smith, Lewis agreed to make his endorsement on October 25 in a nationwide radio broadcast.[79]

Lewis was keeping his actions secret. Until two weeks before the radio broadcast, Lewis was still assuring some of those closest to him that he would not endorse the Republican candidate. He told one of his aides after his private interview with Willkie that he considered the Republican a man of narrow intellectual outlook, with "the mind of a fixer." During the week before his speech, Lewis retreated into almost total isolation and wrote a Willkie endorsement speech without consulting even his close associates. A few days before the speech, Lewis met with several high CIO officials and announced that he was coming out for Willkie and was prepared to take full responsibility for his decision and to stand or fall by it.[80]

On October 21 Davis called the three radio networks to schedule the broadcast and identified himself as a personal representative of Lewis. He arranged for the payment of $55,000 for a thirty-minute radio broadcast in which John L. Lewis would deliver a speech on the national election to more than 362 stations on all three major radio networks. Davis also paid for the printing of millions of copies of Lewis's speech to be distributed across the country after the broadcast.[81]

Davis financed the Lewis broadcast by passing the money to the Democrats for Willkie political committee, which included in its leadership such prominent anti–New Deal Democrats as former presidential candidates Al Smith and John W. Davis. This political committee then paid the radio networks for the broadcast. This indirect arrangement was used to get around the federal campaign finance laws and to hide the source of the contribution. There was a furious exchange of checks to ensure that no one individual would be listed as contributing more than the $5,000 limit of the federal campaign law, and Republican lawyers scanned all the transactions and scrutinized the checks to make sure there were no violations.[82]

The White House was aware of who paid for Lewis's broadcast almost immediately, but chose not to publicize the information until after the election. This behavior at first seems odd because Roosevelt could have exploited the connection to Davis and ruined Willkie's reputation as an anti-Nazi. However, publicizing Davis's connections to Willkie would no doubt have brought Roosevelt's own connections to Davis under public scrutiny. Roosevelt, believing he would probably win without mentioning Davis, deemed it best not to create unnecessary complications.[83]

With a Davis staffer, Arthur Hobson, on hand to take care of last-minute details, Lewis spoke to the nation on the evening of October 25. With an estimated 25–30 million listeners, Lewis delivered in his deep baritone voice a bitter attack on Roosevelt and asked trade unionists to oppose his reelection. He accused the president of not ending unemployment and of neglecting labor, but his most emphatic accusation was that he was leading the nation into war. What was the president's objective, asked Lewis? "It is war. His every act leads to this inescapable conclusion. The President has said that he hates war and will work for peace but his acts do not match his words. The President has been scheming for years to involve us in war." Vehemently denouncing Roosevelt and asserting that his election could very well mean both war and dictatorship, Lewis declared for Willkie.[84]

He praised Willkie's integrity and described Willkie as someone who was not an aristocrat but a common man. "He has the common touch. He was born in the briar and not to the purple. He has worked with his hands, and has known pangs of hunger." This description of Willkie was pure fantasy and was intended for Lewis's labor constituents. Lewis then reviewed the candidate's promises and aims, including the promise that Willkie would give labor full representation in his administration.

Lewis concluded his speech with a dramatic pledge. He placed his personal prestige squarely on the line in support of the Republican nominee by vowing that if Roosevelt received a third presidential term he would consider it a vote of no confidence in his own leadership of the CIO. Therefore, he would resign from his position as president of the CIO if Roosevelt were reelected. He implored his followers: "Sustain me now or repudiate me."[85]

After the speech, Davis and Lewis waited expectantly for labor to move into the Willkie camp. If the CIO vote were captured, it would ensure a Willkie victory. However, virtually all of Lewis's followers, whether they said so or not, were dismayed by his endorsement of Willkie. The pro-Roosevelt faction in the CIO had hoped Lewis would limit himself to vigorous criticism of the president. What had been expected was a vitriolic attack on Roosevelt and a new "plague on both your houses." After his endorsement of Willkie, Lewis pressured union officials to support his stand for Willkie or resign. Several union officials resigned, including the head of labor's Non-Partisan League, Gardner Jackson.[86]

Jackson may have been referring to the Davis dealings in his letter of resignation:

> These are critical days when, more than ever, men seem to become captives of their personal ambition for wealth, social position and influence, and when their adventures in power politics and in finance politics, both at home and in the international field, also make them captives.[87]

It is possible that Jackson's resignation was closely tied to the Lewis-Davis link. Because the radio networks sent the bill for the broadcast to the Non-Partisan League, which then passed it on to the Democrats for Willkie, it is likely that Jackson was aware of the source of funding for the broadcast and that he could not condone taking money from a Nazi sympathizer.[88]

The president and Harry Hopkins, Roosevelt's chief political adviser, had listened to Lewis's speech on the radio and were deeply worried by what they heard. Roosevelt was troubled by Lewis's threat to resign because it was, in effect, an order to every member of the CIO to vote for Willkie. The labor leader, Sidney Hillman, who visited the White House the day after Lewis's speech, said Roosevelt was depressed by Lewis's action. Roosevelt saw Hillman while the president was being shaved in his wheelchair. In a worried tone, he said to Hillman, "What now? What does this mean?" Hillman, who knew the mood of American labor, responded, "What are you worried about? It will be all right!" Hillman insisted that Lewis could not deliver the labor vote to Willkie.[89]

Despite his momentary depression, Lewis's speech had a positive psychological impact on Roosevelt. The president told Adolf Berle on October 26 that until Lewis's broadcast he had little enthusiasm for the election campaign and that he did not greatly care how it came out. After Lewis's line of demagoguery, he, however, wanted to be reelected if only to put Lewis out of public life. Despite his new enthusiasm, Roosevelt was now faced with the delicate political task of reassuring workers that he had not abandoned them while at the same time preparing the United States to withstand the fascist menace abroad.[90]

Praising Lewis for his contribution to unity, Willkie campaigned through the mid-Atlantic seaboard. Frequently departing from his prepared text, he repeatedly charged that if Roosevelt were reelected, American boys would soon be off to fight in Europe. The Republican campaign professionals decided to center the campaign on the charge that the Democrats were the war party and the Republicans were the peace party. In a savage speech in Baltimore at the close of the campaign, Willkie flatly declared, "If you re-elect him you may expect war in April, 1941." Such "warmonger" attacks were paying off, with the Gallup poll of October 27 showing Willkie gaining on the president. It seemed that Willkie had found a winning issue.[91]

In late October, Davis saw to it that copies of his documents on the proposed peace conference of October 1939 reached key figures in the Republican Party, including former president Hoover, Sam Pryor, and Verne Marshall. Verne Marshall, an isolationist newspaper editor and Republican Party activist was outraged by the contents of the documents and was convinced that they proved the duplicity and warlike intentions of President Roosevelt. He brought the documents to Willkie's attention and tried unsuccessfully to persuade Willkie to use the information against Roosevelt in the waning days of the campaign.

Hoover and Pryor also urged using Roosevelt's failure to act on Davis's peace plan as a political weapon, but Willkie decided not to use it, fearing it would backfire.[92]

As Willkie gained in the polls, Democratic leaders became alarmed and the White House was swamped with pleas from the party faithful for Roosevelt to start fighting back. In response to this pressure, Roosevelt campaigned across the northeastern states. To diffuse Willkie's antiwar appeal, Roosevelt made pledges that he knew were disingenuous. For example, he told a Boston crowd, "I have said this before, but I shall say it again and again and again: Your boys are not going to be sent into any foreign wars." On November 2, just before election day, Roosevelt shamelessly declared, "Your President says this country is not going to war." Roosevelt, at that very moment, however, was working with Winston Churchill to destroy Hitler, and Roosevelt knew that to bring down Hitler would almost certainly require the United States to declare war on Germany.[93]

Senator Guffey, now completely back in the Roosevelt camp, triumphantly reported to Democratic headquarters that he had discovered that the tombstones of Willkie's grandparents had the Germanic spelling, Wilcke, and that, therefore, Willkie must be pro-German. This scurrilous accusation only underscores the hypocrisy of the former Mexican-German trade negotiator. Nothing was beneath the senator from Pennsylvania.[94]

Soon, despite Willkie's frenetic campaigning, Roosevelt began to express optimism about his reelection. His crowds were as large and enthusiastic as they had been in 1936 and the rank and file of the CIO did not seem ready to follow Lewis's advice and vote for Willkie. Willkie did not seem able to win the votes of industrial workers, who instinctively distrusted the Republicans, and still often received a hostile reception from working-class audiences. Despite Lewis's endorsement of Willkie, reaffirmation of support for Roosevelt came in from union locals all over the country and messages supporting Roosevelt bombarded the White House.[95]

Finally, the tide of economic events was running against Willkie. The war boom that would end the depression was well under way and thousands of workers were streaming into defense plants. Fewer and fewer Americans had reason to complain about Roosevelt's leadership. Willkie's personal appeal was just not enough to overcome the voters' suspicions of the Republicans.[96]

Roosevelt won reelection with 27 million votes to Willkie's 22 million, his margin of victory coming in the cities. Although he lost, Willkie had cut Roosevelt's plurality to the smallest of any winner since 1916. The votes were divided sharply along class lines, with most of Roosevelt's votes coming from the working class and lower-middle class. If Roosevelt's majority of the popular vote had been cut by just 3.7 percent in every state, Willkie would have won 306 electoral votes, which would have been more than enough for victory. It had been a near thing for the president and he was not about to forget those who had opposed his reelection.[97]

A number of miscalculations, coupled with indecision and poor timing, contributed to the failure of the Lewis-Davis "defeat Roosevelt" campaign. Lewis was asking too much when he asked workers to not only reject Roosevelt but also to line up with the Republicans. After the election a careful study of the repercussions of the Lewis speech concluded that his influence was decisive in only two states: Michigan and Indiana. Overall, only a small number of labor votes went to the Republicans because of Lewis's endorsement.[98]

Lewis and Davis had lost their best opportunity to block Roosevelt by vacillating on forming a third party. Had Lewis or even Wheeler's name been on the ballot as a third-party candidate, many union voters, who would not vote for Republican Willkie, might have turned away from Roosevelt to vote for a labor "peace party." It is unlikely that such a third party candidate could have captured the presidency, but it is likely that such a third-party candidate would have siphoned off enough votes from Roosevelt to put Willkie in first place in a three-way race.[99]

Lewis had abandoned this effort when he could not get the other unions to financially back the "peace party." But why did they not use Hertslet's $5 million secret fund? This money could have been the key seed money needed to get the "peace party" off and rolling. Why it was not used for this purpose is still a mystery. Instead, the secret $5 million fund was frittered away on futile schemes.

The other major mistake was Davis's decision to wait until late in the election campaign to bring out his documents on the secret Goering-Roosevelt peace plan. By the time he brought this plan to the attention of Willkie in late October, there was little time for the Republicans to exploit it. Willkie decided that it was too risky to use these unverified documents with no time to develop a media campaign around them. If Davis had given Willkie the documents in early September, Willkie could have used them as the centerpiece of his "Roosevelt is a warmonger" strategy. Whether a timely exploitation of the documents would have added the extra margin that Willkie needed to win will never be known.

Suppose Davis and Lewis had not fumbled their opportunity and had succeeded in electing Wendell Willkie to the presidency. Would Willkie's election have made a difference for the Germans? If Willkie had been president in December 1941, would the United States have gone to war with Germany? If the United States had stayed out of the war, would that have brought victory to Germany?

These questions are impossible to answer. All one can do is speculate. On the one hand, Willkie was an internationalist who was in favor of assisting the British war effort. He was not a friend of the Germans; therefore, his inclination would no doubt have been to resist Nazi aggression. On the other hand, the Republican Party leadership was rigidly isolationist and would no doubt have discouraged aid to Great Britain and restrained Willkie's interventionist impulses.

Given these circumstances, it is possible that Willkie would have given much less American aid to Great Britain in 1941 than did Roosevelt. It is also likely that the undeclared naval war between Germany and the United States in the summer and fall of 1941 would never have occurred.[100] Without these provocative acts, it is conceivable that Hitler would have decided not to declare war on the United States on December 11, 1941, in conjunction with the Japanese attack on Pearl Harbor. If Hitler had not declared war, it is probable that Willkie would not have declared war on Germany.

After all, the American public was not demanding a war with Germany; a Gallup poll just one month before Pearl Harbor showed that only 26 percent of the American people were willing to unilaterally declare war on Germany. Roosevelt was convinced in the fall of 1941 that he would never get Congress to declare war on Germany. John Kenneth Galbraith, a distinguished economist and a member of the Roosevelt administration in 1941, stated in an interview long after the war:

> When Pearl Harbor happened, we were desperate. I remember, I left Washington and went to the country—to think. We were all in agony. The mood of the American people was obvious—they were determined that the Japanese had to be punished. We could have been forced to concentrate all our efforts on the Pacific, unable from then on to give more than purely peripheral help to Britain. It was truly astounding when Hitler declared war on us three days later. I cannot tell you our feeling of triumph. It was a totally irrational thing for him to do, and I think it saved Europe.[101]

If the United States had stayed out of the European war, it is feasible that either the Soviet Union or Great Britain would have collapsed under the Nazi onslaught in 1942. With the withdrawal of either of these countries from the war, Hitler would eventually have become the master of Europe.

On November 18, with the CIO on the verge of splitting over Lewis's endorsement of Willkie, Lewis went before the annual CIO convention and attempted to stampede the delegates into "drafting" him for reelection. In a tearful, jut-jawed speech to 600 delegates in the ballroom of the Chelsea Hotel in Atlantic City, Lewis reviewed the struggles and triumphs of labor during the last decade. After receiving a forty-five minute ovation by the assembled union leadership, many delegates went up to the rostrum and pleaded with Lewis to reconsider his pledge to resign.[102]

Despite this demonstration of support, Lewis was forced to keep his promise and resigned from the CIO presidency. He was outmaneuvered by Sidney Hillman, who, in a masterful speech, took the wind out of the "draft Lewis" movement. In a master stroke, Hillman lauded Lewis for his contributions to labor and then in the next breath praised Lewis's integrity for keeping his word to resign. Thus, with his road to reelection blocked, Lewis resigned and one of Davis's main sources of political power was shut off.[103]

The decline of Lewis's power within the CIO and the end of his influence with the Roosevelt administration was a major blow to Davis. No longer could Davis use Lewis to gain access to the White House or threaten political retribution on associates who betrayed him. From now on, he would be locked out of the corridors of power. Of even more importance, his behind-the-scenes activities to destroy Roosevelt had not gone unnoticed by the president. Roosevelt was not a man to forgive those who had tried to destroy him. Whatever protection from government harassment that his connection to Lewis had provided, it was now gone. Roosevelt released Berle to get rid of this troublemaker by whatever means was necessary.

eleven

No Foreign Wars

ALTHOUGH HE FAILED to defeat Roosevelt, Davis did not give up his campaign to keep America out of the war, and he would play a critical role in the final attempt by the isolationist movement to stop Roosevelt. Despite Willkie's frenzied antiwar rhetoric during the last weeks of the election campaign, the isolationists did not believe that he had truly challenged Roosevelt's pro-British policies. This left the isolationists without a genuine choice as to whether or not to support the British. As arch-isolationist, Senator Gerald P. Nye said on June 19, 1941, "I shall be surprised if history does not show that beginning at the Republican convention at Philadelphia a conspiracy was carried out to deny the American people a chance to express themselves." The conviction that they had not been defeated fairly and squarely led isolationists to a new surge of political organization.[1]

Even before Roosevelt's reelection, the isolationists had begun forming organizations to halt the movement toward war. One of the earliest of these new organizations, the "No Foreign Wars Committee" (NFW), was first proposed at a dinner in New York City on June 10,

1940. Organized by George T. Eggleston and Douglas Stewart of the ultraconservative *Scribner's Commentator,* the dinner took place at the home of Merwin K. Hart, a public relations expert who listed Franco's fascist government as one of his clients. The guest list included Charles Shipman Payson (a wealthy investment banker), Iowa newspaper editor Verne Marshall, and Charles Lindbergh. The group decided to form a militant isolationist organization if Roosevelt were reelected. They wanted an aggressive committee to oppose British propaganda and keep America out of the war. As the election approached and a Roosevelt victory looked imminent, they began to organize their committee. Among the influential people they asked to join their cause was William Rhodes Davis.[2]

The NFW's leadership—Eggleston, Stewart, and Payson—was closely identified with Charles Lindbergh, and the NFW would soon hire O. K. Armstrong, a close friend of Lindbergh, as its director of organization. Despite the close connection, Lindbergh was never formally a member of the committee. He was influential, but he astutely kept his independence by refusing to allow his name to be used as a supporter of the NFW.[3]

Lindbergh's role in the formation of the NFW highlights his important role in the isolationist movement. By May 1941, his views on foreign policy were known by 58 percent of the American public, and Roosevelt viewed him as the major political threat from the isolationist movement. The youthful folk hero was an ardent spokesman for isolationism and Roosevelt told Morgenthau that he was "absolutely convinced that Lindbergh is a Nazi." Lindbergh had not attempted to hide his admiration for the Third Reich. On several visits to Germany, he was feted by Nazi officials and accepted a decoration from Goering. He pronounced the German air force invincible, and stated that because Great Britain was doomed to defeat, America had no business involving itself with the losing side. As Roosevelt's adviser Rex Tugwell said, "Lindbergh's radio addresses were just next to treasonable but they had an unmistakably receptive audience." Although it is probable that Lindbergh was never a Nazi,[4] supporting him was a group of Nazi and fascist sympathizers.[5]

On October 21 a conference was held in Washington to unite all the isolationist groups into a single powerful anti-Roosevelt bloc. With Lindbergh as the main speaker, fifty representatives of various organizations approved formation of the NFW. The committee was designed to coordinate all non-interventionist efforts, both left and right, but conservative isolationists actually controlled the NFW.[6]

Besides Lindbergh, the NFW's major conservative backers included Henry Ford and Davis. The NFW's public relations were directed from Henry Ford's office in New York City. Davis, however, played an even more important behind-the-scenes role than Ford in the new organization. For example, when the NFW opened its headquarters in Washington, Davis offered to finance a $100,000 nationwide keep-out-of-the-war advertising blitz.[7]

After spending months looking for the right man to lead their new organization, the NFW selected Verne Marshall. He had come to the attention of the isolationist movement after writing an antiwar article that appeared in the June 1940 issue of *Scribner's Commentator*. In that article he took a penultimate isolationist position: "I don't care who wins the war. If Hitler comes to the U.S.A., I'll get myself back to Iowa, get a piece of land and stay there." After meeting Marshall at the isolationist's dinner in June, Lindbergh decided that Marshall might be the man to head the proposed organization.[8]

Verne Marshall, a crusading newspaper editor whose newspaper had won a Pulitzer Prize in 1936, was a slim healthy fifty-one-year-old Iowa native. A lifelong Republican, the cigar-chomping Marshall was famous for his muckraking against graft, illegal gambling, and the use of prison labor. He had a flair for publicity, inexhaustible energy, courage, intense patriotism, and erratic political judgment. The NFW leadership concluded that Marshall had just the right image for the organization.[9]

Stewart had already approached Marshall about the plan to organize a militant new isolationist committee should Willkie's campaign fail, and Marshall had wholeheartedly endorsed the idea. On October 21, the day of the NFW's Washington formation conference, Eggleston and Stewart called Marshall in Iowa and asked him to come to New York and lead the new committee. Although enthusiastic, Marshall did not agree to lead the organization at this time; he agreed only to come to New York to discuss the possibility. Soon after Marshall arrived in New York, Pryor called Davis and asked him to come to his home to meet Marshall. At this meeting, Davis showed Marshall the secret "peace plan" that the Germans had proposed in 1939. After reading the documents, the outraged Marshall agreed to lead the new isolationist committee.[10]

Marshall's first assignment for the NFW was to assist Davis in bringing Wendell Willkie into the isolationist camp. After the election, Wendell Willkie had gone to Florida on December 2 "to read, fish and rest." He stayed at the home of James V. Reed on Jupiter Island in

Hobe Sound, Florida, which was one of Sam Pryor's real estate projects. The trip supposedly was purely for pleasure, as Willkie said to reporters, "I am not even going to talk politics."[11]

Despite this declaration, on December 11, Sam Pryor, Willkie's former campaign manager, invited Davis to Hobe Sound to meet with Willkie. Accompanied by Marshall, Davis went to Florida to persuade Willkie to oppose President Roosevelt's aid-to-Britain policy. There was a long procession of persons, including some of Willkie's most prominent backers, to see Willkie during his vacation stay in Florida. These emissaries tried to convince him that there was still political capital to be made out of denouncing Roosevelt as a warmonger. Tremendous pressure was brought on him to oppose Roosevelt's pro-British policies. According to Willkie, Davis and Marshall were only two of at least fifty people who argued with him on the war issue.[12]

Davis and Marshall stayed two days in Florida, most of the time in the company of Willkie and Pryor. Davis said that he

> talked with Willkie for several hours and the others mostly listened. Willkie seemed most interested in what he should do with regard to the presidential campaign for 1944 and I told him: Wendell you'll have to do something bigger than what everyone else is talking about these days and it will take plenty of courage to do it, but you'll have to do something to bring peace in Europe or we will all be lost and peace can be had. I was, of course, full of my subject, which I feel very deeply, and I know that the United States will not win anything in this war—cannot. Neither can Germany or any other country in the world win through war measures because the economic setup is not such as to assure any kind of peace and it must be altered to that extent. I said to Willkie: if you plan to follow a course that will bring that much desired end, I and all my associates are with you with every dollar I have and that they have and I will take a spade if necessary to bring that about, which is the only salvation of the world.

Trying to entice Willkie, Davis told him that he could arrange a tour for Willkie to every country of Europe (including Germany and Italy), where he could see everyone of importance in those countries at Davis's expense.[13]

However, nothing came of Davis's gambit; Willkie soon turned against the isolationists. This was not surprising because Willkie had never been an ardent isolationist. As early as 1939, he had taken part in the formation of the pro-British "Committee to Defend America by Aiding the Allies" (DAAA). Nevertheless, Roosevelt was clearly concerned about Willkie's trip to Europe, and took swift action to ensure that Willkie did no damage while he was in Europe. The day before Willkie left for Europe on a Pan-American clipper, Willkie was summoned to the Long Island home of Roosevelt's Republican secretary of war, Henry Stimson. There Willkie met with two influential Republicans, Thomas Lamont and Helen Rogers Reid, who talked Willkie out of his original itinerary.[14]

Lamont was a powerful New York banker closely linked to J. P. Morgan and Company and a lifelong Republican. He was one of the most reliable sources of Republican campaign funds and had been a major supporter of Wendell Willkie's campaign. Lamont was not an isolationist and he, like Willkie, had participated in the formation of the DAAA. Helen Reid was a vice president at the *New York Herald Tribune,* was married to Ogden Reid, who was president of the newspaper, and both she and her husband had actively supported Willkie. Like Lamont, they were both Republicans and had consistently supported Roosevelt's foreign policy. They persuaded Willkie to cancel his stops in Germany and Italy. Instead, he visited only England, and Lamont, not Davis, paid for the Willkie trip.[15]

Willkie made his fateful decision just before he left for England. On the verge of departing, Willkie met with reporters on January 12 and told them he was supporting President Roosevelt's new aid-to-Britain congressional bill (Lend-Lease). He denounced the "appeasers, isolationists, or lip-service friends of Britain [who] will seek to sabotage the program for aid to Britain and her allies." Several months later Willkie heard that Davis was circulating the story of Willkie's meeting with Lamont and others. He wrote to Davis inquiring whether it was true that Davis was spreading this information. Davis's answer was a contemptuous brush-off, which aroused Willkie to reply angrily, "I have your very impertinent letter. I had written as one gentleman to another concerning a statement that had been attributed to you. Your replies are merely cheap inferences." So ended Davis's links to Willkie.[16]

At the time of Davis's ploy with Willkie, Ben Smith, a longtime business associate of Davis, was undertaking a covert campaign to arrange a negotiated settlement between Great Britain and Germany. Smith had traveled to Vichy, France, at the beginning of December to sound out leaders of the collaborationist government of Premier Philippe Pétain. Allegedly, Joseph Kennedy, who had just resigned as U.S. ambassador to Great Britain, had sent Smith to see Pétain and find some formula to end the war. Smith had good connections in France because both his wife and daughter had been living in Paris.

He was also a friend of Lord Beaverbrook, who was in the British cabinet and a confidante of Prime Minister Winston Churchill.[17]

Smith's trip caused great anxiety within the British Foreign Office and the British contacted the U.S. State Department for assistance in blocking Smith's endeavor. When informed of Smith's plans, President Roosevelt, through his ambassador in France, Admiral William Leahey, persuaded Marshal Pétain to refuse to meet with Smith. It is not known whether Smith's travels were linked to Davis's attempt to persuade Willkie to travel to Europe under the isolationist banner, but the parallel timing of the two peace ploys is intriguing.[18]

Davis's attempt to lure Willkie into the isolationist camp failed, but Verne Marshall had the idea that Davis would back him 100 percent. However, their relationship quickly became stormy because of Marshall's use of Davis's peace plan documents. They had been discussed at the Marshall-Davis meeting at Sam Pryor's house in October and Marshall later went to Davis's office asking for more information about the plan. Marshall told Davis he needed the facts for a speech he would be making. Davis later said, "Like a fool, I gave him access to my files and the bastard [Marshall] copied from some the correspondence I had had with the White House. If I had known it [the peace plan] was in the files I most certainly would not have let him see it."[19]

On November 4, the day before the presidential election, Marshall's Cedar Rapids, Iowa, *Gazette* broke the story of Davis's peace plan on the front page. The story was rambling and disjointed but it contained one perfectly clear accusation: "President Franklin D. Roosevelt, in October, 1939, was confronted with an opportunity to preside at a peace conference by which this war might have been ended within 10 days," which the president refused.[20]

Davis was furious with Marshall for printing the story. He called him to his office and dressed him down for the unauthorized use of his files. He said "You ain't going to push me around like that, Marshall. Dammit—you violated a confidence and made copies of those files and I want them back." Marshall apologized and for the moment their dispute was defused, but it was reignited soon after their joint December trip to Florida.[21]

On December 17, three days after leaving Florida, Verne Marshall publicly announced formation of the NFW from its new headquarters in New York. The committee was launched in a series of coast-to-coast radio broadcasts and newspaper advertisements. According to Marshall, its one and only purpose was to keep America out of the war. He said, "Our purpose is to prevent the United States from being sucked into the current chapter of Europe's interminable economic, political and ideological war." In regard to Roosevelt's pro-British foreign policy, Marshall said that his committee would "fight it to the bitter end."[22]

On Christmas Day, Marshall, in an editorial in his newspaper, warned President Roosevelt to "take us wholly into his confidence [about his stand on aid to Britain]" in his radio address on the following Sunday or Marshall's organization might release a document detailing "conspiracies" and "deceptions" that had started the European war. Not satisfied with Roosevelt's Sunday radio broadcast, Marshall decided to go on the attack.[23]

In a clever move, Marshall brought the NFW to national prominence with a headline-grabbing press conference. After a Capitol Hill luncheon with important isolationist senators—Clark of Missouri, McCarran of Nevada, and Holt of West Virginia—Marshall announced the existence of Davis's peace plan at a news conference in the National Press Club on December 30, 1940. He said he was making the announcement in the hope that his effort would "keep this country out of the war and to stop the policy of giving away our defenses." Marshall, after giving a detailed and accurate account of Davis's peace mission, challenged the State Department "to let the people of the world decide whether they [the peace documents] are nonsense or not by making them public."[24]

Marshall said the original documents were in a safe-deposit box and that he and a U.S. senator had read a translation of them. He called the peace terms just and said that Germany had wanted to stop the war in 1939. Marshall said he would not "reveal the peace terms. Berle knows them—let him reveal them." However, he said that he had

> every reason to think that if the United States today through some accredited spokesman, either of Congress or the White House, made a sincere proposal to call a peace conference, the belligerents on both sides would be eager to permit a representative of the United States to preside over a peace conference that would begin as soon as their representatives could reach Washington by air. . . . I have every reason to believe that the war would be brought to an end soon after the peace conference began. The best man in the United States should be sent abroad tonight or tomorrow [to set up the peace conference], and, in my opinion, that man would be William Rhodes Davis.[25]

As a newspaper editor, Marshall knew how to make news and to get headlines. He called press conferences almost every day, made radio broadcasts, called U.S. senators insane, denounced Walter Winchell as an idiot, peppered his interviews with "damns" and "hells," announced his life had been threatened, and said he had placed "sensational documents" in a safe-deposit box to be read if he were killed. Everyone Marshall mentioned in his speech was soon asked to comment on his claims.[26]

The State Department and Berle remained officially silent on Marshall's charges. They released only a brief statement, which intimated that Davis's role had been entirely unofficial and made light of the documents he brought from Berlin. Although both the White House and the State Department declined all comment on Marshall's charges, unofficially the Roosevelt administration attempted to discredit Davis.[27]

Vice President Wallace's office announced, "It is obvious that Davis, who has been living off German money for years, wants the war to end as soon as possible in order to resume his operations that were curtailed by the war. Davis wants the war to end on Hitler's terms."

Democratic senator Josh Lee of Oklahoma stated that

> the record of this man Davis shows conclusively the great financial stake he has in a complete Nazi victory in the European war. Much of the gasoline sending showers of fiery death into the defenseless heart of London was sold to the German government by this man Davis in the months before the war started. . . . Davis was attempting to promote a phony peace through the White House to pull Nazi Germany's chestnuts out of the fire.

Nor did the Germans come forward to support Davis. For unknown reasons, the Germans claimed to have no knowledge of Davis's peace plan.[28,29]

Until Marshall's news conference, Davis had been virtually unknown to the public. Marshall's announcement put his name on the front page of the nation's newspapers. Marshall further inflated Davis's notoriety by mentioning his name on a national radio broadcast. The next day, Davis's name became a household synonym for traitor when Walter Winchell, on his popular nationwide radio program, denounced Davis as an agent of the Nazis. Although his friends did not believe that he was a Nazi spy, the charges made Davis extremely uncomfortable.[30]

The same day as the Winchell broadcast, Davis issued a statement in which he declared that

such information as I have transmitted to our government, I believe can best be utilized by officials of the different departments
at [sic] Washington who carry responsibility for the protection of
our national security. I am confident that when, in the opinion of
the present Administration, the best interests of our country can
be served by making public the information which I have from
time to time delivered to it, that information will be made public.

Davis closed his statement defiantly: "It is with emphasis that I endorse all the purposes of the No Foreign Wars Committee in its vigorous effort to keep the United States out of unnecessary wars. That
committee stands for America, first, last and forever."[31]

Irked by the onslaught of unfavorable publicity, Davis struck back.
He called Marshall into his office and gave him hell. Despite his
anger, Davis said he felt sorry for Marshall and "gave him $5,000 and
wished him well."[32] Next, Davis had his friends in Congress threaten
Winchell with a congressional investigation if Winchell did not drop
his attacks on Davis. Finally, he decided to directly counter the bar-
rage of negative publicity by holding a press conference.[33]

On January 5, Davis and Henry Wilson met the press in one of the
inner offices of Davis and Company's New York headquarters in the
RCA Building at Rockefeller Plaza. Wilson passed out copies of a prepared statement to a large group of reporters and photographers and
then announced, "Mr. Davis is coming." Impeccably dressed in a
brown suit with a green tie and white shirt, Davis entered the room,
looked around nervously, and shook hands with a few of the reporters
nearest him. He stood behind a desk, posing patiently for photographers and making good-humored remarks about his associations with
the press. He then made an opening statement.[34]

The affable oilman made public a letter to Senator Wheeler in
which he asked for an opportunity to appear before the senator's new
subcommittee, which was investigating whether national defense production was being affected by foreign (i.e., British) influences. Appointed only a few days before, the Wheeler committee had yet to
hold its first meeting. Davis had been clever in his choice of Senate
subcommittees because Wheeler, an arch-isolationist, would no
doubt be friendly to Davis.[35]

In the letter, Davis asked Senator Wheeler to investigate

inferences that I am engaged in any activity inimical to the best
interests of the country." He asked for "a full and impartial investigation" by Wheeler's committee to clear him "of the grossly unfair and malicious charges that have been lodged against me. He

> declared that he was a "patriotic American . . . [and] these re-
> ports are utterly false, so ridiculous that I would not take the
> trouble to deny them if it were not for the fact that they are being
> circulated in such trying times when the entire world is uneasy.[36]

Davis stated that some of the allegations "have been the workings of a studied and carefully planned publicity campaign instigated by financial and competitive interests [i.e., Big Oil] to besmirch my character and ruin my business enterprises. . . . I am, I always have been and I always will be a true and loyal American citizen. I never expected the day would come when I should have to proclaim it publicly; nevertheless, I do."[37]

After his opening statement, Davis turned the conference over to Henry Wilson to answer questions. Wilson refused to answer questions about Davis's relationship with Joachim Hertslet, however, and lied when he said that Davis had not shipped any Mexican oil to Germany since the war started. Wilson also refused to answer questions about Davis's political contributions to President Roosevelt.[38]

When Wilson refused to answer reporters' questions about Davis's association with Verne Marshall, however, Davis pushed him aside, saying in his Alabama drawl, "Wait a minute. I'm free, white and 21 and of sound mind. I'll speak for myself and answer that question." Davis denied that he was a backer of the NFW. Despite this denial, he admitted that he had offered to finance the NFW with as much as $100,000 and said he favored "all these organizations who hold the same ideas of world tranquility."[39]

Davis told reporters that he wanted "the war to end; it is true. But I do not want the war to end 'on Hitler's terms' as has been so loosely flung at me. I want this war to end by negotiation before the men, women and children of the world are debauched and demoralized; before the wealth and treasures of the world are destroyed, and before human rights and liberties are lost forever." He said his "interest in keeping the United States out of European entanglements is based on the profound conviction that if this war is not soon determined, we shall have in this country that same system of deprivation and regimentation, that same loss of personal liberty and free enterprise, that prevails in the totalitarian countries today." He said that he would be glad to help bring about an end to the war "if proper authorities requested it." He made it plain that he was willing to do anything to aid in bringing about a peace.

When asked if he was a Nazi agent, Davis responded in his fake country style, "I ain't not!" Concluding the press conference, he said, with a faint grin, that he preferred to answer other questions in the congressional inquiry that he was asking Wheeler to initiate.[40]

The next day, Senator Wheeler said he favored an investigation of the German peace offers that Davis had brought from Germany in 1939. He declared he had "never denied anybody a hearing who asked to be investigated. . . . I want to protect businessmen from being unduly harassed or held up to ridicule in times of stress. I think his activities ought to be investigated, and in view of the fact he has asked for one, I feel disposed to give it to him." Wheeler said the subcommittee would question Davis closely about his "peace plan" documents.[41]

However, Wheeler said he would not announce a date for Davis's appearance until he received the letter Davis told newspaper reporters that he had written to Wheeler. Davis said that he had the original German-language copies of Goering's peace proposals in his safe in New York and would bring the documents with him to Wheeler's hearings.[42,43]

But Wheeler never called Davis before his subcommittee because Davis's lawyers asked Wheeler to abandon the investigation. The reason Wheeler agreed to drop his hearings is obvious; no matter how closely Wheeler controlled the questioning there was a substantial risk that the investigation would expose facts embarrassing not only to Davis but also to Wheeler and his political allies.[44]

Although Wheeler's investigation of Davis never occurred, other government officials were less reluctant to scrutinize Davis and his friends. The first to be questioned was John L. Lewis, who had appeared before a federal grand jury in December. The grand jury, which was investigating violations of the federal campaign finance laws during the presidential election, asked Lewis who had paid for his radio broadcast. O. L. Garrison, controller of labor's Non-Partisan League, also testified. Unfortunately, the content of their sworn testimony was never made public.[45]

On January 7, Department of Justice officials, Maurice M. Milligan, special assistant attorney general, and William S. Tarver, assistant U.S. attorney, announced that Davis and Henry Wilson had been subpoenaed to appear before the special District of Columbia grand jury investigating campaign expenditures. Davis was called to find out if he helped pay for John L. Lewis's radio broadcast in which Lewis endorsed Willkie. Accepting the subpoena at his New York office, Davis said he would be "very happy" to tell the grand jury "all I can." "Nothing surprises me any more, I am not only willing to testify, but anxious. I am willing to answer questions on anything they ask me."[46]

Davis and Wilson arrived in Washington on January 8, and the FBI followed them around the city at the request of Milligan, who hoped Davis would visit Lewis, but Davis did not. Erna Wehrle told the author that "we knew people were following us around." The FBI also passed on a report on their extensive investigation of Davis to Milligan. On January 9, Davis testified before the Washington grand jury, but afterward refused to tell reporters about his actual testimony. His only comment was to deny that he had financed Lewis's radio broadcast. U.S. senator Josh Lee told reporters that Davis had admitted to the grand jury that he had been paid $440,000 of German money since the start of the war.[47]

The next week, on January 17, Davis's associate, Ben Smith, was also subpoenaed by the grand jury. No prosecutions resulted from this grand jury, which is curious given Milligan's reputation. He was an excellent prosecutor and had been responsible for the recent conviction of Tom Pendergast, the Kansas City Democratic political boss, on election fraud charges. However, the 1940 federal campaign finance law was basically unenforceable, as Milligan concluded in his final report on the grand jury investigation: "The present existing federal laws . . . are fatally defective . . . and are unenforceable under the conditions which have been presented in this investigation." It is also possible that some of Lewis, Davis, and Smith's testimony involved Roosevelt. If so, the Justice Department would be reluctant to bring their testimony under public scrutiny with an open trial.[48]

Besides the grand jury subpoena, there were calls for a congressional investigation (not controlled by Wheeler) of Davis. Senator Lee introduced a resolution to investigate Davis's foreign propaganda and financial activities. Unfortunately for Senator Lee, the resolution was sent to the Senate Foreign Relations Committee for consideration. Because Joseph Guffey was a member of this committee, it is not surprising that Lee's resolution was never adopted. The House Un-American Activities Committee (HUAC) also sent two investigators to see Davis at his New York offices. Given the right-wing bias of the committee, it is not a surprise that Davis had a pleasant talk with the two men and heard nothing further from HUAC.[49]

Calls for a congressional investigation of Davis did not end in January. After another series of newspaper stories in May on Davis's activities brought renewed demands for hearings on Davis. He and Wehrle always believed that these stories were based on information leaked by Adolf Berle. Hearings were never held, however. The Roosevelt administration discouraged the Senate from proceeding with the hearings because there were too many subjects embarrassing to Roosevelt that Davis could bring up in a public hearing. The ugly newspaper stories were sufficient to destroy Davis's political effectiveness without the uncertainty of a public hearing.[50]

Although the NFW had quickly rocketed to national prominence, it just as quickly disappeared from the political landscape. The media, having been amply irked by Marshall's bombast, amused by his frequent contradictions, and amazed by his championing of Davis, soon dismissed the Iowan. Isolationist leaders began complaining that Marshall was hurting their cause. On January 12, Marshall staged a rally in New York City at which several well-known fascists and anti-Semites addressed the meeting. The newspapers denounced the meeting, and the "respectable" sponsors of the NFW began pulling out. This, coupled with Marshall's crude publicity-seeking blunders, rapidly discredited the NFW in the eyes of the American public.[51]

O. K. Armstrong said, "Our publicity has been terrible, terrible, I don't know what we can do about it. This committee is my baby, I started it. Now Marshall's got us tied up with this Davis and his Nazi connections. We've got to do something. I don't know what we can do—we'll have to see if this thing has torpedoed us." The committee's backers dropped away. On January 16, Lindbergh, the NFW's most important backer, tactfully withdrew his support, announcing that he had no connection with the NFW. At the same time, Armstrong, Lindbergh's friend, resigned from the NFW.[52]

Following the withdrawal of Lindbergh's support, the situation deteriorated rapidly. Despite several reorganizations, the NFW could not be rejuvenated, and, on April 29, 1941, Marshall announced the dissolution of the NFW. Abandoned by other isolationists, Marshall returned to Iowa, but his travails were not over. Embarrassed by Marshall's political blunders, the board of directors of the Cedar Rapids *Gazette* soon forced Marshall from the editorship of the newspaper. Forsaken by everyone, the volatile Marshall had a nervous breakdown and was institutionalized in July.[53]

In March, despite the failure of the NFW, Lewis, Davis, and Wheeler continued their coordinated activities to form an anti-Roosevelt "peace party" to block American participation in the war. Davis and the other isolationists firmly believed that the war would be over by the end of the year. Davis predicted the Germans would soon capture the Suez Canal, overrun Turkey, and take the Iraqi oil fields. His German informants told him that the German high command expected Great Britain to sue for peace by year's end. With a German victory seeming imminent, the isolationists were determined to block Roosevelt from joining the war in alliance with Great Britain.[54]

To reach this goal, the isolationists hoped to capture sufficient congressional seats in the 1942 election to control Congress. They expected to win enough seats so that they would be able to block either the Democrats or Republicans from forming a majority without their support. This was a realistic analysis because 16 percent of the American public said that it would vote for a Lindbergh "keep-out-of-war" party in August 1941. In the long run, isolationists expected to run either Lindbergh or Wheeler for president in 1944 on a platform of cooperating with a by-then victorious Germany.[55]

Though outnumbered in Congress, isolationist groups were both articulate and undismayed. Working side by side in opposition to Roosevelt's policies were conservative Democrats, Republicans, socialists, and communists. For example, Douglas Stuart, an isolationist organizer, considered himself a liberal, while Robert E. Wood was a staunch conservative. Although there was a confusion of motives among this diverse group, they were united in refusing to involve American troops in the European war.[56]

By this time, the mantle of leadership for the isolationist movement had passed from the NFW to another isolationist organization, the "America First Committee" (AFC). In July 1940, a group of midwestern businessmen, including Robert Wood, head of Sears, and Jay Hormel, the meat packer, had begun organizing the AFC. Other original AFC leaders included Henry Ford; Robert McCormick, publisher of the rabidly isolationist *Chicago Tribune*; famous World War I airman Eddie Rickenbacker; Avery Brundage, chairman of the Olympic Games Committee; Kathryn Lewis, John L. Lewis's daughter; and U.S. Senators Wheeler, Gerald P. Nye, and Robert Rice Reynolds. The AFC's chief organizer was R. Douglas Stuart Jr., a Yale Law School student and son of the first vice president of Quaker Oats Company. Stuart got the organization off the ground when he met Senator Burton Wheeler at a student gathering in Chicago. After listening to Stuart's ideas on keeping America out of the war, Wheeler introduced Stuart to Robert Wood.[57]

The organization was formally incorporated in Chicago on September 18, 1940. Wood announced the organization of the new committee on October 4 in his keynote speech to the Chicago Council of Foreign Relations. He contended that a German-dominated Europe would not destroy American foreign trade and that, therefore, there was no need to intervene in the war. Wood publicly stated that he was willing to hand over Europe to Hitler rather than involve American troops in the war. In the same month the AFC announced itself to the public with a full-page advertisement in the *New York Times*. Lindbergh saw the advertisement, was impressed, and soon became a leader in the organization. At one of its earliest meetings, Lindbergh told the group, "We must make our peace with the new powers in Europe."[58]

By the summer of 1941, it was clear that the AFC was not going to be merely another isolationist pressure group, it was becoming a mass political movement. In what was called the "Great Debate," isolationists tried to turn the American public against Roosevelt's foreign policy. Lindbergh and his congressional supporters were stumping the country, not as Democrats or Republicans, but as "America Firsters." They had behind them an enormous propaganda machine and a vast organizational apparatus. They held mass meetings, issued pamphlets, and organized educational meetings. The AFC comprised 250 chapters and a total membership of 5 million members, and millions of dollars were reportedly pouring in to finance the organization. Nothing like it had been witnessed in American politics in a long time.[59]

The AFC's effectiveness had grown so much by 1941 that the temper of the American people toward Europe was difficult to assess. American public opinion gave the impression of being unstable and could potentially move quickly to the side of the isolationists. However, time was running out for the AFC to keep America out of the war. On June 16, 1941, the United States ordered the closing of all twenty-four German consulates, as well as the offices of other German organizations in the United States. This created an international stir because it was recognized as the preliminary step to breaking off diplomatic relations with Germany.[60]

While the leadership of the AFC included some moderate noninterventionists such as Chester Bowles, many of its leaders believed that a Jewish-British-capitalist-Roosevelt conspiracy aimed to plunge the country into war. Operating on a national scale until the Japanese attack on Pearl Harbor, through the medium of the press, radio, mass rallies, street-corner meetings, and other promotional devices, the AFC spread a prodigious amount of anti-British isolationist propaganda.[61]

As 1941 wore on, the anti-Semitic and pro-fascist elements poured into the AFC and became key organizers of the AFC's rallies and fund raising. Less and less was heard from the liberal Douglas Stuart. With the collapse of the NFW, fascists poured into the AFC and the AFC's membership became riddled with fascist agents. It got to the point where it was acceptable for Walter H. Schellenberg (not to be mistaken for Walter Schellenberg, the famous German intelligence operative), the head of the Nazi-controlled League of Germans Abroad in the United States, to sit on the platform in Madison Square Garden at a large rally of the AFC on March 22, 1941.[62]

As a part of this fascist infiltration, Davis and his organization became deeply involved in the AFC. Davis's longtime friend Werner Von Clemm served as a behind-the-scenes propaganda strategist and financial supporter of the important New York branch of the AFC. John L. Lewis also began to spend more time with the isolationist movement. Lewis was shifting to the political right because his leftist allies had abandoned him and had become fervent supporters of Roosevelt's policies when Hitler invaded the Soviet Union on June 22.[63]

Even Davis, on July 26, made a radio appeal for support of Senator Wheeler's all-out attack on Lend-Lease. However, Davis's involvement was primarily behind-the-scenes because his well-known links to the Nazis made it politically impossible for him to play a public role within the AFC. Whether he would eventually have played a more prominent role in the organization will never be known because only days after this broadcast, Davis died suddenly.[64]

Why did Davis stay with the isolationist movement? He had little economic incentive because his oil business was no longer dependent on his German refinery for survival. Berle and the British had made him a pariah through their repeated newspaper attacks on him as a traitor and spy. His campaign to oust Roosevelt from office had failed, yet he continued to play a prominent behind-the-scenes role in the isolationist movement. He may still have had some hope that a negotiated peace would recoup his Mexican-German oil trade, but this remote possibility seems insufficient to explain his behavior. No doubt the Germans were encouraging him to continue combating Roosevelt's foreign policy, but the Germans could exert little influence over him at this point.

Davis's behavior is most likely linked to his bitter hatred of Roosevelt and his conviction that Roosevelt was leading the country to war against his friends in Germany. He could not and would not stop his opposition as long as he could fight against what he saw as an unjust and unnecessary war. Despite the attacks in the media, he would not be intimidated. This fearless but reckless attitude may have cost him his life.

twelve

Banco Continental

By 1941, the American political terrain was changing. American policymakers began to place a high value on inter-American solidarity. In January 1941, President Roosevelt made overtures to President Manuel Avila Camacho of Mexico to allow the construction of U.S. naval bases on Mexico's Pacific Coast. In the spring, the U.S. government contracted to purchase Mexico's entire output of strategic minerals. When Hitler invaded the Soviet Union in June, Mexico moved decidedly into the pro-Allies camp, and only Mexican fascists still supported the Axis. Despite the warming relationship between the U.S. government and Mexico, Roosevelt's administration was still split over the issue of compensating the oil companies for Mexico's nationalization of its oil industry. Secretary of State Cordell Hull wanted full compensation; he was reluctant to compromise with Mexico. This American vacillation left openings for Axis sympathizers in Mexico.[1]

Investment opportunities glittered in Mexico as the worldwide war effort ballooned. Mexico had a developed banking system, huge oil fields, and appeared to be on the verge of vast industrial development in response to war demands. Davis had money to invest because in November 1940 he had sold, for $6 million, half of his interest in the Rincon field to Continental Oil Company, a subsidiary of the financial powerhouse, J. Pierpoint Morgan Company.[2]

Davis, as always seeking new business opportunities, formed a syndicate to take advantage of the Mexican economic boom. It had ambitious plans to construct highways, railways, hotel chains, and service stations. The core of the group included a number of prominent British, American, and Mexican business and political figures. Among these were Serge Rubinstein, a White Russian financier; Harold Christie, a land promoter in the Bahamas; Sir Harry Oakes, a Canadian tycoon; John Ambrose Hastings, a former New York state senator; and Ed Flynn[3] and Bernard Smith.[4]

Through his contacts in Mexico, Davis convinced Maximinio Camacho, the brother of Mexican president Avila Camacho and governor of the Mexican state of Puebla, to smooth the way for the syndicate to get the inside track for lucrative Mexican development projects. To gain Camacho's ear, Davis took advantage of his friendship with John Hastings, who had become a good friend of Maximinio Camacho[5] and whose daughter had married into a wealthy Mexican family. Hastings and Davis had first approached Camacho about their plans in April 1940 in Mexico City.[6]

Maximinio Camacho had a taste for money, was close to his brother Avila, and was friendly with Mexico's fascists. The Mexican fascists were in turn closely tied to the Spanish and German fascist movements, with the Germans having since 1938 poured money into the Mexican fascist movement. After his brother became president, the fascists began to court Maximinio, who admired the dictatorial methods of fascism. A close friend described Maximinio as "ferocious," and the citizens of Puebla were frightened of him. As his friend said, "You don't fool around with Maximinio." With these predilections, it is not surprising that Maximinio was receptive to the fascist cause. The local branch of Spanish fascists held a banquet for him on January 15, 1941. Soon after, the fascists persuaded Camacho to sponsor a move to improve Mexican relations with fascist Spain.[7]

Harold Christie, a former rumrunner who had become the leading real estate dealer in the Bahamas and a prominent figure in the Bahamian assembly, also played a major role in the syndicate's activities. He introduced Harry Oakes to John Hastings while the three were in Mexico looking for business opportunities. Oakes and Christie arrived in Mexico City on July 19, 1940, and soon after visited Maximinio

Camacho. The key player in the syndicate, however, was not Davis, Hastings, or Christie, but Axel Wenner-Gren.[8]

A Swedish citizen, Axel Lenard Wenner-Gren, at age fifty-nine, was said to be the wealthiest man in the world in 1941. Although he had made his fortune through his ownership of the Electrolux vacuum cleaner company, he had interests in many areas: in armament factories (Bofors), Sweden's largest paper company, banks, newspapers, and mines. Wenner-Gren was tall with a powerful frame, white hair, cold blue eyes, bronzed skin, and an erect carriage. He spoke English with a characteristic Swedish accent, and wore expensive tailored clothing.[9]

Always actively opposed to the war against Germany, he acted as a go-between for various German peace overtures. From 1935 on, he carried messages between Goering and British prime minister Neville Chamberlain. After he returned from meeting with German officials in Berlin in March 1940, he met with President Roosevelt in a long intimate conference. As Wenner-Gren explained, "If there should happen to be a stalemate and a negotiated peace, I might be of great use. I have a good standing in Germany."[10]

In February 1940 Wenner-Gren had purchased a Hog Island estate across a narrow channel from Nassau, capital of the Bahamas. On Hog Island, Wenner-Gren built the Paradise Town resort, which became the most popular Bahamian resort of wealthy tourists and is still today very popular. Wenner-Gren also purchased an estate for himself, called Shangri-La, on Hog Island. At the same time as his land purchase, Wenner-Gren founded Bank of the Bahamas, which had connections with the German Stein Bank of Cologne. His partners in the Bahamian bank were Sir Harry Oakes and Harold Christie. This bank soon played a role in Germany's economic warfare against Great Britain.[11]

In June 1940 Roosevelt, by executive order, froze American bank deposits, securities, and other properties of the nations the Germans had just occupied in Europe. The State Department made their transfer subject to license, a tactic the U.S. government hoped would prevent Germany from using the financial resources of its conquests. The Americans were wrong.[12]

The Germans had taken over virtually intact the entire financial structure of Europe, and sought to turn the worldwide European interests and connections to their own ends. They seized important banks, insurance firms, holding companies, and mercantile establishments. They confiscated great sums in gold and foreign exchange from bank vaults in the conquered nations, and, even more important, they secured title to ownership of even larger balances on deposit abroad. Through a series of dummy corporations, they attempted to gain control of these extensive overseas interests and assets.[13]

One of the conduits for this Nazi economic warfare was Wenner-Gren's Bank of the Bahamas. The Germans would send British currency captured in Europe through Lisbon, Portugal, to South America, from South America to banks in the United States, and from the American banks to Nassau. The Germans then exchanged the British currency into another hard currency, such as U.S. dollars. Thus, the Germans could use the money for their own purposes and simultaneously undermine Great Britain's financial position. These activities began to reduce further Great Britain's dwindling reserves of foreign exchange. The maneuver was so successful that Bank of England was forced to limit the number of British pounds that could be exchanged for other currencies. The currency limitation brought to a halt the Wenner-Gren bank's original role in German economic warfare. However, Wenner-Gren's financial shenanigans for Germany were not over.[14]

The Germans still needed money for their activities in Latin America, and it became increasingly difficult for Germany to send money to the Americas after the war began. By the fall of 1940 the German espionage stations in Latin America were running out of money. German agents suspended operations and the Germans had to beg for handouts from wealthy Mexican sympathizers. The Germans tried to solve this crisis by sending money kept in accounts in various American banks to Mexico by courier. However, this solution was eventually thwarted when British intelligence tipped off the Mexican authorities. The Mexicans confiscated a large sum of money in October 1940 from a courier, which ended the courier system.[15]

With the failure of this plan the Germans desperately sought another source of funds. The Germans turned to Wenner-Gren, who devised a plan to use Davis's syndicate of Axis sympathizers who were planning to invest in the Mexican economy. The investors would funnel their money through a bank that would be controlled by the syndicate, and then siphon off money from this bank to fund German espionage operations. To make this bank a success, Wenner-Gren turned to the new governor of the Bahamas, the Duke of Windsor.

Wenner-Gren was among the first to greet the Duke of Windsor when he arrived in the Bahamas in July 1940 to become governor. Wenner-Gren and the duke got on well and were in close and frequent contact. It was on Wenner-Gren's yacht that the Duke and

Duchess of Windsor were to make their first trip to Miami from the Bahamas. The duke and Wenner-Gren agreed in their perspectives on the war. Both believed that the war was a mistake and that the democracies should enter an alliance with Nazi Germany against the Soviet Union. They believed that if the war continued France and Great Britain would go socialist after the war and that communism was a greater menace than Nazism.[16]

The duke was also concerned that his wealth, most of which was frozen in Europe, would be worthless after the war. Wenner-Gren held $2.5 million of the Duke of Windsor's money in his Bahamas bank, but the Duke could not invest his money in the islands because there was nothing in which to invest. Wenner-Gren proposed investing the money in Latin America, but the duke, as a British subject, could not legally transfer his money to Mexico. Thus, the money transfer would have to be done secretly. Later that fall, Wenner-Gren, armed with a letter of introduction from Oakes, arrived in New York and discussed with Hastings a scheme to take over a Mexican bank called Banco Continental. Hastings and Wenner-Gren hoped to get Maximinio Camacho to open the necessary doors for their purchase of the bank.[17]

Camacho needed to be wooed to get him involved in the scheme, and the Windsors were part of this effort, playing host to Camacho at their government residence in Nassau. Oakes and Christie arranged a meeting between the two, which would give the duke an opportunity to encourage Camacho's participation in the scheme. Even though Mexico and Great Britain did not have diplomatic relations, Camacho spent two hours with the Duke of Windsor on March 20, 1941, at Government House in Nassau. The duke and Camacho talked in fluent Spanish about Mexican business opportunities, and agreed to put the Banco Continental scheme in motion.[18]

There was only one problem with the scheme, it was illegal. Neither Oakes, Christie, nor the duke could legally invest in Mexico under British wartime currency controls. To circumvent these controls, the syndicate of investors used Wenner-Gren's Bank of the Bahamas to covertly transfer funds out from under British currency controls. Wenner-Gren's bank manager in Nassau, John H. Anderson, hand delivered the funds to Mexico. By Wenner-Gren's own records, the duke deposited nearly £1 million in the syndicate's Mexican bank, Banco Continental. By this action, the duke was guilty of violating the British Trading with the Enemy Act.[19]

In 1941, Wenner-Gren and Davis were both looking for places in Latin America other than Mexico to invest money. Wenner-Gren visited Rio de Janeiro, where he offered to buy, as the representative of a

German-Swedish consortium of which Krupp was a member, the rich iron ore deposits in the state of Minas Gerais. The deal fell through only because the United States Export-Import Bank stepped in at the last moment with a substantial loan to Brazil. Davis was also active in Brazil in 1941, where he was looking at the prospects of building an aqueduct in Rio de Janeiro. Davis had previously sent Fritz Flanley[20] to Brazil in August 1940 to investigate the possibility of trading oil for manganese, iron ore, and other war essentials. Davis's agents had also been to Uruguay on a similar mission.[21]

After leaving Brazil, Wenner-Gren went to Peru, claiming that he was there to oversee an archaeological expedition. In reality, he was there to purchase Davis's old oil concession in the Peruvian jungle. However, Bertram Lee, who had been cheated out of the concession by Davis, threatened legal action, and Wenner-Gren backed away from the deal.[22]

From Peru, the Swedish industrialist went to Mexico. Davis was also in Mexico City for a week in mid-June 1941. On his first trip to Mexico in many months, Davis interviewed Mexican government officials, including Finance Minister Eduardo Suárez, who said that Davis and he had discussed several unspecified industrial projects, but "nothing definite resulted" from their talks. Wenner-Gren said he was in Mexico "to engage in economic activities in collaboration with American and Mexican financiers." He received a gold key to Mexico City, and was entertained royally by Maximinio Camacho. It was estimated that Wenner-Gren's prospective capital investment for enterprises in that country was $10 million or more. It was reported that he had two projects in mind: forming a joint American-British-Mexican oil trust, and interesting his friend Maximinio Camacho in a road-building enterprise.

Behind the scenes, Wenner-Gren and Davis were both in Mexico to set up their bank. By this time both Davis and Wenner-Gren were notorious as Nazi sympathizers, so Oakes and Hastings were used as front men for the new bank, scheduled to open August 1, 1941, with initial deposits of $7 million. Everything was ready for the bank of Axis sympathizers.[23]

Unfortunately for Davis and Wenner-Gren, the American government and, in particular, Adolf Berle, had been following their activities with growing concern. The FBI had been keeping both Davis and Wenner-Gren under surveillance since early 1940, and there were grave suspicions about what the two were doing. Under Secretary of State Sumner Welles reported that he had received information

that the brother of the new President of Mexico, General Maximinio Camacho, is due to arrive in Nassau early in February
1941, apparently to confer with Mr. Wenner-Gren. Reports have
reached me that Mr. Wenner-Gren is anxious to participate in an
American consortium planning the investment of a considerable
amount of new capital in Mexico.[24]

The British government was also extremely disturbed by the Duke
of Windsor's friendship with Wenner-Gren, and Churchill wrote to
the duke in March 1941 pleading with the former king to break off his
business dealings with the Swedish tycoon because of the damage the
relationship could do to Great Britain's war effort. When his pleading
had no effect on the duke, Churchill turned the matter over to
William Stephenson, Britain's chief of intelligence in the Western
Hemisphere and the mastermind behind Great Britain's secret operations throughout the Americas. He had arrived in New York in July
1940 and was entrusted by British intelligence with the task of col-
lecting information on Axis activities aimed against Great Britain's war
effort and countering them. Further, he was to use his contacts
among American business and government leaders to help Great
Britain obtain essential war supplies. Finally, Stephenson was to do all
he could to promote a climate of public opinion favorable to American
intervention in the war.

It was a big task, but Stephenson, a self-made millionaire, was not
daunted by challenges. He had been a flying ace in World War I and
been responsible for several important intelligence reports on the
German steel industry in the late 1930s. The forty-four-year-old
Stephenson was a small, slim man with a ruddy complexion and graying hair, was a good listener, and was called "Little Bill" by his close
associates because of his short stature.[25]

Stephenson quickly expanded his efforts beyond the mere collection of information to an active campaign of highly illegal dirty tricks
and secret warfare. Through his official capacity as head of the British
Security Coordination (BSC), he oversaw the functions of various
British government departments, such as the Ministry of Information,
Economic Warfare, Supply, War Transport, Intelligence, and the military. The BSC was responsible for destroying the vast German espionage network in Latin America, as well as blocking the Axis smuggling routes from the Americas.

The BSC was aware of the Banco Continental arrangement because it had been monitoring Davis's activities since the beginning of

the war. H. Montgomery Hyde, one of Stephenson's agents, was in Nassau at the time of the Windsor-Camacho talks and was concerned about the implications of the talks. To counter Davis and Wenner-Gren's activities, Stephenson reinforced his Latin American organization with additional staff. With the tacit approval of the FBI, he developed a scheme to disrupt the Wenner-Gren and Davis syndicate's plans.[26]

thirteen

Strange Death

AT THE SAME TIME Davis was trying to rebuild his Mexican business, he was also rapidly expanding his Texas oil empire. Already possessing the largest oil reserves in South Texas, Davis was forging ahead. In November 1940, he opened a new oil field in Goliad County, Texas (near Corpus Christi). A boomtown sprang up on the mesquite-covered plains and hundreds of men were employed in his oil field; his friends and workers named the place Davis City. Not content with 51 wells and a big tank farm, he planned 100 more wells, a large refinery, a recycling plant, and a 120-mile pipeline from his Rincon field to Brownsville. Davis opened negotiations with the head of the Brownsville port to bring oil tankers to the port to carry Davis's oil.[1]

To realize his plans, Davis held a meeting with bankers to finance his constructions plans. Dodging reporters, he invited twenty-three guests to tour his Brownsville facilities in late January 1941. Given Davis's notoriety, the guests' identities and the reason for their visit were kept secret. Hotel workers and Davis employees were under strict orders not to divulge any information. This effort at secrecy proved futile, however, and the newspaper reporters hounding Davis soon had the names of most of his guests.[2]

The sixteen businessmen, seven accompanied by their wives, included high officials of several independent oil companies of Texas, Oklahoma, and New York as well as Davis's bankers. The visitors included Guy E. Reed, director of Harris Trust & Savings Bank of Chicago (Harris Trust had already made a substantial loan to finance Davis's Rincon facilities); Wilbur E. Hightower, president of First National Bank of Oklahoma City; Davis's favorite banker, Latimer Gray of Bank of Boston; and other Davis cronies, Nils Hansell, C. E. MacDonald, Austin Taylor, and Fritz Flanley.[3]

After entertaining his guests in Matamoros, Mexico, Davis invited them to the nearby Double D Ranch, owned by Douglas Davenport, a colorful oil tycoon and friend of Davis. Meeting the guests at the Double D Ranch were Davenport, Davis, his wife, and Erna Wehrle. While there, Davis made his standard sales pitch in which he described the vast fortune to be made from investing in his new projects.[4]

The bankers and oilmen must have liked what Davis told them, because soon Davis was expanding his Texas holdings. He took out options to drill on another 100,000 acres in the lower Rio Grande valley. Davis's Rio Grande valley oil field was rich, and drilling continued long after his death. To further his plans for an oil pipeline from the Rincon field, Davis bought the Valley Pipe Line Company in May. By this time he had built up such an impressive set of oil holdings and facilities that he ranked among the top individual oilmen in the state of Texas. With his new wealth, he began to look for new oil fields in other states. He made several trips to California to survey possible oil deals in the Long Beach area, and he opened an office in Seattle to manage a shale oil operation in Washington State.[5]

Everything was going so well in Texas that Davis, on April 30, moved his New York office from its palatial 30 Rockefeller Plaza location to a smaller office in the Chrysler Building. The Davis office lease had come up for renewal and someone—either Big Oil, the British, or the FBI—put pressure on the Rockefeller Plaza people to refuse to renew the Davis lease. However, this did not really bother Davis, whose oil prospects in Texas were looking so good that he moved the main activities of the company to the Houston office in June. Almost all of the company's assets were then in Texas and the international operations were for the most part closed down because of the war. Most of the company's staff moved to Houston and only Davis, Wehrle, Kauffman, and Morris Geye, who took care of Davis's personal finances, remained in the New York office.[6]

Because the New York office was being closed down, Werner Von Clemm decided to leave Davis and Company. He had too many ties in New York to move to Houston. His New York import business was keeping him busy and he was active in the America First Committee in New York. There were also clandestine reasons for Von Clemm to stay in New York. In addition, it was becoming a political embarrassment for Davis to have Von Clemm on the payroll. In May, a British cabinet minister, Hugh Dalton, accused Von Clemm's Pioneer Import Corporation of being the outstanding evader of the British economic blockade of Germany. Von Clemm issued a statement denying the charge, but it was still best for Davis to distance himself from Von Clemm.[7]

Davis knew the FBI was still following him and that it would be best if he did not provide them with any more detrimental information with which to harass him. The FBI and British intelligence were both harassing him through the newspapers, but it did not stop him. It just made him more circumspect. He did not like the surveillance and intimidation, nor did his staff, but it did not frighten him or interfere with his activities. It was just something he had to tolerate. This may have been a fatal mistake on his part. The harassment was a warning to cease his behavior. To ignore such a warning was dangerous.[8]

Davis's activities continued until August 1, 1941, when he died suddenly and unexpectedly in Houston, Texas. To supervise his expanding Texas oil business, Davis and Wehrle had flown to Houston on July 23 from New York. After taking care of some business there, including a radio broadcast endorsing Senator Wheeler's attack on Lend-Lease, he drove with Austin Taylor to San Antonio on July 31. Davis and Taylor returned to Houston that evening, arriving about eight o'clock. Taylor said that Davis "was in as excellent spirits and health as I have ever seen him."[9]

On returning to Houston, Davis tried to telephone his son Joe, who was in Houston with his fiancée, so that he could take them out to dinner. Unable to reach Joe, Davis and Wehrle went to dinner at a little crab and fish restaurant that they frequented when in Houston. Davis was tired when he returned to the hotel, but he tried once more to reach his son. However, his son had gone over to the neighbors' for a barbecue and Davis never reached him.[10]

Davis and Wehrle were staying in his apartment at the Lamar Hotel. Since 1936, both he and Wehrle had stayed at the Lamar when in Houston, and Davis had retained the apartment on a permanent basis since 1939. The apartment consisted of five rooms (kitchen, living room, and three bedrooms) connected by a long corridor that extended through the suite. Davis's wife, as usual, had stayed in New York.[11]

According to Wehrle, at about two o'clock in the morning on August 1, a very agitated and talkative Davis knocked on her bedroom door and said excitedly, "Miss Wehrle, I am really sick this time." Wehrle immediately called Davis's Houston doctor, who said he would be right over. In the meantime, Davis went to the kitchen to get a glass of water, claiming to be very thirsty. After hanging up the telephone, Wehrle went to the door of her room and looked down the corridor. At that moment, Davis was coming down the corridor from the kitchen toward her. As he reached the door to his bedroom and turned to enter, he dropped to the floor at her feet. Wehrle says that, "He didn't say anything and as I looked down, he had blood coming out his mouth and nose. He was dead."[12]

The doctor arrived soon after, examined Davis, and pronounced him dead. The doctor recorded the cause of death as a coronary occlusion and had the body taken to the county morgue. The next morning the body was transferred to a funeral home, where the Davis family and Davis's Houston employees viewed the body. The same day Wehrle rented a plane from Eastern Airlines and, accompanied by Joe Davis and his fiancée, flew with the body back to New York late that evening. Davis's wife, Marjanna, had the funeral home people meet the plane and they immediately took his body to be cremated. After Davis was cremated, Mrs. Davis took his ashes and spread them over the rosebushes at their Scarsdale home. There was no funeral.[13]

Davis was dead in the prime of his life, even though as far as his friends knew he was in the best of health. Wehrle said, "It was a shock. . . . He was only 52. He was a very young man." Wehrle felt Davis's last words, "I am really sick this time," were strange. "Very often he would say he wasn't feeling well or he was sick but it was as if he really felt this was something very serious."[14]

According to Wehrle, Davis had only one symptom that indicated he might have heart problems. In April, on his way to Mexico City, Davis was taken ill in Brownsville, Texas. He had a blood clot in his shoulder and his arm had gone numb. He checked into the local hospital for a couple of days until the blood clot had broken up. After the Brownsville incident, Davis had a complete physical examination by his doctor in New York, after which the doctor said that Davis was fine and as far as he could tell there was nothing wrong with him. Davis told Wehrle that the doctor had told him that "he was like a young man." When Wehrle returned to New York after Davis's death she talked with his New York doctor and asked, "How on earth could you not know something was wrong?" The doctor could say only that you could not always catch a heart problem.[15]

Davis's New York doctor may have been correct in his original diagnosis that there was nothing wrong with Davis's heart. At the request of the author, a physician reviewed Davis's symptoms and concluded that it was unlikely that Davis died from a coronary occlusion. If Davis had a coronary occlusion, he probably would not have fallen over and immediately died. Most likely he would have been in great pain and lingered for some time before expiring. Further, blood coming out of Davis's mouth and nose is not consistent with a heart attack because when the heart stops blood will not flow. Therefore, Davis probably did not die from a heart attack.[16]

Davis's sudden death naturally raised rumors of foul play, but the FBI discreetly discouraged any official inquiry at the request of the BSC. If Davis's death was due to natural causes why would the BSC discourage an inquiry? Adding to the uncertainty is the following curious event. Some time after Davis's death, Wehrle received a telephone call from Davis's doctor in Houston, saying that he had received a strange telephone call from someone who refused to identify himself. The person wanted to know if Davis had died a natural death or if he had been poisoned.[17]

After telling the caller that Davis died of a heart attack, the doctor began having second thoughts. He had not performed an autopsy and he really was not certain what had killed Davis. The doctor realized that it was possible that someone might have put something in his drinking water. Indeed, some of the symptoms of poisoning by atropine (commonly known as belladonna) are similar to those exhibited by Davis just before his death. Atropine causes a great thirst and often the victim becomes agitated and talkative.

After mulling over this possibility, the doctor called Wehrle to ask her what she thought of the possibility that Davis was poisoned. Wehrle thought the idea was absurd because Davis always drank tap water and they had not eaten in the hotel the night of his death. Therefore, she felt that "there was no possible way for anyone to have the opportunity to poison Davis." As she told the doctor, "I am the only one who could have poisoned Davis." Nor could she see why anyone would want to kill Davis. As she told the author, "Why would the British Secret Service or the FBI kill Davis? Did they think he was that important?"[18]

Despite Wehrle's disbelief and although there is no definitive evidence that anyone killed Davis, there were a number of people and organizations that would have benefited from his death. The list of potential suspects is long, and the following discussion explains why most of these can be eliminated and why only one, British intelligence, would have murdered Davis.

The Germans clearly had a motivation to kill Davis. Davis's death probably averted a full congressional inquiry of Davis's alliance with John L. Lewis. On April 30, 1941, Representative Francis Walter (Democrat, Pennsylvania) had asked on the House floor for a congressional investigation of Davis "to find out what he did in return for this tremendous fee [$440,000 from the Germans]." If Davis had cooperated with such an inquiry, John L. Lewis, Senators Wheeler and Guffey, and other powerful Americans would have been at least embarrassed and possibly arrested on criminal charges. Further, Davis had extensive knowledge about German activities in the Americas. Therefore, the Germans and their sympathizers had reasons to keep Davis quiet. Adolf Berle considered it a possibility that Erna Wehrle was an important German espionage agent. If so, then she, as she herself admits, had the opportunity to poison Davis. Moreover, it seems odd that Davis's body was immediately flown back to New York and cremated, which made it impossible to ever definitively prove the cause of death.[19]

As Senator Josh Lee (Democrat, Oklahoma) said on the Senate floor on November 4, 1941,

> . . . a strange thing happened. I make no charges; I simply refer to facts. It was known then, and published, that . . . when this investigation was pending, suddenly a man who had never had heart disease in his life, according to all the information I could get, suddenly died from heart disease, or else it was suicide. Certainly he was a man who was absolutely in good health. You say, oh, you have a good imagination. The Nazis do stranger things than that. They reached their long arm down into South America and rubbed out a FBI star witness. . . . There is also evidence that they reached their long arm into the United States and rubbed out a man who used to be a newspaper man in Germany.[20]

However, it is unlikely that the Germans eliminated Davis as a preventive measure. The Germans, as standard procedure, had limited Davis's knowledge of their clandestine activities. Moreover, the Germans knew that Davis would not be able to tell a congressional committee much about their activities that was not already known by the American government. Nor is there any reason to believe that the various American isolationists would need to murder Davis. There is little that Davis could tell anyone about the isolationists that was not already known to the public.

A less sinister set of suspects would be Davis's own wife, Marjanna, and Erna Wehrle. Each had motivation: Marjanna would inherit his wealth and Wehrle would take over control of the company. They had the opportunity: Wehrle was the person who had the best opportunity to poison Davis. In addition, if Wehrle and Marjanna were in league to kill Davis, it would explain the abrupt movement of his body from Houston to New York and the immediate cremation of the body on arrival in New York.[21]

Despite this circumstantial evidence, there are several problems with this scenario. First, there is no evidence that either Mrs. Davis or Wehrle were other than completely devoted to Davis. The conjecture that Wehrle would have killed Davis seems implausible. She had spent the past seven years of her life with Davis and everything indicates that she was utterly devoted to him. Second, although it is possible that Marjanna and Wehrle could be accomplices in his death, if money and power were their motivation, then the theory falls apart. It is possible that Marjanna Davis was unaware of her husband's tax problems, but Wehrle would certainly have known of the company's looming tax liabilities. Further, Wehrle also had to know that the viability of Davis and Company was directly linked to William Davis. Without his brilliant business sense, the company would quickly collapse.[22]

A much more likely suspect would be the FBI at the behest of Adolf Berle. The following is a list of circumstantial evidence for such a scenario:

1. Roosevelt placed Berle in charge of coordinating U.S. counterespionage activities and Berle was the State Department's liaison with the FBI.
2. Both Roosevelt and Berle hated Davis because of his moves to stop Roosevelt's reelection and his attempt to entrap the president in Hitler's peace ploys.
3. Roosevelt gave Berle license to stop Davis's activities.
4. Berle instigated the FBI surveillance of Davis, which was still in place at the time of Davis's death.
5. Roosevelt was personally interested in the Davis surveillance.
6. Berle was behind much of the harassment campaign against Davis.
7. The FBI, despite all of its surveillance and harassment of Davis, had been unable to gather evidence of any crime for which it could arrest Davis.

Given his rising wealth and pro-German activities, Berle and the FBI must have been frustrated that they were unable to stop him from continuing his anti-Roosevelt operations.[23]

Yet there is no evidence that the FBI ever contemplated killing Davis. For example, FBI internal memoranda indicate that the Texas office was completely surprised by Davis's death. In addition, as described in the next chapter, the FBI was assisting the Internal Revenue Service to bring Davis down through tax evasion charges. Why would the FBI look at Davis's taxes if it intended to kill him? Finally, it was completely out of character for J. Edgar Hoover to approve an illegal murder. Hoover was at heart a policeman and, despite his various illegal chicaneries, would probably never had sanctioned the FBI carrying out a murder. Moreover, the FBI had been "taken out of the loop" by Roosevelt in the execution of "dirty" operations.[24]

By far the most plausible candidate to kill Davis was British intelligence. William Stephenson, in his authorized biography, *A Man Called Intrepid*, implied that his organization killed Davis. There is little question that the British had a few scores to settle with Davis. His organization had for many years been under surveillance by British intelligence throughout the world. During those years the British had taken note of the following activities by Davis:

1. Built the Germans one of their best oil refineries.
2. Tried to undermine British domination of the European oil market in the 1930s to the benefit of Germany.
3. Provided Mexico with the means to successfully destroy the British exploitation of Mexican oil fields.
4. Obtained for Germany the vital oil supplies that the German war machine needed before the war.
5. Tried to stop the war in 1939, which would have benefited only Germany.
6. Smuggled oil and other war materials through the British blockade to Germany.
7. Gathered espionage information for Germany through his business contacts.
8. Tried to defeat Roosevelt in his 1940 reelection campaign. Churchill considered Roosevelt's reelection vital to the British war effort.
9. Provided financial backing to the isolationist movement that was trying to limit American support of the British war effort.
10. Helped entangle the Duke of Windsor in the fascist-controlled Banco Continental.[25]

There was no likelihood that Davis was going to stop his anti-British activities, especially given his highly successful Texas oil fields, which were providing him with the means to intensify these activities. The British had no legal way to get their hands on Davis, so if they were going to stop him, they would have to use other means. Although there is no definitive evidence that the British assassinated Davis, the BSC papers record that "the swiftest way to put a stop to [Davis's schemes] was to remove Davis from the scene." There is also substantial circumstantial evidence that supports British involvement in Davis's death.[26]

First, British intelligence had close links to the Roosevelt administration and had wide latitude from the U.S. government to operate in the United States. Stephenson was very aware that his liaison with U.S. authorities was critical to his mission and he succeeded brilliantly in gaining their trust. In 1940, the British had established a close working relationship with the FBI.[27]

To forge this link, Stephenson had a mutual friend, boxing champion Gene Tunney, set up a meeting with J. Edgar Hoover in April 1940 at Hoover's home in Washington. Hoover listened to Stephenson's plea for cooperation on intelligence matters, then said he could do nothing without a specific order from Roosevelt. Stephenson replied, "And if I get it?" Hoover said, "Then we'll do business directly. Just myself and you. Nobody else gets in the act." Stephenson told him, "You will be getting presidential sanction."[28]

Soon afterward, following a meeting between Stephenson and Roosevelt, the president ordered "the closest possible marriage between the FBI and British Intelligence." Roosevelt was running a great risk, perhaps even of impeachment, by ordering such cooperation while America remained at peace. Hoover knew it was risky and insisted that the liaison be kept secret from the State Department.

An armchair warrior, Hoover at first impressed the British. He provided the radio transmitter that gave Stephenson direct communication with London and the FBI helped prevent sabotage of British ships in American ports. FBI agents intercepted letters from the U.S. mail that Stephenson wanted to see and passed on documents captured from German spies. In return for his assistance, the British passed on information they obtained from opening other people's mail and shared with Hoover information collected by British agents in Latin America. A year after cooperation began, Stephenson had sent no fewer than 100,000 reports to the FBI.[29]

Eventually the British became disillusioned with Hoover, however, because he made such poor use of the information that they supplied him. For example, Hoover loved publicity, and the British had to be very careful what information they passed on to the FBI because British methods depended on concealment and they dared not confide in him certain plans for fear of leaks.[30]

To replace Hoover, the British pushed Roosevelt for someone who had better instincts for intelligence work. On July 11, 1941, Roosevelt appointed a coordinator for the new Office of Information (soon to be renamed the Office of Strategic Services [OSS], forerunner of the Central Intelligence Agency [CIA]) to oversee U.S. foreign intelligence activities. His appointment to direct the OSS was William Donovan, a longtime enemy of Hoover. Well aware of Stephenson's efforts on Donovan's behalf, Hoover stopped cooperating with the BSC in the summer of 1941.[31]

Because of Hoover's limitations, Roosevelt, through Berle, who was his intermediary with British intelligence, used the BSC to conduct a number of secret operations. Roosevelt either did not wish to entrust these operations to the FBI or he felt the FBI director might refuse to go along with the operations. For example, Stephenson was the moving force behind a campaign to discredit Senator Burton Wheeler. The British also, as Hoover discovered, were carrying out surveillance and wiretapping operations against Americans. These activities required a considerable staff and at one time the BSC employed 3,000 men and women from its New York headquarters at 630 Fifth Avenue in Rockefeller Plaza.[32]

Even more amazing, Stephenson had people killed in the United States with the acquiescence of the American government. The BSC had "disposal squads" to handle disagreeable duties. These squads were trained at a secret camp that Stephenson had established just across the border in Canada in the fall of 1940. Recruits were instructed in intelligence and espionage techniques, including assassination methods. The normal formula for the British assassinations was that the victim would be declared "has departed for Canada," a fate more final than these innocuous words imply.[33]

As one of Stephenson's agent's, Ian Fleming, later the author of the James Bond novels, said about a traitorous British seaman, "killing him quickly perhaps saved hundreds of sailors' lives . . . [and] saved his Majesty's Government a lot of time and money, too." The sailor was found dead in the basement of a New York apartment building. In response to an FBI agent's comment that it might be good if the sailor were killed, Stephenson "glanced down at his right hand. He lifted it and chopped at an angle against the hardwood surface of his desk. I already have," he said.[34]

On another occasion a captain in German intelligence, Ulrich Von Der Osten, was knocked down by a taxi and then run over by another vehicle while crossing Broadway in Times Square in New York City on the evening of March 18, 1941. He died the next day without regaining consciousness. By a supposed "lucky" tip from the man's hotel manager, the FBI found letters in his luggage that helped them round up a German spy ring. More than one account has implied that the death was not accidental.[35]

Of course, U.S. authorities were often irritated by such British activities and Stephenson did everything he could to keep his illegal activities secret and thereby not embarrass the American government. This leaves matters very murky. Did Roosevelt request that the British eliminate Davis or did the British act on their own volition? Did the British have American acquiescence for the killing? In fact, did they even tell the Americans about the assassination? These questions remain unanswered.[36]

Despite the circumstantial evidence, it is not possible to prove that British intelligence assassinated Davis. First, Davis had a blood clot only a few months before his death, which could have been a symptom of ill health. Indeed, the physician that the author consulted believes that Davis's symptoms are consistent with a blood clot in the lungs. This type of clot would cause Davis to quickly pass out due to lack of blood flow to the brain. Second, despite his doctor's clean bill of health for Davis, medical science's ability to diagnose a heart problem in the 1940s was limited. Third, although Davis did not drink, his life-style was conducive to heart problems: he smoked, he was at the age when men typically have heart attacks, and he worked very hard. Fourth, as Wehrle said, how could the British have poisoned Davis? The opportunities were limited for the British to have gotten Davis to consume poison on the night of his death. Fifth, despite Davis's many offenses in British eyes, was stopping Davis truly worth the risk of killing a well-known wealthy American businessman? If they were concerned about Banco Continental and its link to the Duke of Windsor, why not kill Wenner-Gren, the key conspirator, rather than the lesser light, Davis? Finally, not even William Stephenson's ambiguous statements that imply that the British eliminated Davis can be believed with certainty. There have been criticisms of Stephenson's biography as having many inaccuracies and exaggerations. In the end, as with most things about Davis's life, his death is just another mystery.[37]

fourteen

Collapse and Cover-Up

ERNA WEHRLE'S COMPLETE knowledge of all aspects of the various Davis enterprises made her the logical successor to be head of Davis and Company. Despite the male prejudice against career women, and with the recommendation of Bank of Boston, a meeting of company officials in Houston in October 1941 made Erna Wehrle president of the company and James Lee Kauffman executor of the Davis estate. Because Davis and Company revolved completely around Davis, it was obvious to all that the company could not continue to exist without him. Thus, closure of the company was a foregone conclusion. However, Davis and Company was not closed down immediately because it had many ongoing contracts.[1]

Davis left virtually all his estate (initially valued at up to $10 million) as a trust fund for his wife and two sons. His wife was to receive almost half of the income from the estate during her lifetime and his two sons were to split the rest. With Kauffman as executor and Wehrle as an agent for the executor, the two insiders controlled the company's assets. Kauffman recommended that since everything was in Davis's name, the corporation's assets be transferred to an estate trust to avoid taxes.[2]

After the assets were transferred, Kauffman and Wehrle soon realized that the income from the Texas oil fields was not sufficient to cover the company's operating expenses. Because the operating expenses were financed with bank loans, something had to be done to generate more cash flow or the banks would seize the company. Latimer Gray estimated that Davis owed Bank of Boston $4 million and other banks at least another $1 million.[3]

To prevent foreclosure, Wehrle laid off staff and the New York office was closed at the end of January 1942. Next, Kauffman and Wehrle began selling off company assets. In July, Erna Wehrle sold Davis's interests in some of the Texas oil fields to a business group that included former Davis employee, Henry Wilson. However, the Treasury Department brought Wehrle and Kauffman's efforts to a dead stop.[4]

The Treasury Department, in conjunction with the FBI, had been investigating Davis's tax returns since December 1940 and had uncovered massive tax liabilities. Davis had never paid taxes on his overseas earnings. The magnitude of his tax problems were such that Davis had gone to Washington early in the summer of 1941 to discuss the status of the inquiry with Secretary of the Treasury Morgenthau. Soon after his death, the federal government put a lien on the estate for $5 million in tax claims. Placed in charge of settling the tax claims against the estate was Judge Roy Hofheinz, who was later mayor of Houston.[5]

The estate was tied up for a long time after Davis's death because of the tax claims. If the company was to keep paying off its bank loans, something needed to be done quickly. After Kauffman discussed the situation with Judge Hofheinz, the judge proposed that the Davis half of the Rincon oil field be sold to the Rice Institute, a subsidiary of Rice University. The deal went through and Kauffman was able to preserve a 5-percent interest in the oil field for the Davis estate. The 5-percent interest was worth a significant sum and the sale of the Rincon field provided sufficient cash to pay off the company's various bank loans.[6]

However, this did not resolve the tax problems of the company. By this time, government accountants had complete access to Davis's financial accounts and had uncovered total tax claims on the Davis estate that came to the enormous sum of $45 million. However, Kauffman was able to settle these claims for just $850,000 in March 1948, less than 3 percent of the original assessment. This generous settlement came after Charles Oliphant and Daniel A. Bolich of the Internal Revenue Service recommended the settlement to Internal Revenue commissioner Joseph D. Nunan.

Four years later, Senator John J. Williams (Republican, Delaware) charged that the case smacked of "influence-peddling" because Kauffman in 1945 hired former Democratic National Committee chairman William M. Boyle and a former Treasury official, Daniel J. Hanlon, to "fix" the case. Senator Williams charged that Boyle and Hanlon bribed Oliphant and Bolich to recommend the settlement. Although never proven, Senator Williams's accusation is quite possibly true because Nunan, Oliphant, and Bolich were later found guilty of similar offenses.[7]

Ironically, Davis's sons thought that Kauffman connived with Bank of Boston to steal the company's assets and leave the heirs with only crumbs. However, according to Wehrle, Kauffman "did everything he could and was very conscious of the beneficiaries and held out for the five percent interest in Rincon. Mrs. Davis got $1 million out of the settlement of the estate." No doubt what infuriated the Davis boys was that when Kauffman transferred the assets from the company to the estate trust, he received a significant portion of the assets as a fee for his job as executor of the will. There was nothing illegal about this, but Kauffman, embarrassed about his fee, postponed claiming it for some time. Wehrle contends that the asset transfer saved the estate a lot of money by avoiding inheritance taxes. As she said, "I think the boys were lucky with what they got."[8]

Despite Davis's death, the Germans wanted to continue their collaboration with Davis and Company. The high command of the German navy had the German Foreign Office send the following cable to Wehrle via the German embassy in Washington on August 29, 1941.

> For Miss Wehrle. Suggest a meeting with (you) . . . in Lisbon or Madrid to discuss important pending matters in connection with WR death. We expect you not to dispose of any of your European interests in connection with Eurotank, especially Crusader, without previously consulting us on long term. Please confirm cable. Power of attorney regarding Skanditank imperative to protect its and Eurotank's interests. Bockelmann (Eurotank plant manager), Dr. Sarre send their sincerest condolences to Mrs. Davis. [Signed Fetzer]

Wehrle knew she would not be able to go to Europe because she knew the U.S. State Department would not give her a passport. She also wanted to back away from the Germans because it was too dangerous to continue the collaboration. However, she had to be careful or the Germans would seize the company's European assets. She accordingly sent the following cautious reply, which went as a coded cable on September 20, 1941.

> Appreciate your messages. We have innumerable problems which must be solved before any attention can be paid to foreign holdings. I have been made president of companies and so long as I hold this position you can count on continued collaboration as in the past, and I can assure you now no moves will be made regarding European interests for many months to come and without advising you previously. Meeting abroad impossible in near future.

Although Wehrle would not come to Europe, Davis's German friends protected the company's German assets. After Davis's death, Fetzer oversaw Eurotank's operations, while Bockelmann continued as plant manager. However, Davis's German friends could not protect the Davis cabal in the Americas.[9]

In early 1942 federal agents arrested a member of Davis's inner circle, Werner Von Clemm. In February 1941, a lucky find by Treasury agents in New York eventually led to Clemm's arrest. Treasury agents had been watching a neutral ship, which had just docked. When two American sailors of German origin got off the boat carrying a Budweiser beer box, the Treasury agents stopped them. The box was searched and found to have a false bottom, under which were one hundred letters as well as valuable government bonds. The hidden documents were addressed to Werner Von Clemm and described a diamond smuggling operation.[10]

The Germans had seized a large quantity of diamonds when they occupied Belgium and Holland in 1940. Although it was never proven, there were suspicions that some of these diamonds were sent to the United States to be used to fund German espionage in the Americas. Because the war was going on, shipping these diamonds to the United States was in direct contravention of U.S. law. To evade U.S. customs, Von Clemm, with the help of his brother, Karl, and other accomplices, set up a complex smuggling operation that involved routing the diamonds through several countries. The diamonds were shipped from Brussels and Amsterdam to Rome, were put aboard an Italian airliner and flown via Lisbon and Dakar to Rio de Janeiro, and from South America went to New York by parcel post or courier.[11]

The hidden documents tipped the government off to Von Clemm's activity. After a long investigation, the Treasury Department finally pieced Von Clemm's smuggling operation together, and, on January 28, 1942, Treasury agents arrested him for smuggling diamonds into the United States. Von Clemm was eventually convicted and sentenced to prison for the maximum two-year term.[12]

At the same time as Von Clemm's arrest, Davis's activities in Mexico collapsed. First, under pressure from Roosevelt, the British government reestablished diplomatic relations with Mexico on October 22, 1941, a fitting end to Josephus Daniels's distinguished career. In the same month, Daniels resigned his post and returned home because of his wife's ill health.

Daniels's replacement was George Messersmith, another ardent anti-fascist, who would soon shut down the Davis and Wenner-Gren Mexican business syndicate.[13] During his first months in Mexico, Messersmith discovered that the Davis and Wenner-Gren business syndicate was financing Maximinio Camacho to bring about a coup d'état against his brother, the president of Mexico. With this evidence, Messersmith urged Treasury secretary Henry Morgenthau to act against Wenner-Gren. In January 1942, Morgenthau placed Axel Wenner-Gren on Washington's official blacklist of individuals in neutral countries doing business with the Axis powers. This made it a crime for any American firm to do business with Wenner-Gren or his companies. Wenner-Gren protested the State Department's action as unfair and tried through his powerful friends in Congress to have his name removed from the list, but the State Department stood firm.[14]

The blacklisting was not a complete disaster for Wenner-Gren because he had learned about it enough in advance to get his money out of Mexico before the Mexican government could freeze his funds. Nevertheless, the blacklisting was a severe blow to the pro-fascist business syndicate in Mexico because Wenner-Gren was to have been the principal source of capital for the syndicate. John Hastings endeavored to get New York bankers to take the place of Wenner-Gren, but failed, and the syndicate's contracts were canceled. Soon thereafter, Banco Continental was sold to local interests and the syndicate collapsed.[15]

With the collapse of the business syndicate, there was no further need for a Davis and Company office in Mexico, so in early 1942 Wehrle left for Mexico City to close the company's office. U.S. border police stopped her and thoroughly questioned her before they let her proceed to Mexico. They held up her plane and Wehrle thought they must have had her name on a list. While in Mexico, she was followed, and when she returned to the United States she was again stopped and questioned. It is not surprising that the FBI continued to investigate Davis and Company, because the FBI suspected that Wehrle was continuing to communicate with the Germans. It was clear to Wehrle that she needed to act if she were to end the harassment and get on with her life.[16]

To improve the image of Davis and Company, Wehrle decided that a public relations effort was in order. She had confidence in John L. Lewis and went to see him about an idea to placate the British. She asked him if it would be a good idea to donate oil to the British war effort to mitigate the charges that Davis was a German spy. Lewis was against the idea and the donation was never made. Soon after, the Davis estate purchased $400,000 in U.S. war bonds. On June 23, 1943, at a press conference, Wehrle formally bought the bonds with various local dignitaries present.[17]

While Wehrle was making her peace with the American authorities, Joachim Hertslet was having his own change of heart about the Nazi regime. After returning to Germany in the spring of 1941, Hertslet continued to negotiate trade contracts for the German military. However, the economic blockade around Germany tightened steadily during 1941–42, and the scope of Hertslet's trade functions gradually faded. After the German army's defeat at Stalingrad in February 1943, German manpower was fully mobilized and Hertslet, no longer indispensable to trade, was drafted into the German army.

By the time Hertslet was drafted, he had become completely disillusioned with Hitler. Like many other right-wing Germans who had once enthusiastically supported Hitler's drive for world domination, Hertslet now saw Hitler as the cause of Germany's coming defeat. Hertslet was always a man of strong convictions, and his complete loss of faith in Hitler led him to commit a dangerous protest.[18]

Soon after joining the army, Hertslet, in the presence of other soldiers, pulled down a portrait of Hitler from the barracks wall and smashed it to pieces. He declared that there was no way to win the war anymore. He was quickly arrested and was sentenced to death on October 30, 1943, for "seditious actions while in the army." However, by one of the war's random acts, Hertslet did not die. While awaiting execution in Berlin, the British massively bombed the city on November 23, 1943, destroying the official document that contained his death sentence. The German military decided that without proper documentation, the execution could not proceed and that Hertslet's court-martial would have to be repeated.

For some unknown reason, in his second trial in April 1944, Hertslet was sentenced to only a one-year suspended sentence. Instead of being executed, Hertslet was put in a probation battalion composed of soldiers who had committed offenses against the Reich. Hertslet spent the rest of the war under this hard-labor regime, and was captured by the Russians in 1945.[19]

With the liquidation of Davis and Company, the collapse of the Davis and Wenner-Gren syndicate, Von Clemm's arrest, Wehrle's attempts to get into the government's good graces, and Hertslet's imprisonment, Davis's conspiracy ended. However, there is one more episode in the story.

In the early spring of 1946, John Rogge, assistant U.S. attorney general, was preparing for the trial of thirty Americans, who were Nazi sympathizers, on charges of sedition. Unexpectedly, he received from U.S. Army captain Sam Harris, a member of the U.S. prosecution at the Nuremberg trials, information that there existed in Germany concrete proof of former ties between the Nazi government and certain important U.S. citizens.

Rogge immediately urged Attorney General Tom Clark to send him to Germany to obtain evidence of the Nazi-American connection. Clark authorized Rogge's mission and provided him with a four-person staff. Rogge flew to Europe on April 4 and stayed in Germany for eleven weeks. Rogge had the ideal background for this assignment because he had an intense interest in prosecuting American fascists. He had failed in the prosecution of fascist crackpots in 1943 because he lacked hard evidence of crimes, and he was determined not to fail this time.[20]

John Rogge was a forty-three-year-old midwesterner who had grown up on a farm. His parents were German immigrants and he had spoken only German until he entered school. A gifted scholar, he was the youngest graduate of Harvard Law School in modern times and was admitted to the bar at the age of twenty-one. Rogge worked for a variety of U.S. government agencies in the 1930s: Reconstruction Finance Corporation, Securities and Exchange Commission, Treasury Department, and Justice Department.

He had successfully prosecuted both corporate and criminal cases, and was a progressive New Deal liberal who talked enthusiastically about the prospects of democratic capitalism in America. He was utterly fearless in rooting out corruption and illegality, regardless of the political label of the malefactor. His politics and character would combine to make it impossible for him to back away from his own destruction.[21]

During their investigation in Germany, the Rogge team questioned sixty-six people, including two of the defendants in the main war crimes trial: Goering and Ribbentrop. He also interrogated dozens of other former top-ranking German officials, including Davis's friends,

Friederich Fetzer and Joachim Hertslet. With information from Fetzer and Hertslet, Rogge pieced together the basic outlines of Davis's pro-German activities.

The Rogge mission painstakingly scrutinized thousands of confidential documents from the files of the German War Ministry, Foreign Office, Propaganda Ministry, and Abwehr. Rogge later said,

> Our investigation showed us that we had completely underestimated the scope and scale of Nazi activities in the United States. When I went to Germany I felt that the biggest threat to American democracy emanated from the machinations of persons like the defendants in the sedition trial [i.e., Fascist crackpots]. I found that a far more dangerous threat lay in the inter-connections between German and American industrialists, and that some of the best known names in America were involved in Nazi intrigue.

When Rogge returned to Washington toward the end of June, he was confident that he had uncovered sufficient evidence to warrant federal prosecution of a number of Americans. Working at fever pitch, Rogge began preparing a comprehensive report to Attorney General Clark on the voluminous data he had collected in Germany. In early July, Rogge submitted to Clark a draft of the first section of his report.

To Rogge's surprise, the report's references to links between the Germans and American business and political leaders clearly disturbed Clark. He specifically commented on the mention of Senator Burton K. Wheeler in the report (Wheeler was a friend of Clark). After reading the report, Clark declared that it could not possibly be published and would have to remain a secret document. Rogge was not happy with Clark's proposal and asked that Clark hold off on a final decision until the report was completed. Rogge continued to work on the report through August. As he neared the end, one of Clark's aides proposed that Rogge omit all names of American politicians and businessmen. Rogge refused.[22]

By the time Rogge finished writing the report, he knew that the Department of Justice would never agree to publish his findings. Accordingly, he decided that he might as well put everything in the report regardless of whether it was politically expedient. The incendiary final recommendation of the report was for the Justice Department to begin an investigation of the collaboration between German and American industrialists before the war. On September 17, 1946, Rogge delivered his 396-page report to Attorney General Clark. As Rogge expected, Clark told him "the report would not be made public."[23]

Within days, however, Drew Pearson, the noted political muck-raker, published excerpts from Rogge's report in his column. Rogge said, "They appeared to be word for word from the report. I don't know where Mr. Pearson obtained them. I did not give the report to him." Despite Rogge's denial, it is curious that it was Drew Pearson who arranged the opening date for Rogge's national speaking tour a few weeks later.[24]

There were suspicions that Attorney General Clark had leaked excerpts from the report to Pearson, as Clark was one of Pearson's principal sources in the Justice Department. It was also reported that Clark had given the report to a well-known lawyer, who may have passed the report to Pearson. If Clark leaked the report, it may have been to give him the excuse he needed to fire Rogge by accusing Rogge of leaking the report to Pearson. Pearson indirectly confirmed the Clark leak story when he said that he did not receive his information from Rogge. He told Clark that "if you check your own files you will find that you yourself sent one of them (the Rogge report) out of Washington."[25]

Shortly afterward, Rogge obtained permission to take a two-week leave of absence to make a lecture tour on the fascist menace in the United States. Rogge told Attorney General Clark that he was going to make a speech on Nazi penetration of the United States. Rogge said Clark "asked me whether I would say that the department had not attempted to restrain me in any way. He again stated that my report was not going to be made public. I told him that I would not mention the report."[26,27]

But in a Swarthmore College speech, Rogge revealed to his college audience some of his report's discoveries. He stated that Goering and Ribbentrop had told him that John L. Lewis, William Rhodes Davis, Senator Burton Wheeler, former vice president John Garner, former postmaster general James Farley, and former president Herbert Hoover had all conspired with the Germans in an attempt to defeat Roosevelt in 1940 and keep the United States out of the war. He also mentioned that Hertslet played a key role in the German scheme to prevent Roosevelt's reelection in 1940.[28]

On the morning of October 25, Rogge left New York by plane for a speaking engagement in Seattle, Washington. Due to bad weather, the plane made an unscheduled stop in Spokane. At the airport Rogge was informed that there was no room for him on the next leg of the flight. Stuck in Spokane, he was told that a Mr. Savage was on his way to the airport to see him. Soon afterward, a man approached Rogge at the airport and said, "My name's Savage, I'm from the Federal Bureau of Investigation." He handed Rogge an envelope. The envelope contained a letter to Rogge from Attorney General Clark. The letter curtly notified Rogge that he was dismissed from the Justice Department immediately. Clearly the FBI had been following Rogge and had arranged to keep him in Spokane so that he could be handed his termination letter. Attorney General Clark wanted Rogge's authority as a federal official stripped away before he could speak at another college.

On October 24, the day before Rogge was fired, Senator Wheeler had visited the White House and conferred privately with President Harry Truman for two hours. Wheeler was concerned that the Rogge report made it seem as if Wheeler's speeches and activities were linked to Nazi propaganda plans. Wheeler also hoped that Truman would soon appoint the senator to a federal judgeship and knew that Rogge's accusations might put an end to this appointment because it required Senate confirmation. Although John L. Lewis had refused to comment publicly on Rogge's accusations about Lewis's German connections, he supposedly gave Wheeler off-stage prompting to meet with President Truman.[29]

Wheeler and Truman were old friends. In the 1930s Wheeler had treated Truman, the then-junior senator from Missouri, with generosity. He had been a teacher of sorts to Truman and had given him his first major responsibility, a railroad investigation. In return, Wheeler was the only Democratic senator that President Truman had openly supported for renomination in 1946. Unfortunately, Truman's support had not been enough to overcome Montana Democrats' dislike of Wheeler's isolationist policies, and Wheeler had failed to win the Democratic primary that summer. Although their political views were now far apart, Truman felt compelled to stand by Wheeler.[30]

That evening the president telephoned Attorney General Clark and summoned him to the White House, where he gave Clark direct orders to fire Rogge. A few hours later, the attorney general called a midnight press conference and announced that Rogge was being dismissed from the Justice Department. Clark said Rogge was being fired because he had "willfully violated" department regulations by publicly quoting from his confidential report.[31]

Rogge's dismissal seems particularly ironic in that J. Edgar Hoover was traveling around the country giving speeches that denounced Americans for being communists, and Hoover's sources were confidential FBI files. The newspapers and radio commentators had a field day denouncing Attorney General Clark and President Truman for firing Rogge. Walter Winchell went so far as to call for Clark's impeachment by Congress. Progressives complained that Truman's action was yet another indication that the president placed friendship above the public interest.

However, nothing came of it. Too many important Washington political figures, both left and right, would be embarrassed by a public airing of Rogge's report, and despite heated demands, Clark never released the report to the public. Rogge went on a speaking tour denouncing fascist infiltration of America, but the media soon lost interest and the story disappeared from public discussion. It was the beginning of the Cold War and the U.S. government was interested in making friends with "acceptable" Germans. No one wanted to bring up anyone's Nazi connections. When later asked why he was fired, Rogge said, "Wheeler was closer to President Truman than I was."

Despite Wheeler's ouster of Rogge, it did Wheeler no good. The political furor over Rogge's firing had ended any possibility of a political appointment for Wheeler by Truman. The man who had been touted as the likely next president of the United States in 1940 had no political future. In 1947, he left his seat in the Senate after twenty-four years. With no political prospects, he took up a law practice with his son in Washington, D.C., disappeared from the political spotlight, and died in obscurity in 1975.

So ended the Davis intrigues. Only a few of the participants ever suffered for their activities. Their deeds had been a major contribution to the Nazi war effort, but it was impossible to prove that any of them had done anything illegal. Most disappeared from the headlines and went on with their lives. For example, all of Davis's many partners in the Nazi oil trade died in their beds. Walter Jones barely outlived Davis, dying on September 3, 1943, at his home in Washington, D.C., at the age of sixty-nine after a short illness. Like Wheeler, Joseph Guffey lost his Senate seat in the 1946 election and returned to the oil business. He died in Washington, D.C., in 1959. Latimer Gray, Davis's banker, continued with Bank of Boston. He had a distinguished banking career and was added to the board of directors of Bank of Boston in 1953. He retired from the bank in 1959 and died in 1985 at the age of ninety-one.[32]

John L. Lewis continued to lead the United Mine Workers union for many years and died a labor icon. In 1960, Adolf Berle sat next to Lewis at an award dinner. Berle said of the event, "He was all smiles and velvet and we chatted and nobody said a word about his negotiations with Hitler. He has done a great deal for a great many people." It must have galled Berle that someone he knew had collaborated with the Nazis on several occasions was now lionized as a great hero of democracy.[33]

Lord Inverforth died in 1955 at his home at the age of ninety, leaving his heirs a vast fortune. His funeral was a magnificent event. The archdeacon of Hampstead officiated and more than one hundred heads of major British corporations, as well as Prince Axel of Denmark, attended. Nothing surfaced about his German connections until many years after his death. Similarly, Axel Wenner-Gren was never prosecuted for his pro-Nazi activities. After the war, he devoted his time to industrial enterprises in Mexico and Canada and to various philanthropic activities in Sweden. He died a wealthy and well-respected businessman in 1961 at the age of eighty.[34]

Charles Lindbergh served in a distinguished manner in the Pacific Theater during World War II and, after the war, wrote several well-received books. In the 1950s, a popular movie (starring James Stewart) about his famous flight to Paris glorified Lindbergh as a true American hero. Nothing was said about his pro-Nazi leanings or his anti-Semitism. He died a well-respected American legend in 1974.

As for Davis's German conspirators, they, like most Germans of the period, tried to forget about the war and the Nazis. The Von Clemms went into private banking after the war. Helmuth Wohlthat married an American in 1953 and spent much of his life in the United States. He joined the Henkel Corporation and eventually became a member of the board of directors. He died in Düsseldorf, Germany, in 1983.[35]

As for Joachim Hertslet, his linguistic abilities (he spoke Russian) stood him in good stead with the Soviets, who quickly released him from a prisoner-of-war camp. He became an interpreter for the Soviet army for several years before moving to West Germany. He joined a financial firm in Bonn and spent the remainder of his career as a foreign trade and currency adviser. In his role as an international businessman, he visited the United States in the early 1950s and met with Kauffman and Wehrle. He played a role in German-Arab trade policy in the 1950s and 1960s and was one of the first German businessmen to open economic relations with Gamal Abdel Nasser's Egypt. Indicative of his anti-Semitic past, he opposed the German Holocaust reparation treaty with Israel because it might damage trade relations with the Arab world. He died of kidney disease in Munich, Germany, in 1970 at the age of fifty-seven.[36]

As for Davis's personal staff, Nils Hansell went to Sweden after the war to sell off Davis's Swedish assets. With the liquidation of Davis and Company assets, he retired. He later moved to Hawaii and died in the 1950s. Austin Taylor went to work for the billionaire oilman, H. L. Hunt, until Taylor's death. James Lee Kauffman returned to

Japan after the war as part of the American occupation government, and played a major role in establishing a new legal system for Japan. He remained in Japan and rebuilt his Japanese law firm until his death.[37]

As might be expected, Davis's personal secretary and confidant, Erna Wehrle, "landed on her feet." After the war she traveled to Hamburg to sell the European assets of Davis and Company and sold the Eurotank refinery to British Petroleum in 1946. Thus, Big Oil at long last had "done in" Davis. Erna Wehrle married in the late 1940s and later retired to a comfortable life in a California resort town. She was still living there at the time of this writing.[38]

This story does not have a happy conclusion, and few of the principal actors come across as shining examples for humanity. Nor do most of the evildoers get their comeuppances in the end. It is a tale of greed on all sides, with only a handful of the players standing up for democratic principles. However, if there is anything to learn from the Davis story, it is that some people can and will take a stand for what is just and right. Certainly, Daniels, Berle, Morgenthau, Messersmith, and Rogge were willing to fight against the evil that fascism represented, despite the consequences. For this stand we must honor them, regardless of other mistakes in their lives. Acts of courage, when most people were silent, are what foiled Davis in the end. These acts should be honored and remembered.

Notes

In citing works in the notes, the following shortened titles have been used:

NYT New York Times.
SD   U.S. State Department.
FO   Foreign Office.

Chapter One: High Roller

[1] First interview with Erna Frieda Wehrle, Nov. 11, 1995, p. 14; William Rhodes Davis Federal Bureau of Investigation File # 65-1128 Part One, p. 71; *Houston Post*, Aug. 2, 1941.

[2] Davis FBI File Part One, p. 290; Thirteenth Census of the United States, Census Roll 33, vol. 46, ED 95, Sheet 4, Line 55, 1900; *New York Times (NYT)*, Aug. 2, 1941; *Newsweek*, Jan. 13, 1941; *Fortune*, Jan. 1941, p. 86.

[3] Davis FBI File Part One, p. 290; *New York Herald Tribune*, Jan. 6, 1941; *Houston Post*, Aug. 2, 1941.

[4] Massachusetts Department of Public Health Marriage Records.

[5] *Houston Post*, Aug. 2, 1941; *PM* (New York), May 6, 1941, p. 11.

[6] *New York Herald Tribune*, Jan. 6, 1941; Davis FBI File Part One, p. 290; Wehrle interview one, p. 20.

[7] *Houston Post*, Aug. 2, 1941; U.S. Department of State (SD) File 812.6363 W. R. Davis & Co.

[8] SD File 812.6363 W. R. Davis & Co.; Davis FBI File Part One, p. 291.

[9] *New York Herald Tribune*, Jan. 6, 1941; *National Cyclopedia of American Biography*, vol. 32, p. 217; *Fortune*, Jan. 41, p. 86; Mallison, Sam T., *The Great Wildcatter* (Charleston, W. Va.: Education Foundation of West Virginia, 1953), pp. 356–357; *Fortune*, Jan. 41, p. 86.

[10] Wehrle interview one, pp. 7, 13, 15; *PM*, Apr. 29, 1941, p. 22.

[11] Davis FBI File Part One, pp. 78, 114, 184.

[12] Ibid., p. 334.

[13] *Petroleum Times* (London), Oct. 2, 1920, p. 332; Davis FBI File Part One, p. 114; *New York Herald Tribune*, Jan. 6, 1941.

[14] Davis FBI File Part One, p. 67; Wehrle interview one, p. 16; SD File 812.6363 W. R. Davis & Co.

[15] Davis FBI File Part One, p. 78.

[16] *Great Wildcatter*, pp. 356–357; Davis FBI File Part One, pp. 292, 296.

[17] *NYT*, Apr. 27, 1924.

[18] *NYT*, Aug. 11, 1929; S.D. File 823.52 W. R. Davis & Co., p. 57; *Fortune*, Jan. 41, p. 86.

[19] *Fortune*, Jan. 41, p. 86.

[20] Townsend, Peter, ed., *Burke's Peerage: Baronetage and Knightage* (London: Burke's Peerage Limited, 1970), p. 1428; File E1368 1936, Correspondence of the Foreign Office (FO), Public Record Office, Great Britain, pp. 152–153.

[21] Davis FBI File Part One, pp. 10–11, 438; *Who Was Who*, vol. 3.

[22] *St. Louis Post-Dispatch*, Apr. 7, 1940.

[23] *Fortune*, Jan. 41, p. 86; SD File 823.52, pp. 73, 77.

[24] *PM*, May 6, 1941; SD File 823.52, p. 77; *NYT*, Aug. 21, 1928.

[25] SD File 823.52, p. 144; *Fortune*, Jan. 41, p. 88.

[26] *Fortune*, Jan. 41, pp. 86, 88; *PM*, May 6, 1941, pp. 11, 339; SD File 823.52; *NYT*, Aug. 11, 1929.

[27] SD File 812.6363 W. R. Davis & Co., p. 117; *NYT* 6/3, 1930; Davis FBI File Part One, pp. 63, 86; *Fortune*, Jan. 41, p. 86; SD File 823.52, pp. 119–120; *NYT*, Dec. 14, 1929.

[28] Davis FBI File Part One, p. 297; *Fortune*, Jan. 41, p. 88.

[29] *NYT*, Dec. 14, 1929, pp. 10–11, Aug. 26, 1930, Aug. 2, 1941; *PM*, May 6, 1941, p. 11.

[30] Davis FBI File Part One, pp. 63, 87, 76; *Fortune*, Jan. 41, pp. 86, 88.

[31] SD File 812.6363 W. R. Davis & Co., p. 117; Davis FBI File Part One, p. 290.

Chapter Two: Eurotank

[1] *Moody's Manual of Investments*, 1934, p. 203; SD File 812.6363 W. R. Davis & Co , p. 3.

[2] Davis FBI File Part One, p. 651; *Moody's*, 1936.

[3] During this period, he remarried. His new wife, Marie Marjanna Tomkunas, was a beautiful woman twenty years younger (Wehrle interview one, p. 1; *NYT*, Sept. 4, 1941; Davis FBI File Part One, p. 107).

[4] Davis FBI File Part Four, p. 44.

[5] Stevenson, William, *A Man Called Intrepid: The Secret War* (New York: Harcourt, Brace Jovanovich, 1976), p. 289.

[6] Davis FBI File Part Five, p. 176; Breuer, William B, *Hitler's Undercover War: The Nazi Espionage Invasion of the U.S.A.* (New York: St. Martin's Press, 1989), pp. 126–127.

[7] Childs, Marquis W., *I Write from Washington* (New York: Harper and Brothers, 1942), p. 179; Rogge, O. John, *The Official German Report: Nazi Penetration 1924–1942 Pan-Arabism 1939–Today* (New York: A. S. Barnes, 1961), p. 239; Davis FBI File Part One, p. 200; *Petroleum Times*, June 9, 1934, p. 634; Farago, Ladislas, *The Game of the Foxes: The Untold Story of German Espionage in the United States and Great Britain During World War Two* (New York: Donald McKay, 1971), p. 353; Rogge, p. 239.

[8] Childs, p. 179; Weyl, Nathaniel, and Weyl, Sylvia, *The Reconquest of Mexico: The Years of Lazaro Cárdenas* (New York: Oxford Univ. Press, 1939), p. 306; Martin, James Stewart, *All Honorable Men* (Boston: Little, Brown, 1950), p. 120; Guerin, Daniel, *Big Business and Fascism* (New York: Pathfinder Press, 1973), p. 232.

[9] Weyl, p. 306; Childs, p. 179; Davis FBI File Part Three, p. 52.

[10] *Moody's* 1938, p. 446; *Boston Evening Transcript*, Jan. 28, 1936; SD File 812.6363 W. R. Davis & Co., pp. 9, 32; Davis FBI File Part Four, p. 376;

New York Herald Tribune, Jan. 6, 1941; Daniels, Josephus, *Shirt-Sleeve Diplomat* (Chapel Hill, N.C.: Univ. of North Carolina Press, 1947), p. 251; Williams, Ben Ames Jr., *Bank of Boston 200: A History of New England's Leading Bank 1784–1984* (Boston: Houghton Mifflin, 1984), pp. 331–332; *Current Biography*, 1941, p. 211.

[11] SD File 812.6363 W. R. Davis & Co., p. 9; Williams, pp. 331–332.

[12] FO Paper FO371/22776 35696, p. 148.

[13] *NYT*, Feb. 12, 1940, Jan. 19, 1953; Williams, pp. 331–332.

[14] Williams, pp. 331–332.

[15] Farago, p. 353; Wehrle interview one, p. 15.

[16] Wehrle interview one, p. 17; Higham (A), Charles, *Trading with the Enemy: An Expose of the Nazi-American Money Plot 1937–1949* (New York: Delacorte Press, 1983), pp. 63–65; *NYT*, Jan. 23, 1942; Metcalfe, Philip, *1933* (Sag Harbor, N.Y.: Permanent Press, 1988), p. 225.

[17] Davis FBI File Part One, 9/25/1939, pp. 2–3; *NYT*, Jan. 23, 1942.

[18] Davis FBI File Part Five, p. 85; Davis FBI File Part One 9/25/1939, pp. 2–3; See *NYT*, Jan. 23, 1942.

[19] Higham (A), pp. 63–65.

[20] Martin, p. 120.

[21] Riess, Curt, *Total Espionage* (New York: G. P. Putnam's Sons, 1941), p. 201.

[22] Higham (A), p. 65; Farago, p. 353.

[23] Breuer, pp. 126–127; Davis FBI File Part Five, p. 85.

[24] Higham (A), p. 65.

[25] Rogge, p. 249; *PM*, Apr. 30, 1941, p. 22.

[26] Laquer, Walter, ed., *Fascism: A Reader's Guide: Analyses, Interpretations, Bibliography* (Berkeley, Calif.: Univ. of California Press, 1976), p. 419.

[27] Childs, p. 179.

[28] Weber, Eugen, *Varieties of Fascism: Doctrines of Revolution in the Twentieth Century* (Princeton, N.J.: D. Van Nostrand Company, 1964), pp. 15–16, 53–54, 64; Guerin, p. 82.

[29] Higham (A), pp. 63–65; Riess, p. 201.

[30] Stevenson, p. 289; Davis FBI File Part Five, p. 177; Higham (A), pp. 63–65.

[31] Davis FBI File Part Four, p. 377; Breuer, pp. 126–127; *Petroleum Times*, Nov. 24, 1934, p. 573; Davis FBI File Part Four, p. 377.

32 Davis FBI File Part One, 9/22/1939, pp. 16, 208; *Petroleum Times*, Aug. 3, 1935, p. 131; Davis FBI File Part Four, p. 376.

33 Ross, Hugh, "John L. Lewis and the Election of 1940," *Labor History* (Spring 1976), p. 163; Farago, p. 353; *PM*, Apr. 30, 1941, p. 22.

34 Davis FBI File Part Five, p. 176; Berle (A), Adolf Augustus Jr., *The Diary of Adolf Augustus Berle Jr. 1939–1941*, Yale Univ., p. 44.

35 Wehrle interview one, pp. 3, 19.

36 Davis FBI File Part Five, p. 34; Davis FBI File Part One, p. 208.

37 The company's headquarters was moved to New York in June 1936.

38 Davis FBI File Part One 9/22/39 65-128, pp. 10–11, 15.

39 Davis FBI File Part Five, pp. 220, 252.

40 Davis FBI File Part One, p. 418; *Petroleum Times*, Aug. 3, 1935, p. 131; Ross, p. 163; Wehrle interview one, pp. 4, 11.

41 SD file 812.6363 Scott Appeal Review; *Petroleum Times*, Feb. 15, 1936, p. 215.

42 SD file 812.6363 Scott Appeal Review; *NYT*, July 16, 1938; Wehrle interview one, p. 8; *New York Herald Tribune*, Jan. 6, 1941.

43 Higham (A), p. 65; *Foreign Office Correspondence Index (Index)*, 1936, Public Records Office, p. 377; Childs, pp. 179–180; *London Times*, Apr. 6, 1939; Davis FBI File Part One 9/22/39 65-128, pp. 10–11, 438; *Who Was Who*, vol. 3; *Petroleum Times*, Mar. 20, 1937, p. 381.

44 FO Paper E956/479/93 1936, p. 111; FO Paper E1368 1936, pp. 154-155.

45 FO Paper J542/20/1 1936, p. 185; Davis FBI File Part Three, p. 83; Davis FBI File Part Two, p. 179; *Index*, 1936, p. 825; Rhodes, Anthony, *The Vatican in the Age of the Dictators 1922–1945* (New York: Holt, Rinehart and Winston, 1973), p. 77.

46 FO Paper J542/20/1 1936, p. 185.

47 Childs, pp. 179–180.

48 FO Paper J542/20/1 1936, p. 185.

Chapter Three: Big Oil and Parent

1 Yergin, Daniel, *The Prize: The Epic Quest for Oil, Money and Power* (New York: Simon & Schuster, 1991), pp. 263–268.

2 Sampson, Anthony, *The Seven Sisters: The Great Oil Companies and the World They Shaped* (New York: Viking Press, 1975), p. 73.

[3] Yergin, pp. 263–268.

[4] *Petroleum Times*, Aug. 3, 1935, p. 131, May 9, 1936, p. 614.

[5] *Petroleum Times*, July 23, 1938, p. 122.

[6] SD file 812.6363 Scott Appeal Review; *Petroleum Times*, Feb. 15, 1934, p. 216.

[7] *Petroleum Times*, Apr. 25, 1936, p. 351.

[8] Higham (A), p. 65; *New York Herald Tribune*, Jan. 6, 1941; *Petroleum Times*, Mar. 20, 1937, p. 381.

[9] *Petroleum Times*, May 25, 1940, p. 484; Davis FBI File Part One 9/22/39 65-128, p. 11; *World Petroleum* (New York), Aug. 1938, p. 33; Childs, pp. 179–180.

[10] *Petroleum Times*, July 15, 1933, p. 107, Mar. 9, 1935, p. 283, Oct. 15, 1938, p. 505.

[11] *Petroleum Times*, June 22, 1940, p. 564.

[12] *London Times*, Apr. 6, 1939; *New York Herald Tribune*, Jan. 6, 1941.

[13] Dearborn was Bank of Boston's man in Davis's operations. Dearborn had formerly been with Bank of Boston and had gone to Davis and Company to protect the bank's interests (Davis FBI File 11-168 Part Two, p. 178).

[14] *Petroleum Times*, June 22, 1940, pp. 564, 570; *London Times*, Mar. 30, 1939, Apr. 6, 1939.

[15] Parent Petroleum Interests controlled the Eurotank refinery through Crusader Petroleum Industries.

[16] *Petroleum Times*, Sept. 19, 1936, p. 570, June 22, 1940, p. 378.

[17] *London Times*, Mar. 30, 1939, Apr. 6, 1939; *Petroleum Times*, Mar. 12, 1938.

[18] Sampson, pp. 76–77.

[19] *Petroleum Times*, Apr. 25, 1936, p. 531, Mar. 12, 1938, p. 341; *New York Herald Tribune*, Jan. 6, 1941.

[20] Childs, pp. 179–180; *Petroleum Times*, June 27, 1936, p. 836; Davis FBI File Part One 65-125 9/25/1939, p. 1.

[21] *Petroleum Times*, May 25, 1940, p. 484; *London Times*, Mar. 23, 1937.

[22] Davis FBI File Part One 65-128 9/25/1939, p. 1.

[23] SD File 812.6363 W. R. Davis & Co., p. 11; Wehrle interview one, pp. 2, 3; *Houston Post*, Aug. 2, 1941.

[24] *NYT*, Aug. 2, 1941; Davis FBI File Part One 65-128, p. 164.

[25] Van Allen was married to Davis's sister, and was Davis's brother-in-law (Davis FBI File 65-128, p. 7).

[26] Davis FBI File Part Five, p. 252; Wehrle interview one, p. 29.

[27] Davis FBI File Part Five, p. 62; Wehrle interview one, p. 1.

[28] Farago, p. 352; *New York Herald Tribune*, Jan. 6, 1941; Wehrle interview one, p. 2.

[29] Wehrle interview one, p. 1.

[30] Davis FBI File Part One 65-128 9/27/1939, p. 2.

[31] Farago, p. 352; Wehrle interview one, p. 9; Higham (A), p. 67; Davis FBI File Part Five, p. 332.

[32] Wehrle interview one, p. 1; *PM*, Apr. 29, 1941, p. 22; Davis FBI File 65-128 Part One, pp. 211–212; Davis FBI File Part Two, p. 273; Davis FBI File Part Five, p. 330.

[33] Wehrle interview one, p. 14; *PM*, Apr. 29, 1941, p. 22.

[34] *London Times*, Mar. 29, 1938.

[35] *Petroleum Times*, Apr. 24, 1937, p. 536.

[36] *Petroleum Times*, July 25, 1936, p. 119, Mar. 20, 1937, p. 384, Mar. 27, 1937, p. 402; *London Times*, Mar. 29, 1938, Apr. 6, 1939; *St. Louis Post-Dispatch*, Apr. 7, 1940.

[37] *Petroleum Times*, May 25, 1940, p. 484; *London Times*, Apr. 6, 1939.

[38] *Petroleum Times*, June 22, 1940, p. 570.

[39] Schröder Bank was closely linked to the Nazis. For example, the agreement that made Hitler chancellor of Germany in January 1933 was worked out in Herr Von Schröder's Cologne home (Guerin, Daniel, *Fascism and Big Business* [New York: Pathfinder Press, 1973], p. 40).

[40] Latimer Gray returned to Germany in the summer of 1939 to collect the last of the money owed by the German banks on the Hamburg oil refinery operation. When he left Germany on the last train before the German invasion of Poland, on September 1, 1939, he had in his pocket a draft for about $500,000, which completed the recovery of all that was owed to Bank of Boston (Williams, Ben Ames Jr., *Bank of Boston 200: A History of New England's Leading Bank 1784–1984* [Boston, Mass.: Houghton Mifflin, 1984], pp. 331–332).

[41] *Moody's*, 1937, p. 642.

[42] *Petroleum Times*, Feb. 19, 1938, p. 241, July 30, 1938, p. 159; *London Times*, Mar. 17, 1938.

[43] No significant destruction was caused by an oil tanker berthed at Purfleet during World War II. Ironically, an oil tanker docked at Thames Haven precipitated one of the largest disasters on the Thames River during the war. In April 1941, the tanker, SS *Lunula,* docked at Thames Haven, set off a German magnetic mine while shifting berth. The ship, cargo, crew, jetty, and adjacent tugboat, *Persia,* went up in flames. The resulting fire burned for ninety-seven hours before it was put out. Patches of burning oil floating on the river, showers of red-hot debris, and cascades of blazing oil partially closed passage on the river (Bates, L. M., *The Thames on Fire: The Battle of London River 1939-1945* [Levenham, Suffolk: Terence Dalton Limited, 1985], pp. 14, 88).

[44] *Petroleum Times,* March 24, 1938, pp. 424–425.

[45] *London Times,* June 30, 1938, Mar. 30, 1939, Apr. 6, 1939; *PM,* May 4, 1941, p. 19; *National Cyclopedia Supplement Three,* vol. 32, 1966, p. 227.

[46] *London Times,* Dec. 3, 1938, Mar. 31, 1939.

[47] *Petroleum Times,* Mar. 30, 1940, p. 573, June 22, 1940, p. 562; *London Times,* June 30, 1938, Apr. 6, 1939.

[48] SD File 812.6363 W. R. Davis & Co. Lockett letter to Daniels, Dec. 5, 1938, p. 2.

Chapter Four: Mexico—Preparing the Way for Germany

[1] Although Wehrle told the author that she accompanied Davis on every trip to Mexico, her name will be mentioned only when she played a role in the action (Wehrle interview one, p. 4).

[2] Davis FBI File Part One 9/22/39 65-128, p. 15; Davis FBI File Part Four, p. 206; Davis FBI File Part Five, p. 219.

[3] *Petroleum Times,* June 9, 1934, p. 634, Mar., 27, 1948, p. 520; *St. Louis Post-Dispatch,* Apr. 7, 1940.

[4] Daniels, Josephus, *Shirt-Sleeve Diplomat* (Chapel Hill, N.C.: Univ. of North Carolina Press, 1947), p. 253; *Franklin D. Roosevelt and Foreign Affairs: Second Series January 1937–August 1939 Volume Five: April-June 1937 and Volume Twelve: November-December 1938,* edited by Donald B. Schewe (New York: Clearwater Publishing, 1969; Daniels letter, Apr. 16, 1938; *NYT,* Aug. 2, 1941.

[5] Dollars in the 1930s were worth approximately 10 times current dollars.

[6] Following Roosevelt's election, Benedum was at first very close to the Democratic administration. His chartered yacht was the scene for many conferences of administration officials. However, much like Davis, Bene-

dum drifted away from Roosevelt as the Democrats shifted their policies to the left.

[7] *New York Herald Tribune*, Jan. 6, 1941; SD File 812.6363 W. R. Davis & Co. /3, p. 1; Daniels letter; Meyer, Lorenzo, *Mexico and the United States in the Oil Controversy, 1917–1942* (Austin, Tex.: Univ. of Texas Press, 1972), p. 211.

[8] Overacker, Louise (A), "American Government and Politics," *American Political Science Review*, Oct. 1933, p. 781.

[9] *National Cyclopedia*, vol. 49; Mallison, p. 420; Guffey, Joseph F., *Seventy Years on the Red-Fire Wagon: From Tilden to Truman Through New Freedom and New Deal*, (privately printed, 1952), p. 78; *Current Biography*, 1941, p. 212.

[10] Jesse Holman Jones was chairman of the Reconstruction Finance Corporation (RFC), a government-chartered corporation that purchased the preferred stock of U.S. banks. These purchases bolstered the capital structure of the banks, which in turn created a base for credit expansion in the U.S. economy. Under Jones, the RFC became the nation's largest bank and largest single investor (Leuchtenburg, William E., *Franklin D. Roosevelt and the New Deal 1932–1940* [New York: Harper & Row], p. 71).

[11] *New York Herald Tribune*, Jan. 6, 1941; *St. Louis Post-Dispatch*, June 14, 1939.

[12] *PM*, Dec. 12, 1940; *Current Biography*, p. 211; *New York Herald Tribune*, Jan. 6, 1941.

[13] Wehrle told the author that Davis contributed as much as $100,000 to Roosevelt in 1936 (Wehrle interview one, p. 16).

[14] Leuchtenburg, William E., *Franklin D. Roosevelt and the New Deal 1932–1940* (New York: Harper & Row, 1963), pp. 254–255.

[15] *St. Louis Post-Dispatch*, Apr. 7, 1940; Alinsky, Saul, *John L. Lewis: An Unauthorized Biography* (New York: G. P. Putnam's Sons, 1949), pp. 202–203.

[16] Overacker, Louise (B), "American Government and Politics," *American Political Science Review*, June 1937, pp. 481, 487; Ickes, Harold L., *The Secret Diary of Harold L. Ickes: Volume Two 1936–1939* (New York: Simon & Schuster, 1954), p. 27; *St. Louis Post-Dispatch*, Apr. 7, 1940; Davis FBI File Part One, p. 131.

[17] Ross, p. 186; *Current Biography*, 1941, p. 212; Alinsky, pp. 202–203; Wehrle interview one, p. 16.

[18] Davis later purchased the rest of Sabalo (*St. Louis Post-Dispatch*, Apr. 7, 1940; *PM* [New York], Apr. 29, 1941, p. 22).

[19] Yergin, p. 267.

[20] *Petroleum Times*, June 22, 1940, p. 484.

[21] Childs, p. 181; Cronon, E. David, *Josephus Daniels in Mexico* (Madison, Wis.: Univ. of Wisconsin Press, 1960), p. 234.

[22] Ward, Geoffrey C., *First Class Temperament: The Emergence of Franklin Roosevelt.* (New York: Harper & Row, 1989), p. 216.

[23] *Current Biography*, 1944, p. 175.

[24] SD File 812.6363 W. R. Davis & Co./1, p. 1; Daniels letter; Camp, Roderic Ai, *Mexican Political Biographies 1935–1975* (Tucson, Ariz.: Univ. of Arizona Press, 1976), p. 311; SD File 812.6363 W. R. Davis & Co./1, pp. 2–3.

[25] Daniels letter; SD File 812.6363 W. R. Davis & Co./1, pp. 2, 3.

[26] SD File 812.6363 W. R. Davis & Co./4, p. 1.

[27] Daniels remained an active opponent of German economic penetration into Mexico. In the fall of 1937, the U.S. embassy attempted to block German efforts to create a German oil base in Mexico. It was reported that Daniels told Mexican president Cárdenas that the United States was prepared to take all of Mexico's oil exports if the Germans were denied access to Mexican oil (*Documents on German Foreign Policy 1918–1945: Volume Five, Series D, Poland, Balkans, Latin America, The Small Powers 1937–1939* [Washington D.C.: U.S. Government Printing Office, 1953], p. 828).

[28] Wehrle interview one, p. 5; Camp, p. 311.

[29] Cronon, p. 234; Daniels letter.

[30] Cronon, p. 234; Williams, William Appleman, *The Tragedy of American Diplomacy* (New York: Dell Publishing, 1972), p. 168.

[31] *PM*, Apr. 30, 1941, p. 22; *St. Louis Post-Dispatch*, Apr. 7, 1940.

[32] Cumberland, Charles C., *Mexico: The Struggle for Modernity* (New York: Oxford Univ. Press, 1968), pp. 307–308.

[33] Green, David, *The Containment of Latin America: A History of the Myths and Realities of the Wood Policy* (Chicago, Ill.: Quadrangle Books, 1971), p. 28; Cumberland, pp. 308, 310; Meyer, Michael C., and Sherman, William L., *The Course of Mexican History* (New York: Oxford Univ. Press, 1979), p. 603.

[34] Cumberland, p. 309; Meyer L., p. 154.

[35] *NYT*, Feb. 21, 1937, p. 1; SD File 812.6363 W. R. Davis & Co., p. 3, Reed letter; Green, p. 28.

[36] Daniels letter; Meyer, L., p. 211.

[37] SD File 812.6363 W. R. Davis & Co./8+15, pp. 4, 1; Daniels letter.

[38] Davis FBI File Part One 65-128 9/22/1939; Higham (A), p. 66; *PM*, Apr. 29, 1941, p. 22.

[39] *National Cyclopedia*, vol. 49, p. 85.

[40] Childs, p. 182; *St. Louis Post-Dispatch*, Apr. 7, 1940.

[41] SD File 812.6363 W. R. Davis & Co./1, p. 1; SD File 812.6363 W. R. Davis & Co./11.

[42] *NYT*, May 18, 1937; Davis FBI File Part One, p. 155; *St. Louis Post-Dispatch*, June 14, 1939; SD File 812.6363 W. R. Davis & Co./16, p. 1; Davis FBI File Part Four, p. 219.

[43] *St. Louis Post-Dispatch*, June 14, 1939; Kirk, Betty, *Covering the Mexican Front*, (Norman, Okla.: Univ. of Oklahoma Press, 1942), p. 174; *NYT*, May 22, 1938; Davis FBI File Part One, p. 374.

[44] *St. Louis Post-Dispatch*, June 14, 1939, Apr. 7, 1940; *NYT*, Dec. 14, 1937.

[45] Green, p. 29; Millon, Robert Paul, *Mexican Marxist: Vicente Lombardo Toledano*, (Chapel Hill, N.C.: Univ. of North Carolina Press, 1966), p. 125; Powell, J. Richard, *The Mexican Petroleum Industry 1938–1950*, (Berkeley, Calif.: Univ. of California Press, 1956), pp. 22, 1076; *Encyclopedia of World History*, Meyer, M., p. 604.

[46] Davis FBI File Part One, p. 374; Wood, Bryce, *The Making of the Good Neighbor Policy* (New York: Columbia Univ. Press, 1961), p. 204; Childs, p. 176; Meyer, L., p. 170; Powell, p. 22.

[47] Davis FBI File Part Four, p. 218.

[48] This plan was probably a topic of conversation at Smith's meeting with Roosevelt at the White House on January 25, 1938 (*NYT*, Jan. 26, 1938).

[49] Kirk, p. 166; *Petroleum Times*, May 25, 1940, p. 475.

[50] FO Papers FO371/23099 35695, p. 88; *St. Louis Post-Dispatch*, Apr. 7, 1940.

[51] *Petroleum Times*, May 25, 1940, pp. 483–484.

[52] Farago, pp. 383, 384; Wehrle interview one, p. 4.

[53] Higham (A), p. 66; Davis FBI File Part Two, p. 119.

[54] This shipment of German goods was sent eventually to the United States, arriving in New Orleans on January 19, 1939. Through arrangements made by Davis and Company, the goods were sold for cash to Sinclair Oil Company to be used in the Louisiana oil fields. Amazingly, Davis had got-

ten American oil interests to buy German goods to pay for the Mexican nationalization of Davis's Sabalo oil field (*NYT*, Jan. 21, 1939; Davis FBI File 11-168 Part Four, p. 10).

[55] Wehrle interview one, p. 5.

[56] Childs, p. 176; *NYT*, May 15, 1938; *PM*, Apr. 30, 1941, p. 22.

[57] *Petroleum Times*, Dec. 10, 1938, p.769.

[58] Childs, p. 177; *NYT*, May 15, 1938; *PM*, Apr. 29, 1941, p. 22.

Chapter Five: Mexican Oil for Germany

[1] *Encyclopedia of World History*, p. 1076; Childs, p. 176.

[2] Powell, p. 23; Childs, p. 176; *NYT*, May 22,1938; *Saturday Evening Post*, July 29, 1939, p. 49.

[3] Big Oil was right to be worried about the effect of the Mexican nationalization on Venezuela. In January 1939, Davis would send a representative to Venezuela to open negotiations to set up a Davis and Company refinery in Venezuela. Although nothing came of it, Shell and the British government were in a panic over the negotiations (FO Papers FO371/22851 35695, p. 4).

[4] Bratzel, John F., and Rout, Leslie B., *The Shadow War: German Espionage and United States Counterespionage in Latin America During World War Two* (Frederick, Md.: University Publication of America, 1986), p. 53; Meyer, Lorenzo (B), and Vazquez, Josefina Zraida, *The United States and Mexico* (Chicago, Ill.: Univ. of Chicago Press, 1985), p. 151.

[5] Childs, pp. 177, 203; Meyer, L. Kirk, pp. 171, 203.

[6] Wood, p. 231; Childs, p. 182.

[7] Daniels, p. 251; *Oil and Gas Journal*, June 30, 1938, p. 42.

[8] *Oil and Gas Journal*, June 30, 1938, p. 19; Kirk, p. 170.

[9] Meyer, M., p. 604; Kirk, p. 170.

[10] Meyer, L., p. 176.

[11] Bratzel, p. 53; Camp, p. 54; Daniels, p. 251.

[12] Weyl, p. 307; *NYT*, Oct. 10, 1939; Weyl, p. 307; Davis FBI File Part Four, p. 206; Davis FBI File Part Five, p. 62; *Petroleum Times*, June 22, 1940, p. 571.

[13] Daniels, p. 251.

[14] *London Times*, July 2, 1938; U.S. State Department, *Documents on German Foreign Policy 1918–1945: Volume Five, Series D, Poland, Balkans,*

Latin America, and the Small Powers 1937–1939, 1953, p. 829; Meyer, L., p. 209.

[15] *St. Louis Post-Dispatch*, Apr. 7, 1940; Camp, p. 64; U.S. State Department, *Foreign Relations of the United States (A), 1938, Volume V: The American Republics*, 1956, p. 728; Meyer, L., p. 309; *Foreign Relations (A)*, p. 728.

[16] FO Papers A2703/10/26 1938, p. 252; FO Papers FO371/24216 35695, p. 91; Camp, p. 160; FO Papers, FO371/21465 1938, p. 255.

[17] *Petroleum Times*, May 25, 1940, pp. 483–484.

[18] *NYT*, Apr. 13, 1938; FO Papers, A2711 1938, p. 260; *London Times*, June 30, 1938, Apr. 6, 1939; *London Times*, Apr. 6, 1939.

[19] *New York Herald Tribune*, Jan. 6, 1941; Rogge, p. 239; Ross, p. 163; Farago, p. 354.

[20] *NYT*, May 22, 1938; Daniels, p. 252; *Foreign Relations (A)*, p. 745.

[21] *NYT*, Apr. 10, 1938; *PM*, Apr. 29, 1941, p. 22.

[22] Meyer, M., p. 604.

[23] SD File 812.6363 W. R. Davis & Co./59, p. 1.

[24] *Current Biography*, 1940, pp. 516–517; *NYT*, Aug. 2, 1941; *PM*, Apr. 29, 1941, p. 22.

[25] Davis FBI File Part Four, p. 219.

[26] *St. Louis Post-Dispatch*, June 14, 1939; Guffey, p. 129; Davis FBI File Part One, pp. 130, 306; Farago, p. 354.

[27] Wehrle interview one, p. 15; *St. Louis Post-Dispatch*, June 14, 1939; Dubofsy, Melvyn, and Van Tine, Warren, *John L. Lewis: A Biography* (New York: Quadrangle, 1977), p. 331.

[28] FBI Davis File Part One, 5-1168-14X, p. 181; *Oil and Gas Journal*, June 30, 1938, p. 42.

[29] There is a record of this conversation because the FBI had a wiretap on Lewis's Washington office. The FBI also had a wiretap on Davis's New York and Mexico City offices during part of 1938 (Davis FBI File 11-168 Part One, p. 308).

[30] Davis FBI File Part One, p. 182, 65-1168-14x.

[31] While negotiations were proceeding with Davis on shipping oil to Germany, Toledano called lies the reports that Mexico would sell oil to Germany, Italy, and Japan. He said that Mexico would not sell oil to any fascist country (*NYT*, June 3, 1938). This prevarication and similar falsehoods by

other Mexican officials were an indication of their anxiety about the American response to a possible German trade deal.

[32] Meyer, L., p. 211; Wechsler, James A., *Labor Baron: A Portrait of John L. Lewis* (New York: William Morrow, 1944), p. 111.

[33] *National Cyclopedia, Supplement Five*, 1966, p. 376; MacFarland, Charles K., *Roosevelt, Lewis, and the New Deal* (Fort Worth, Tex.: Texas Christian Univ. Press, 1970), p. 105; *Current Biography*, 1942, p. 513.

[34] Wechsler, p. 111; Dubofsky, p. 332; Higham (A), p. 66.

[35] At the Carleton Hotel in Washington, D.C., on December 17, 1948 (Alinsky, Saul, *John L. Lewis: An Unauthorized Biography* [New York: P. Putnam's Sons, 1949], p. 202).

[36] Alinsky, pp. 202–203; Childs, p. 183.

[37] Davis FBI File Part One, p. 281.

[38] Karl Von Clemm managed the German end of Davis's arrangement with Mexico (*NYT*, Jan. 29, 1942; *PM* (New York), May 4, 1941, p. 19).

[39] Alinsky, pp. 202–203.

[40] In fact, the Mexicans complained about the high prices the Germans were quoting for their machinery in the barter agreement and held up the oil transfers until this issue was resolved (*London Times*, Sept. 12, 1938).

[41] *London Times*, July 8, 1938; *PM*, Apr. 30, 1941, p. 22; Meyer, L., p. 211.

[42] *NYT*, July 24, 1938; Powell, p. 113.

[43] *Oil and Gas Journal*, July 7, 1938, p. 42, June 1, 1939, p. 18; *NYT*, July 24, 1938.

[44] *NYT*, Aug. 2, 1941; *London Times*, July 8, 1938.

[45] Kennedy, Paul, *The Rise and Fall of The Great Powers: Economic Change and Military Conflict from 1500 to 2000* (New York: Random House, 1987), pp. 307, 332; *NYT*, Apr. 7, 1983, July 24, 1938; Farago, p. 355.

[46] *NYT*, Aug. 2, 1941; Kennedy, *The Rise and Fall of the Great Powers*, pp. 307, 332; Carroll, Bernice A., *Design for Total War: Arms and Economics in the Third Reich* (The Hague, Netherlands: Mouton, 1968), p. 144.

[47] Bernice, *Petroleum Times*, May 25, 1940, p. 297.

[48] *New York Herald Tribune*, Jan. 6, 1941.

[49] *PM*, Apr. 29, 1941, p. 29.

[50] Rogge, p. 240.

[51] Icaza was linked to Toledano through his membership on the board of directors of the Workers University (Camp, Roderic Ai, *Mexican Political Biographies 1935-1975*, [Tucson: Univ. of Arizona Press, 1976], p. 172).

[52] Wehrle interview one, p. 4; Childs, pp. 176–177; Daniels, p. 252.

[53] Rogge, p. 240; *PM*, May 5, 1941, p. 22; Davis FBI File Part Five, p. 239.

[54] Millon, p. 131; *PM*, May 5, 1941, p. 22.

[55] FO Papers 1938, FO371/21465 35695, p. 266.

[56] Belknap, John, *American Appeasement: United States Foreign Policy and Germany 1933–1938* (Cambridge, Mass.: Harvard Univ. Press, 1969), p. 176; Green, p. 29; Belknap, p. 176.

[57] In Roosevelt's administration, the conflict between the State Department's policies and the policies of other executive branches was not unusual. Roosevelt frequently stated his belief in a competitive bureaucracy with himself as arbitrator (*The National Cyclopedia of American Biography: Supplemental Three*, 1966, p. 325).

[58] The fact that silver production in Mexico was largely controlled by American interests no doubt influenced the decision to make these purchases (Meyer, Lorenzo, *Mexico and the United States in the Oil Controversy, 1917-1942* [Austin: Univ. of Texas Press, 1972], p. 205).

[59] Wood, pp. 223, 229–230; SD File 812.6363 W. R. Davis & Co./42, p. 2.

[60] Belknap, p. 176; Scroggs, William O., "Mexican Anxieties," *Foreign Affairs*, vol. 18, no. 2 (Jan. 1940), pp. 270–273.

[61] Wood, p. 228; *NYT*, Jan. 21, 1939, Dec. 10, 1938; Davis FBI File Part One, p. 295.

[62] Belknap, p. 176; Meyer, L., p. 192.

[63] Davis FBI File Part One, p. 295.

[64] Green, p. 31; Meyer, L. (B), p. 146; Hearden, Patrick J., *Roosevelt Confronts Hitler: America's Entry into World War Two* (DeKalb, Ill.: Northern Illinois Univ. Press, 1987), p. 111; Green, p. 31; Williams, W., p. 180.

[65] SD File 812.6363 W. R. Davis & Co./42, pp. 1–2.

[66] Overacker (B), pp. 487–488; Wood, p. 294.

[67] Wood, pp. 207, 225; *Oil and Gas Journal*, Dec. 15, 1938, p. 31.

[68] Hearden, p. 111.

Chapter Six: Mexico—Making War Possible

[1] *London Times*, July 8, 1938; Wehrle interview one, p. 5.

[2] Ironically, it is possible that the real motivation of the U.S. and British oil companies in denouncing Mexico's dealings with the fascist powers was the fear that the oil companies would permanently lose to Mexico the lucrative fascist states' oil market (Weyl, Nathaniel, and Sylvia Weyl, *The Reconquest of Mexico: The Years of Lazaro Cárdenas* [New York: Oxford Univ. Press, 1939], p. 306).

[3] Daniels, p. 252; Kirk, p. 169.

[4] Kirk, pp. 173–174.

[5] Dutch authorities seized the 10,000-ton oil tanker, *Lundgren*, on July 18, 1938, on the Scheldt River (*Petroleum Times* [London], July 23, 1938, p. 115). French authorities seized 12,600 tons of oil held in the Cie. Industrielle Maritime (CIM) tank farm in Le Havre on October 7, 1938. CIM was a subsidiary of Thames Haven, which had until recently been connected to Davis through Parent (*Petroleum Times* [London], Oct. 29, 1938, p. 559).

[6] Childs, p. 182; Wood, p. 227; Kirk, p. 173.

[7] Davis FBI File Part Five, p. 343; Meyer, L. (A), p. 202.

[8] The major oil companies had tremendous leverage in Sweden where they completely controlled the oil market (Sampson, Anthony, *The Seven Sisters: The Great Oil Companies and the World They Shaped* [New York: Viking Press, 1975], pp. 76–77).

[9] FO Papers FO371/22776 35696, p. 149; Wehrle interview one, p. 6.

[10] F.O. A6302/10/26 1938, p. 231.

[11] The FBI was asked by the War Department to investigate Davis in September 1938 and began the investigation in January 1939. It found nothing to indicate that Davis was involved in espionage and closed the investigation in June 1939 (Davis FBI File 11-169 Part One, pp. 1, 24). The FBI's conclusion was correct, Davis's assistance in Mexico for Germany, although certainly pro-Nazi, never involved stealing secrets.

[12] Wood, pp. 223, 229–230; Davis FBI File Part One, p. 289; Meyer, L. (A), pp. 203, 209.

[13] Wehrle interview one, p. 6; Meyer, L. (A), pp. 9, 210.

[14] SD File 812.6363 W. R. Davis & Co., Lockett letter to Daniels Aug. 3, 1938.

[15] From Winkler Koch of Topeka, Kansas, which built Eurotank (*Covering the Mexican Front*, p. 158).

[16] SD File 812.6363 W. R. Davis & Co./1023, p. 2.

[17] *Petroleum Times*, Dec. 15, 1938, p. 769.

[18] *NYT*, Dec. 10, 1938; Wood, p. 228; Meyer, L. (A), p. 203; SD File 812.6363 W. R. Davis & Co., Lockett letter to Daniels Aug. 7, 1939, p. 3.

[19] It is also revealing that the U.S. Treasury issued an order on October 25, 1938, permitting the oil sent from the Mexican oil fields to the Eastern States Petroleum Company to enter Houston under bond for refining and reshipping abroad. Thus, the company avoided having to pay custom duties on the oil. This Roosevelt administration assistance is another example of Roosevelt's aid to the Cárdenas government (*NYT*, Dec. 10, 1938).

[20] *Petroleum Times*, June 23, 1939, p. 85; *Saturday Evening Post*, July 29, 1939, p. 48.

[21] *PM*, Apr. 30, 1941, p. 22; Meyer, L. (A), p. 213; *PM*, Apr. 30, 1941, p. 22; SD File 812.6363 W. R. Davis & Co., Daniels letter June 17, 1939, p. 2.

[22] *NYT*, Oct. 21, 1938, Jan. 1, 1939.

[23] *NYT*, Jan. 1, 1939; Williams, A., pp. 331–332.

[24] *World Petroleum*, p. 78; *London Times*, Aug. 13, 1938; Ashby, Joe C., *Organized Labor and the Mexican Revolution Under Lazaro Cárdenas* (Chapel Hill, N.C.: Univ. of North Carolina Press, 1963), p. 92; Rogge, p. 240.

[25] Dubofsy, p. 331; Ashby, p. 94.

[26] Ross, p. 164.

[27] Dubofsky, p. 331; Cronon, p. 234.

[28] Given his relationship with Davis, Lewis would seem an unlikely figure to deliver this message to Roosevelt. However, Cárdenas believed that Davis and Lewis had substantial influence with President Roosevelt because Cárdenas had several times used Davis to send special coded messages to high officials in the U.S. State Department (Davis FBI File Part One, p. 419).

[29] Daniels, p. 208.

[30] Bratzel, p. 54; *Oil and Gas Journal*, Dec. 15, 1938, p. 31.

[31] Weyl, p. 307.

[32] Just before this new German deal, an Italian commission led by Commendatore Viotto arrived in Mexico in October 1938. The Italians in quick succession signed two oil barter deals with the Mexican government for the Italian company, Azienda Generale Italian Petroli. The agreements, signed October 28 and later in November, arranged to exchange 7 million barrels of oil worth $5 million for three 10,500-ton tankers to be built in

Italy and other merchandise. In addition, Mexico informed Italy that it would supply an unlimited quantity of oil to Italy. This commitment foreshadowed a series of barter deals between Mexico and Italy until Italy entered the war. Unfortunately for the Mexicans, these three tankers were never delivered (due to the British blockade) and were confiscated by the Italian government in April 1941 (Kirk, Betty, *Covering the Mexican Front* [Norman: Univ. of Oklahoma Press, 1942], pp. 167–168, 176; *NYT*, Apr. 6, 1939; *Petroleum Times* [London], Nov. 5, 1938, p. 595).

[33] Wood, p. 229.

[34] Green, p. 33; Meyer, L. (A), p. 193.

[35] Daniels letter, Dec. 9, 1938.

[36] Despite these assurances to Daniels, the Mexican government, unhappy that the size and nature of the new German contract had been publicized, expelled the *New York Times* reporter who wrote the story that exposed the contract (*Oil and Gas Journal*, Jan. 26, 1939, p. 69).

[37] Kirk, p. 168; *London Times*, Feb. 17, 1939; *NYT*, Oct. 10, 1939.

[38] *NYT*, Feb. 24, 1939.

[39] Cronon, pp. 235–236; Meyer, L. (A), p. 193.

[40] *New York Herald Tribune*, Jan. 2, 1941.

[41] Meyer, L. (A), p. 211; Davis FBI File Part One 62-1000; Davis FBI File Part One, p. 468.

[42] *London Times*, Feb. 17, 1939; Meyer, L. (A), p. 211.

[43] In the early years of the Nazi regime, Wohlthat had been chief of the Foreign Exchange Office. Among his duties was supervising the distribution of foreign exchange funds that were to be used for the purchase of imported raw materials. In this capacity, he may have already had dealings with Davis (Riess, Curt, *Total Espionage* [New York: G. P. Putnam's Sons, 1941], p. 204).

[44] Riess, pp. 203–204; Wohlthat interview.

[45] Davis FBI File Part Five, p. 382; Higham (A), pp. 4, 67.

[46] Farago, p. 353; Rogge, pp. 239–242.

[47] Higham (A), p. 67; *NYT*, Apr. 6, 1939.

[48] Weyl, p. 307; *NYT*, Apr. 6, 1939.

[49] Higham (A), p. 67.

[50] The Mexican government was also exerting pressure on hardware merchants in Mexico, most of whom were Germans, to purchase some of the German barter goods at a discount so that the Mexican government could

increase its cash reserve (*NYT*, Apr. 6, 1939). Nearly all of this barter trade was carried out through Davecom. The German firms in Mexico complained that their barter business was forced to "clear through" Davecom; at a nice profit for Davis (Davis FBI File 11-168 Part One, p. 468; Davis FBI File Part Three, p. 362).

[51] *London Times*, May 29, 1939; *NYT*, Oct. 10, 1939; Meyer, L. (A), p. 210.

[52] SD File 812.6363 W. R. Davis & Co./199, p. 1.

[53] SD File 812. 6363 W. R. Davis & Co./199, pp. 2–3; Wohlthat interview; Bratzel, p. 54.

[54] Wehrle interview one, p. 11.

[55] SD File 812.6363 W. R. Davis & Co./225, p. 4; Wehrle interview one, p. 10.

[56] Rogge, p. 242; Davis FBI File Part One, p. 374; Bratzel, p. 54.

[57] Higham (A), p. 67; SD File 812.6363 W. R. Davis & Co./195, p. 1; *PM*, May 2, 1941, p. 9; Davis FBI File Part One, p. 419; *London Times*, Aug. 14, 1939; Rogge, p. 242.

[58] SD File 812.6363 W. R. Davis & Co./195, p. 1.

[59] Wood, pp. 229–230; SD File 812.6363 W. R. Davis & Co./198, p. 2.

[60] Richberg, a labor lawyer, was a New Dealer who had been the head of the National Recovery Administration, the centerpiece of the early New Deal. He was also the former law partner of Harold Ickes, the secretary of the interior (Watkins, T. H., *The Great Depression* [New York: Little, Brown, 1993], pp. 141, 144).

[61] Ickes, p. 626.

[62] Wehrle interview one, p. 5.

[63] Rogge, p. 242; Bratzel, p. 54.

[64] *NYT*, Oct. 10, 1939, Aug. 2, 1941.

[65] *Petroleum Times*, Mar. 18, 1939, p. 356; Powell, p. 79; Freeburg, Russell W., and Goralski, Robert, *Oil and War: How the Deadly Struggle for Fuel in World War Two Meant Victory or Defeat* (New York: William Morrow and Company, 1987), pp. 26, 343; Kirk, p. 169.

[66] The French aircraft industry was expanding rapidly and was capable of building 3,000 planes per year by 1940. In addition, the French had ordered 4,700 planes from the United States. However, only 554 of these U.S. planes had arrived by the time of the French collapse in June 1940 (Shirer, William L., *The Collapse of the Third Republic: An Inquiry into the Fall of France in 1940* [New York: Simon & Schuster, 1969], pp. 407, 616).

[67] Kennedy, p. 341.

[68] In May 1940, when the Germans attacked France, they actually had slightly fewer soldiers and many fewer tanks than the Allies. Even in the air, the German superiority was not overwhelming, with the Allies actually having more fighter aircraft than the Germans. The Germans won despite this near equality in armaments and men due to their superior tactics. Whether better tactics would have succeeded if the Germans had been markedly inferior in armaments and soldiers is an entirely different matter. For example, these were the exact conditions that prevailed in the German invasion of Russia in 1941. During the Russian campaign the German advance eventually ground to a halt because of insufficient resources (Shirer, William L., *The Collapse of the Third Republic: An Inquiry into the Fall of France in 1940* [New York: Simon & Schuster, 1969], pp. 608–617).

Chapter Seven: Peace Plan

[1] Wehrle interview one, p. 8; *PM*, Apr. 28, 1941, p. 22; Cole, Wayne S. (A), *Roosevelt and the Isolationists 1932–45* (Lincoln, Neb.: Univ. of Nebraska Press, 1983), p. 334.

[2] Wehrle interview one, pp. 8, 10.

[3] FO Papers FO371/22776 35696, p. 3.

[4] Breuer, p. 128.

[5] Geye carried with him a secret code that Davis and Erna Wehrle had devised to keep in touch with Berlin. Using a code would prevent the British from reading Davis's telegrams when the telegrams passed through Bermuda. In Davis's code Hitler had the code name "Heron," Goering was "Harold," Davis was "Baron," Lewis had the peculiar code name "Dung," and Wehrle had the name "Chrysanthemum." The FBI would label this code the "Chrysanthemum" code. Thus, with the war barely started, Davis's German affairs already were taking on a clandestine aura.

[6] Wehrle interview one, p. 11; *PM*, Apr. 28, 1941, p. 22; SD File 812.6363 W. R. Davis & Co./003; Ross, p. 164; Breuer, p. 128; Gleason, Everett, and Langer, William L., *Challenge to Isolation 1937–40* (New York: Harper and Brothers, 1952), p. 347.

[7] Dallek, Robert, *Franklin D. Roosevelt and American Foreign Policy 1932–1945* (New York: Oxford Univ. Press, 1979), p. 206.

[8] Roberts, Andrew, *Holy Fox: A Biography of Lord Halifax* (London: Weidenfeld and Nicolson, 1991), p. 176; Gilbert, Martin, and Gott, Richard, *The Appeasers: The Decline of Democracy from Hitler's Rise to Chamberlain's Fall* (Boston: Houghton Mifflin, 1963), p. 345; Lash, Joseph P., *Roosevelt and Churchill 1939–1941: The Partnership That Saved the West* (New York: W. W. Norton & Company, 1976), p. 75.

[9] Gleason, p. 347.

[10] There were many other attempts to arrange peace negotiations through neutral businessmen sympathetic to the Germans. Unlike Davis's intrigue most of these other schemes had little chance of success.

[11] Gilbert, p. 341; Dallek, p. 206.

[12] Wehrle interview one, p. 10; *PM*, Apr. 28, 1941, p. 22; Childs, p. 185.

[13] Wehrle interview one, pp. 10, 11.

[14] *PM*, Apr. 28, 1941, p. 22; Weschler, p. 112; Higham (A), p. 68; Weschler, p. 112; *PM*, Apr. 28, 1941, p. 22; Davis FBI File Part One, p. 279.

[15] By not guaranteeing secrecy, Roosevelt could publicize the meeting at his discretion. Nevertheless, the White House kept the meeting secret for more than a year.

[16] Childs, p. 185; Davis FBI File Part Four, p. 303; Berle (A), 1939, p. 43.

[17] Dubofsy, p. 332; Davis FBI File Part One, p. 282.

[18] *PM*, Apr. 29, 1941, p. 22; Williams, W., pp. 187, 196.

[19] Schmitz, David F., ed., *Appeasement in Europe: A Reassessment of U.S. Policies* (New York: Greenwood Press, 1990), pp. xix–xxi.

[20] Davis contended that Roosevelt called him to the White House on this occasion and gave him authority to speak for the U.S. government in Europe, but the author has found no substantiation for this claim (*PM* [New York], Apr. 28, 1941, p. 22).

[21] Davis FBI File Part Five, p. 401; Berle (A) 1939, pp. 2, 44; Davis FBI File Part Four, p. 303.

[22] Berle (A), 1939, pp. 2, 44.

[23] Ibid., pp. 45–46.

[24] This was possibly a reference to the activities of Davis's friends—Lord Inverforth, Bernard Smith, and Francis Rickett—which will be discussed at the end of chapter seven.

[25] Berle (A), 1939, pp. 45–46.

[26] *PM*, Apr. 28, 1941, p. 22; Breuer, p. 128; Berle (A) 1939, pp. 47–48; Davis FBI File Part One, p. 456.

[27] Berle (A) 1939, pp. 46, 48; Cole (A), p. 335.

[28] Dallek, p. 207.

[29] Moseley, Leonard, *Reich Marshall: A Biography of Hermann Goering* (New York: Doubleday, 1974), p. 240; Berle (A) 1939, pp. 49–50.

[30] Cole (A) p. 331; Davis FBI File Part Two, p. 219.

[31] Berle (A) 1939, pp. 59–60; Davis FBI File Part One 65-1168-108, pp. 1–2.

[32] At the beginning of the war, the passport office ordered the invalidation of all passports and instituted a review procedure before issuing a new passport. Full details of the background and business of each applicant were required before a passport was issued. In particular, passports for travel to belligerent countries or a combat zone were difficult to obtain (*Current Biography*, 1947, p. 572).

[33] SD File 800.20211 Davis, William Rhodes/11/2; Berle (A) 1939, pp. 56–57; Davis FBI File Part One, p. 312; Rogge, p. 246.

[34] Berle (A) 1939, pp. 56–57; Davis FBI File Part One, p. 273; Gentry, Curt, *J. Edgar Hoover: The Man and the Secrets* (New York: W.W. Norton & Company, 1991), p. 267.

[35] The Logan Act forbade contact by a U.S. citizen with a foreign government for the purpose of influencing its conduct in a controversy with the U.S. government without authorization from the U.S. government. The act had been on the books since 1799, but had seldom been used (Rogge, O. John, *The Official German Report: Nazi Penetration 1924–1942 Pan-Arabism 1939–Today* [New York: A. S. Barnes, 1961], p. 247).

[36] Rogge, p. 247; Berle (A) 1939, pp. 56–57; Davis FBI File Part One, pp. 271, 274; Ross, pp. 165–166.

[37] Liberal, pp. 169–170; Higham (A), p. 68.

[38] Schwartz, Jordan A., *Liberal: Adolf A. Berle and the Vision of an American Era* (New York: Free Press, 1987), pp. 169–170.

[39] Davis was one of the first passengers on the transatlantic flying boat, which had begun regular service only a few months before.

[40] Davis FBI File Part One, p. 278; SD File 812.6363 W. R. Davis & Co./202A; SD File 800.20211 Davis, William Rhodes/11/2.

[41] The British government was curious about Davis's purpose in Germany. The British ambassador in Washington, Lord Lothian, asked the State Department about Davis's mission. Berle's embarrassment about Roosevelt's involvement in the Davis affair is evident in the State Department's reply. The British were told that Davis's peace plan was "moonshine" and that Davis had not the slightest chance of getting even to the White House doorstep (FO Papers, FO371/23099 35695, p. 83).

[42] Daniels, p. 252; Davis FBI File Part One 65-1168-11X,14; Davis FBI File Part Four, p. 303.

[43] Davis FBI File Part One, p. 285–286; SD File 812.6363 W. R. Davis & Co., Daniels letter, Nov. 1939, p. 2; *PM*, Apr. 22, 1941, p. 22.

[44] Davis FBI File Part One, p. 279; Davis FBI File Part One 65-1128-26, p. 285; Berle (A) 1939, p. 186; Moffat, Jay Pierrepont, *The Moffat Papers: Selections from the Diplomatic Journals of Jay Pierrepont Moffat*, edited by Nancy Harvison Hooker (Cambridge, Mass.: Harvard Univ. Press, 1956), p. 274.

[45] Davis's story of the soccer game may have been apocryphal, but it was true that there was almost no fighting on the Franco-German border in 1939.

[46] Berle (A) 1939, pp. 186–187; SD File 812.6363 W. R. Davis & Co., Daniels letter, Nov. 1939, p. 2.

[47] Either Davis lied when he described what he saw from above Warsaw or the Germans completely fooled him. German bombing had devastated Warsaw. Walter Schellenberg, future chief of the Abwehr, described Warsaw after its surrender on September 27: "I was shocked at what had become of the beautiful city I had known—ruined and burn-out [sic] houses, . . . everywhere there was the sweetish smell of burnt flesh" (Sulzberger, C. L., *World War II* [New York: American Heritage, 1966], p. 58).

[48] Moffat, p. 274; Berle (A) 1939, p. 187.

[49] Roberts, p. 177.

[50] Fisher, David E., *Race on the Edge of Time: Radar—The Decisive Weapon of World War Two* (New York: Paragon House, 1989), p. 140.

[51] Moseley, p. 241; Shirer, William L., *Collapse of the Third Republic: An Inquiry into the Fall of France in 1940* (New York: Pocket Books, 1971), p. 520.

[52] Rogge, p. 247; Farago, p. 358.

[53] *NYT*, Dec. 31, 1940; U.S. State Department, *Documents on German Foreign Policy 1918–1945: Volume Eight, Series D, Poland, Balkans, Latin America, and The Small Powers 1937–1939* (1953), pp. 270, 829; Churchill, Winston Spencer, *The Gathering Storm: Volume One—The Second World War* (Boston: Houghton Mifflin, 1948), p. 537; Farago, p. 358.

[54] Cole (A), pp. 335–336.

[55] Rogge, p. 249; Farago, pp. 360–361; Cole (A), pp. 335–336.

[56] Farago, pp. 360–361.

[57] Rogge, pp. 247–248.

[58] Ross, p. 165; Stevenson, p. 290.

[59] Rogge, p. 250.

[60] Ross, p. 166; Breuer, pp. 128–129; Rogge, p. 250; Cole (A), p. 336.

[61] Tansil, Charles Callan, *Back Door to War: The Roosevelt Foreign Policy 1933–1941* (Chicago: Henry Regnery Company, 1952), p. 560; Moseley, p. 241.

[62] Friedlander, Saul, *Prelude to Downfall: Hitler and the United States 1939–1941* (New York: Alfred A. Knopf, 1967), pp. 37–38; Tansil, p. 560; Cole (A), p. 336; Friedlander, pp. 37–38.

[63] Ross, p. 166.

[64] SD File 812.6363 W. R. Davis & Co./211, p. 1; *PM*, Apr. 28, 1941, p. 22.

[65] SD File 812.6363 W. R. Davis & Co./214, p. 1; SD File 812.6363 W. R. Davis & Co./211, p. 1.

[66] Gilbert, p. 341; Tansil, p. 560.

[67] Shirer, p. 520.

[68] Gilbert, p. 341; Roberts, p. 180.

[69] Shirer, p. 521; Gilbert, p. 341; Moseley, p. 242.

[70] Gleason, p. 249.

[71] Moffat, p. 272; Moseley, p. 242.

Chapter Eight: Peace Plan Collapses

[1] Breuer, p. 129; Dallek, p. 207.

[2] Morgenthau, Henry F., *From the Morgenthau Diaries: Years of Urgency 1938–1941*, edited by John Morton Blum (Boston: Houghton Mifflin, 1965), entry dated Oct. 3, 1939.

[3] Berle (A) 1939, pp. 117–118; Davis FBI File Part Two, pp. 220, 320.

[4] Berle (A) 1939, pp. 117–118; Davis FBI File Part Two, p. 220.

[5] Leuchtenburg, pp. 294–295; Lash, p. 77.

[6] Friedlander, p. 39.

[7] *Current Biography*, 1940, pp. 78–79.

[8] Higham (A), p. 68; *Current Biography*, 1940, pp. 78–79.

[9] Other versions of this incident (see Childs, Farago, Stevenson, Breuer) assert that British intelligence exposed the fraud and informed the U.S. consulate, which then denied Hertslet a visa. Although the British tip-off story

is plausible, U.S. State Department records do not indicate that the British tipped off the American government. Nor do any of the above authors explain how the British knew that Hertslet was traveling with Davis.

The origin of the British interception story was likely a bit of subterfuge on the part of Adolf Berle. The State Department had broken Davis's private code using the decoded September 19 telegram from Hertslet to Davis that Lewis had provided to the State Department. Berle had been monitoring Davis's activities in Europe by decoding Davis's telegrams to his New York headquarters. Using the information gleaned from the decoded telegrams, Berle told Pan-American Airways in Lisbon to watch for Hertslet. To avoid the discovery of his role in sabotaging Davis's peace mission, Berle was also likely the originator of the British intelligence story. This origin is given credence by the first rendition of the British interception story, coming from newspaper reporter Marquis Childs. Childs's story of the event was published a few years later based on information provided to him by Berle (Stevenson, William, *Intrepid*, p. 290; Childs, Marquis W., *I Write from Washington*, p. 185; U.S. State Department File 812.6363 microfilm 388; U.S. State Department File 800.20211 Davis, William Rhodes/11/2).

[10] Davis FBI File Part Two, pp. 379, 382.

[11] SD File 812.6363 W. R. Davis & Co./213, p. 1; SD File 812.6363 W. R. Davis & Co./220, p. 1, 5.

[12] Farago, p. 363.

[13] SD File 812.6363 W. R. Davis & Co./225, p. 2.

[14] Berle (A) 1939, p. 174.

[15] SD File 812.6363 W. R. Davis & Co., p. 6; SD File 800.20211 Davis, William Rhodes/2-F.

[16] Someone from the German consulate in Washington could have represented Germany, but Goering was keeping his entire peace scheme secret from Ribbentrop and the German Foreign Ministry. Therefore, Goering did not notify the German consulate in Washington about Davis's activities (Davis FBI File Part Two 11-168, p. 383).

[17] SD File 812.6363 W. R. Davis & Co./225, p. 3; Childs, p. 185.

[18] SD File 812.6363 W. R. Davis & Co./215, p. 2; Breuer, pp. 128–129; Weschler, p. 112; SD File 800.20211 Davis, William Rhodes/2-G; Farago, p. 363; Davis FBI File Part One, pp. 370, 376.

[19] Breuer, pp. 128–129; Davis FBI File Part Two, pp. 273, 300, 391; Ross, pp. 166–167; Berle (A) 1939, pp. 180, 187; Tansil, p. 561.

[20] *NYT*, Dec. 31, 1940; Berle (A) 1939, p. 181; Ross, p. 167.

[21] Moffat, p. 273; *New York Herald Tribune*, Jan. 2, 1941; Davis FBI File Part Four, p. 303.

[22] Berle (A) 1939, pp. 183–186, 188–189.

[23] Berle (A), pp. 190–191; Moffat, p. 275.

[24] Berle (A), pp. 190–191.

[25] Davis FBI File Part Two, p. 265; *NYT*, Dec. 31, 1940.

[26] Wehrle interview one, pp. 12, 28; SD File 800.20211.

[27] Berle (A) 1939, pp. 191–192, 200, 204; Farago, p. 363; Stevenson, p. 290.

[28] Berle (A) 1939, p. 204.

[29] Moseley, p. 242.

[30] SD File 800.20211 Davis, William Rhodes/11/2; Berle (A) 1939, p. 204.

[31] Dallek, p. 207; SD File 800.20211.

[32] Berle (A) 1939, pp. 215–216; Ross, p. 167.

[33] Berle (A) 1939, pp. 216–219.

[34] Ibid., pp. 220, 233.

[35] Ickes, p. 61; Weschler, p. 112.

[36] SD File 800.20211 Davis, William Rhodes/11/2.

[37] Wehrle interview one, pp. 12, 14.

[38] FO Papers FO371/23099 35695, pp. 78–79.

[39] Berle (A) 1939, p. 238, 247; FO Papers C18201 1939, p. 158.

[40] Lash, p. 74.

[41] Wehrle interview one, p. 14.

Chapter Nine: Breaking the Blockade

[1] Wehrle interview one, p. 8; Davis FBI File Part One, pp. 365, 453–455; SD File 812.6363 W. R. Davis & Co./200.

[2] Davis FBI File Part Five, p. 335; *Oil and Gas Journal*, Nov. 2, 1939, p. 27; *NYT*, Oct. 10, 1939, Oct. 27, 1939.

[3] Fodor, Denis J., *The Neutrals* (New York: Time-Life Books, 1982), p. 13; Pratt, Julius W., *Cordell Hull* (New York: Cooper Square Publishers, 1964), p. 328; Davis FBI File Part Five, pp. 335, 373; *Oil and Gas Journal*, Nov. 2, 1939, p. 27; *NYT*, Oct. 10, 1939, Oct. 27, 1939.

4 Davis FBI File Part One, pp. 450, 466, 473; SD File 812.6363 W. R. Davis & Co., p. 410.

5 Davis FBI File Part One, pp. 365, 453–455.

6 Davis FBI File Part One, pp. 288, 469; Davis FBI File Part Two, p. 139; SD File 812.6363 W. R. Davis & Co., p. 410.

7 NYT, Oct. 7, 1939; Farago, p. 355; SD File 812.6363 W. R. Davis & Co./206, /211, /243.

8 SD File 812.6363 W. R. Davis & Co./206; Rogge, p. 249; Davis FBI File Part Five, pp. 287, 335–336, 338; Moffat, p. 275.

9 The Swedish refinery was never built because the British blockade was too tight.

10 Wehrle interview one, p. 2; SD File 812.6363 W. R. Davis & Co., p. 411.

11 Moffat, p 275; Davis FBI File Part Four, p. 229; NYT, Oct. 7, 1939.

12 Davis FBI File Part Two, p. 192; Wehrle interview one, p. 17; Higham, p. 71 (A).

13 Werle interview one, p. 17.

14 Werle interview one, p. 4; Newsweek, Jan. 13, 1941; Wehrle interview one, p. 10.

15 Rogge, pp. 130, 325.

16 Farago, p. 234.

17 Ibid., p. 362.

18 Stevenson, p. 295; Farago, pp. 234, 383

19 Davis may also have enlisted Ben Smith in his espionage network. In the spring of 1940, just before the German invasion of France, Smith held a series of cocktail parties for British air force officers at his wife's apartment in Paris. British intelligence suspected that Smith was using these parties to collect military information and/or was spreading "peace" propaganda to undermine these officers' morale (FO Papers, FO371/24405 35695, p. 308).

20 Stevenson, p. 295; Burkes Peerage 1970, p. 1428; Farago, pp. 383, 384; Wohlthat interview.

21 FO Papers C17220, 1939, p. 89.

22 NYT, Oct. 7, 1939, Oct. 10, 1939; Foreign Relations, 1939, vol. 5, p. 707.

23 Scroggs, p. 270.

24 Wood, p. 232; Green, p. 52; Foreign Relations, 1939, vol. 5, p. 707.

[25] The *Emmy Friedrich* was the last German tanker to leave Tampico, Mexico, for Malmö, Sweden. It left on October 20, was discovered by a British cruiser four days later, and was scuttled by its crew to avoid capture (*Foreign Affairs*, 1939, p. 271).

[26] Pratt, p. 328; *NYT*, Aug. 2, 1941.

[27] Scroggs, p. 270.

[28] Powell, p. 99.

[29] Scroggs, p. 270.

[30] *NYT*, Oct. 7, 1939; Davis FBI File Part Three, p. 61.

[31] Davis FBI File Part One, p. 386.

[32] Higham (A), p. 72; *PM*, Apr. 25, 1941, p. 20.

[33] *NYT*, Oct. 10, 1939; Davis FBI File Part One, p. 452; Davis FBI File Part Two, p. 185; *Index*, 1940, p. 828; FO Papers FO371/25048 35696, p. 344.

[34] Davis FBI File Part One, p. 13; Wehrle interview one, pp. 3, 26; *Newsweek*, Jan. 20, 1941, p. 12; Davis FBI File Part Four, p. 7.

[35] *Houston Post*, Aug. 2, 1941; Davis FBI File Part Four, pp. 7, 9; Davis FBI File Part Five, p. 336; *Oil and Gas Journal*, Sept. 14, 1939, p. 83; Davis FBI File Part One, p. 13.

[36] *Current Biography*, 1941, pp. 211–212; *Oil and Gas Journal*, Nov. 30, 1939.

[37] Buhite, Russell D., *Patrick J. Hurley and American Foreign Policy* (Ithaca, N.Y.: Cornell Univ. Press, 1973), p. 94; Meyer, L. (B), p. 150; Green, p. 53.

[38] Cronon, p. 237; *Foreign Relations*, 1939, vol. 5, p. 680.

[39] Hurley may already have known Davis because Hurley had been an oilman in Tulsa, Oklahoma, in the early 1920s when Davis was also in the oil business in that small city (*Current Biography*, 1944, p. 320).

[40] Rogge, pp. 251, 252; Buhite, p. 94.

[41] *PM*, May 5, 1941, p. 22.

[42] Buhite, p. 94.

[43] *NYT*, May 8, 1940.

[44] Davis FBI File Part One, p. 419; *PM*, May 5, 1941, p. 22; Green, p. 54; Powell, p. 114.

[45] In fact, the Abwehr seems to have recruited Davis's entire circle of German contacts: Hertslet, Wohlthat, Fetzer, and the Von Clemm brothers. In an interview many years after the war, Wohlthat admitted that he met with

Canaris, chief of the Abwehr, as many as one hundred times and that he conferred with Canaris before and after every trip he took abroad. Wohlthat said that he provided Canaris with information for Abwehr intelligence operations. Fetzer was in the Canaris circle and dealt in black market oil. The Von Clemms were also Abwehr agents (Wohlthat interview).

[46] Farago, p. 372; German Documents, vol. 9, series D, p. 30; Bratzel, p. 54; Rogge, p. 253.

[47] Davis FBI File Part Four, p. 206; Bratzel, p. 55.

[48] Riess, p. 240; Bratzel, p. 55.

[49] Thomas Hertslet, son of Joachim Hertslet, telephone call June 3, 1997; Farago, p. 306; Wehrle interview one, p. 8.

[50] New York Herald Tribune, Jan. 1, 1941.

[51] New York Herald Tribune, Jan. 2, 1941.

[52] There were accusations that James Lee Kauffman, Davis's attorney, was involved in these Japanese deals. For many years, Kauffman had operated a successful law practice in Tokyo. Since returning to America in the early 1930s, he had represented many Japanese firms on American legal matters (Wehrle interview one, p. 4). Kauffman still had extremely good contacts in Japan through his Japanese law firm, McIvor, Kauffman, Smith, & Yamamoto (Davis FBI File Part Four 65-1128, p. 235).

[53] Bratzel, p. 54; Powell, p. 114; Farago, p. 307; New York Herald Tribune, Jan. 2, 1941; PM, Dec. 12, 1940.

[54] Rogge, p. 249; Farago, p. 389.

[55] FO Papers FO371/24212 35696, p. 132.

[56] Davis FBI File Part Three, p. 9; Index, 1940, p. 828.

[57] Chase, Allan, Falange: The Axis Secret Army in the Americas (New York: G. P. Putnam's Sons, 1943), pp. 248–249; Fodor, p. 79.

[58] Chase, Falange, pp. 248–249; Higham (A), p. 36.

[59] Index, 1940, p. 828; Morgenthau, pp. 324–325.

[60] Current Biography, 1940, p. 139; Meyer, L. (A), p. 176; Camp, p. 16.

[61] Current Biography, 1940, p. 14; Camp, p. 16.

[62] Current Biography, 1940, pp. 15, 139; The New Republic, May 13, 1940, p. 629.

[63] FO papers FO371/24216 35695, p. 7.

[64] Higham (A), p. 77; Riess, pp. 238–239.

[65] Meyer, M., pp. 606, 628; Meyer, L. (B), p. 177.

[66] Camp, p. 23; *Current Biography*, 1940, p. 139.

[67] Ibid., pp. 13–14, 138; Camp, p. 23; Meyer, L. (B), p. 178; Cronon, p. 256.

[68] *NYT*, Oct. 2, 1940, pp. 1, 4.

[69] *Current Biography*, 1940, p. 14.

[70] Ibid., pp. 14, 140.

[71] *NYT*, Jan. 7, 1941.

[72] *NYT*, Jan. 4, 1941.

[73] SD File 800.20211 Hertslet, Joachim/59 Nov. 29, 1940; Riess, p. 206.

[74] Davis FBI File Part One, pp. 374, 420.

[75] Rogge, p. 257; Davis FBI File Part One, p. 400.

[76] Bratzel, p. 55; Williams, W., pp. 181–182.

[77] Bratzel, p. 55.

[78] Higham (A), p. 72.

[79] Farago, p. 389; U.S. Military Intelligence Department, File 10602-207 Apr. 30, 1942; Heinz Hertslet, brother of Joachim Hertslet, letter Apr. 28, 1997.

[80] Wehrle interview one, p. 10.

Chapter Ten: Defeat Roosevelt

[1] Friedlander, p. 36; Lee, Albert, *Henry Ford and the Jews* (New York: Stein and Day, 1980), p. 123.

[2] Friedlander, p. 36.

[3] Daniels, p. 253.

[4] Daniels, p. 253; Frye, Alton, *Nazi Germany and the Western Hemisphere 1932–1942* (New Haven, Conn.: Yale Univ. Press, 1967), p. 143.

[5] Ickes, vol. 2, pp. 694–695.

[6] Farago, p. 369; Ross, pp. 165–166.

[7] Stevenson, p. 290; Ross, p. 166; Rogge, pp. 248–249.

[8] Rogge, pp. 248–249; Ross, p. 166; Farago, p. 369.

[9] Ickes, vol. 3, pp. 61–62.

[10] Wehrle interview one, pp. 17, 20.

[11] Ross, p. 167.

[12] MacFarland, p. 104.

[13] Donahoe, Bernard F., *Private Plans and Public Dangers: The Story of FDR's Third Nomination* (South Bend, Ind.: Univ. of Notre Dame, 1965), p. 121.

[14] How well Wheeler knew Davis is unknown. Wheeler admitted that he had at least one meeting with Davis (*Congressional Record*, 1941, p. 8497).

[15] Donahoe, *Private Plans*, pp. 133, 134.

[16] Berle may have been the State Department official who tipped off Childs (Berle Papers, 1939, p. 229).

[17] *St. Louis Post-Dispatch*, June 14, 1939.

[18] *St. Louis Post-Dispatch*, July 30, 1939; *Chicago Tribune*, July 30, 1939; *NYT*, Aug. 6, 1939; *Washington Post*, July 30, 1939.

[19] *St. Louis Post-Dispatch*, Aug. 5, 1939.

[20] Davis FBI File Part Two, pp. 272, 287.

[21] Ibid., p. 273.

[22] Ibid., pp. 274, 286, 294.

[23] Farago, p. 368.

[24] Farago, p. 368; German Documents, Series D, vol. X, 1940, p. 160; *NYT*, Mar. 5, 1940, Mar. 13, 1940.

[25] FO Papers FO371/24212 35696, p. 129.

[26] Ross, p. 174; Frye, p. 143.

[27] Davis FBI File Part Two, pp. 340, 342, 388; Davis FBI File Part Three, p. 6; Davis FBI File Part Five, p. 234.

[28] Davis FBI File Part Two, p. 395; Davis FBI File Part Three, pp. 5, 388.

[29] Farago, p. 373.

[30] Rogge, p. 257.

[31] Ross, p. 173; Farago, p. 374; Ross, p. 173.

[32] Davis FBI File Part Three, p. 19; Rogge, p. 252.

[33] The FBI had both Davis and Hertslet under surveillance. Therefore, both the FBI and Roosevelt may have been aware of the German contacts with Lewis. Hecht, Marie B., and Herbert S. Parmet, *Never Again: A President Runs for a Third Term* (New York: Macmillan, 1968), p. 256.

[34] Farago, pp. 307–308, 371.

[35] Luigi Podestá was a delegate of the Italian National Institute of Exchange and manager of the Italian government's exchange control in New York City (*NYT*, Dec. 30, 1938). He was also a longtime organizer of Italian Fascist Party activities in the Italian-American community of New York (Salvemini, Gaetano, *Italian Fascist Activities in the United States* [New York: Center for Migration Studies, 1977], p. 203).

[36] Farago, pp. 307–308; Rogge, pp. 248–249.

[37] Rogge, p. 252; Documents of German Foreign Political Series D, vol. IX 1940, p. 30; Frye, p. 144.

[38] Documents of German Foreign Political Series D, vol. IX 1940, p. 30.

[39] Ross, p. 173; Davis FBI File Part Two, p. 391; Davis FBI File Part Three, p. 219.

[40] Davis FBI File Part Two, p. 9; Davis FBI File Part Three, p. 194.

[41] Davis FBI File Part Two, p. 374; Davis FBI File Part Three, p. 13.

[42] Leuchtenburg, pp. 310–312; Breuer, p. 166.

[43] Leuchtenburg, pp. 310–312; *NYT*, Dec. 31, 1940.

[44] MacFarland, p. 104; Donahoe, p. 134; Hecht, Marie B., and Parmet, Herbert S., *Willkie: A President Runs for a Third Term* (New York: MacMillan Company, 1968), p. 234; Farago, p. 371.

[45] MacFarland, p. 104; Donahoe, p. 134.

[46] *Current Biography*, 1940, p. 859.

[47] Donahoe, p. 156; *Current Biography*, 1940, p. 859.

[48] Farago, p. 384; Ross, p. 171.

[49] Frye, p. 144; Ross, p. 173; Davis FBI File Part Three, p. 65.

[50] Rogge, p. 87; Ross, p. 174; Lee, p. 123.

[51] German Documents Series D, vol. X 1940, p. 102.

[52] Ross, p. 171; Donahoe, p. 158.

[53] Leuchtenburg, p. 314.

[54] Farago, p. 382; Davis FBI File Part Four, p. 18.

[55] Frye, pp. 142, 144; German Documents Series D, vol. X 1940, p. 160.

[56] Frye, p. 142.

[57] Leuchtenburg, pp. 312–313.

[58] Barnes, Joseph, *Willkie: The Events He Was Part Of—The Ideas He Fought For* (New York: Simon & Schuster, 1952), p. 223.

[59] Leuchtenburg, pp. 317–318.

[60] Rogge, p. 90.

[61] *NYT*, Oct. 23, 1946; German Documents Series D, vol. X 1940, p. 126; Rogge, p. 249; Overacker, 1940, p. 713.

[62] *PM*, Apr. 25, 1941, p. 20; Davis FBI File Part Five, p. 186; *St. Louis Post-Dispatch*, Jan. 17, 1941; *NYT*, Jan. 18, 1941.

[63] Davis FBI File Part Three, pp. 187, 188.

[64] Hecht, pp. 233–234; Ross, p. 184; Davis FBI File Part Three, pp. 187, 188; Hecht, pp. 233–234; Childs, p. 206.

[65] Childs, p. 207; Hecht, pp. 233–234.

[66] Johnson, Donald Bruce, *The Republican Party and Wendell Willkie* (Urbana, Ill.: Univ. of Illinois Press, 1960), p. 154; Wehrle interview one, p. 21.

[67] Barnard, Ellsworth, *Wendell Willkie: Fighter for Freedom* (Marquette, Mich.: Northern Michigan Univ. Press, 1966), p. 559.

[68] The presence of Gene Tunney is odd. As discussed in chapter thirteen, Tunney was a good friend of both the head of British intelligence in New York and of J. Edgar Hoover of the FBI. Further, Tunney was a friend of Franklin Roosevelt Jr. None of these relationships was expected of a Willkie supporter. Could it be that Tunney was a "mole" inside the Willkie organization for Roosevelt? (Tunney, Gene, *Arms for Living* [New York: Wilfred Funk, 1941], p. 1).

[69] Wehrle interview one, p. 20.

[70] Ross, p. 184; Hecht, pp. 233–234.

[71] Ross, p. 184; Hecht, p. 234.

[72] Willkie, p. 220.

[73] Josephson, Matthew, *Sidney Hillman: Statesman of American Labor* (Garden City, N.Y.: Doubleday & Co., 1952), p. 486; Hecht, p. 255; Ross, p. 185; *PM*, Dec. 11, 1940, p. 8.

[74] Hecht, p. 256; Lash, p. 238.

[75] Josephson, p. 486; Gentry, p. 237; Lash, p. 239.

[76] Hecht, p. 256; Lash, p. 239.

[77] Hecht, p. 256; Dubofsy, p. 356.

[78] Ross, p. 185; Dubofsy, p. 357; Berle, Adolf Augustus Jr. (B), *Navigating the Rapids 1918–1971: From the Papers of Adolf A. Berle*, edited by Beatrice Berle and Travis Beal Jacobs (New York: Harcourt, Brace, Jovanovich, 1973), p. 346; *PM*, Dec. 11, 1940, p. 8.

[79] Ross, p. 185.

[80] *The Nation* (Washington), Nov. 2, 1940, p. 414; Dubofsy, p. 357.

[81] Farago, p. 387; Willkie, p. 221; Davis FBI File Part Three, p. 188.

[82] Davis FBI File Part Three, p. 171; *PM*, Dec. 11, 1940, p. 8; Davis FBI File Part Three, p. 171; Childs, p. 206.

[83] Berle (A), 1940, p. 11; Childs, p. 207.

[84] Davis FBI File Part Three, p. 187; Dubofsy, p. 357; Johnson, p. 154; Hecht, p. 255; Goodwin, Doris Kearns, *No Ordinary Time: Franklin and Eleanor Roosevelt—The Home Front in World War* (New York: Simon & Schuster, 1994), p. 183; Frye, p. 144.

[85] Johnson, p. 154; Frye, p. 144; Rogge, p. 256.

[86] *The Nation*, p. 414.

[87] Weschler, pp. 111–112.

[88] Farago, p. 387; *PM*, Dec. 12, 1940, p. 10.

[89] Goodwin, p. 184; Josephson, p. 488.

[90] Berle (B), p. 346; Ross, p. 160.

[91] Johnson, p. 155; Lash, p. 234; Leuchtenburg, p. 320.

[92] Cole (A), p. 338; Cole, Wayne S. (B), *Charles A. Lindbergh and the Battle Against American Intervention in World War Two* (New York: Harcourt, Brace, Jovanovich, 1974), p. 110.

[93] Farago, p. 385; Johnson, p. 155; Leuchtenburg, p. 321.

[94] Lash, p. 229.

[95] Leuchtenburg, pp. 319–320.

[96] Leuchtenburg, pp. 319–320; Childs, p. 207.

[97] Leuchtenburg, p. 321.

[98] Ross, p. 189; Johnson, p. 154; Childs, p. 206.

[99] Ross, p. 189.

[100] The U.S. Navy escorted ship convoys across the Atlantic and engaged in numerous battles with German submarines. Several U.S. warships were sunk or damaged.

[101] Gallup, George H., *The Gallup Poll: Volume One 1935–1948* (New York: Random House, 1972), p. 307; Goodwin, p. 283; Sereny, Gitta, *Albert Speer: His Battle with Truth* (New York: Alfred A. Knopf, 1995), p. 268.

[102] Farago, p. 388.

[103] Josephson, p. 493.

Chapter Eleven: No Foreign Wars

[1] Hoke, Henry, *It's a Secret* (New York: Pamphlet Press, 1946), p. 58.

[2] *NYT*, Dec. 31, 1940; Hoke, p. 58; *PM*, Jan. 12, 1941, p. 12.

[3] Hoke, p. 58; Cole (B), p. 110; *NYT*, Dec. 31, 1940.

[4] However, it should be noted that Lindbergh had a cordial relationship with America's leading fascist intellectual, Lawrence Dennis. Dennis considered himself a friend of Lindbergh and saw Lindbergh often in 1940–41. Dennis took credit as the inspiration for most of the ideas in Lindbergh's isolationist articles and books (The Official German Report, 1961, p. 282).

[5] Gallup, vol. 1, p. 278; Gentry, p. 226; Lash, p. 234.

[6] Kahn, Albert Eugene, and Sayers, Michael, *Sabotage (A)!: The Secret War Against America* (New York: Harper & Brothers, 1942), p. 165; Cole (B), p. 110.

[7] *PM*, Jan. 12, 1941, p. 12; Hoke, p. 58; Breuer, p. 167.

[8] *Current Biography*, 1941, p. 561; Hoke, p. 58; Kahn (A), p. 165.

[9] *Current Biography*, 1941, p. 561; Cole (B), p. 110; *PM*, Jan. 12, 1941, p. 12.

[10] *NYT*, Dec. 31, 1940; *PM*, Jan. 12, 1941, p. 12, Apr. 27, 1941, p. 18.

[11] *NYT*, Dec. 3, 1940; Davis FBI File Part Four, p. 149.

[12] Davis FBI File Part Four, p. 149; Davis FBI File Part Five, p. 6, *St. Louis Post-Dispatch*, Jan. 17, 1941; Barnes, p. 243.

[13] *St. Louis Post-Dispatch*, Jan. 17, 1941; Davis FBI File Part One, pp. 410–411.

[14] Barnes, p. 223; Davis FBI File Part Five, p. 6.

[15] *Current Biography*, 1940, pp. 477–478; *Current Biography*, 1941, p. 699; *Cyclopedia*, vol. 33, p. 35; Davis FBI File Part Five, p. 6.

[16] Barnes, pp. 242–243; Barnard, p. 560.

[17] FO Papers FO371/24405 35695, p. 308.

[18] FO Papers FO371/24405 35695, pp. 310–311; Beschloss, Michael R., *Kennedy and Roosevelt: The Uneasy Alliance* (New York: W. W. Norton & Company, 1980), p. 231.

[19] Davis FBI File Part One, pp. 410–411.

[20] Ibid.

[21] Ibid.

22 Davis FBI File Part One, p. 375; Breuer, p. 167; *NYT*, Dec. 18, 1940; *Current Biography*, 1941, p. 562.

23 *NYT*, Dec. 26, 1940.

24 Davis FBI File Part One, p. 375; *NYT*, Dec. 31, 1940.

25 Davis FBI File Part One, p. 375. *NYT*, Dec. 31, 1940.

26 *PM*, Jan. 12, 1941, p. 12.

27 *NYT*, Dec. 31, 1940, Jan. 1, 1941.

28 What is curious about the massive publicity received by Marshall's disclosure is that the story was not new. Drew Pearson had broken the story of Davis's peace plan almost a year before in a February 18, 1940, newspaper report. For some reason the newspaper story did not make front-page news then and was officially denied by the State Department at the time (Davis FBI File Part Four, p. 303).

29 Davis FBI File Part One, p. 394; *NYT*, Jan. 1, 1941.

30 *PM*, Apr. 25, 1941, p. 20; Wehrle interview one, pp. 17, 27; Davis FBI File Part Four, p. 166.

31 *NYT*, Jan. 1, 1941.

32 Marshall later claimed that Davis gave the NFW $41,000 (Davis FBI File Part One, p. 383).

33 Davis FBI File Part One, pp. 410, 411; Davis FBI File Part Five, p. 126.

34 Davis FBI File Part One, pp. 390, 393–394.

35 Ibid., pp. 382–383, 388, 393, 402, 410.

36 Ibid., p. 391.

37 Ibid., pp. 383, 390.

38 Ibid., pp. 374, 383, 393.

39 Ibid., pp. 374, 385, 390.

40 Ibid., pp. 374, 383, 390, 394.

41 *NYT*, Jan. 7, 1941, Jan. 8, 1941; Davis FBI File Part One, p. 388.

42 This document was later given to John L. Lewis for safekeeping and was never returned to Davis (Davis FBI File Part Five, p. 203). One of the mysteries of Davis's intrigues is what happened to these documents.

43 Davis FBI File Part One, p. 402; Davis FBI File Part Five, p. 177.

44 Davis FBI File Part One, p. 410.

[45] *PM*, Dec. 12, 1940, p. 7; Davis FBI File Part Five, p. 186.

[46] Davis FBI File Part One, pp. 399–401.

[47] Wehrle interview one, p. 21; Davis FBI File Part Four, pp. 32, 42; Davis FBI File Part One, pp. 404–405; *Congressional Record*, vol. 87, part 8, p. 8497.

[48] *NYT*, Jan. 18, 1941; Overacker, 1940, pp. 703, 725; *PM*, Dec. 11, 1940, p. 8.

[49] Davis FBI File Part One, p. 434; Wehrle interview one, p. 21.

[50] Wehrle interview one, p. 28; Davis FBI File Part One, p. 417.

[51] *Newsweek*, Jan. 13, 1941, p. 16; Hoke, p. 59; Kahn (A), p. 167.

[52] Hoke, p. 59; Kahn (A), p. 167.

[53] *Current Biography*, 1941, p. 560; Hoke, p. 58.

[54] Davis FBI File Part Five, pp. 8, 196; Wehrle interview one, p. 22.

[55] Gallup, p. 298; Davis FBI File Part Five, p. 196.

[56] Hoke, p. 59; *Life*, Jan. 20, 1941, p. 826.

[57] Leuchtenberg, p. 311; Higham, Charles (B), *American Swastika* (Garden City, N.Y.: Doubleday, 1985), p. 13; Kahn, Albert Eugene (B), *High Treason: The Plot Against the People* (New York: Lear Publishers, 1950), p. 220; Leuchtenberg, p. 311; *Congressional Record*, vol. 87, part 8, p. 8497.

[58] Kahn (A), p. 166; Higham (B), p. 13; Hoke, p. 59.

[59] Sulzberger, C. L., *World War II* (New York: American Heritage Publishing, 1966), p. 140; Stevenson, p. 292; Higham (B), p. 14, Kahn (A), p. 238.

[60] Stevenson, p. 292; Riess, p. 287.

[61] Leuchtenberg, p. 311; Kahn (B), p. 219.

[62] Hoke, p. 60; Riess, pp. 292–293.

[63] Kahn (A), p. 220; Stevenson, pp. 293–294.

[64] Higham (A), p. 73.

Chapter Twelve: Banco Continental

[1] Green, pp. 54–55; Meyer, M., p. 630; Williams, W., pp. 181–182.

[2] Pye, Michael, *The King Over Water: The Scandalous Truth about the Windsors' War Years* (New York: Holt, Rinehart and Winston, 1981), p. 100; *NYT*, Nov. 10, 1940; Davis FBI File Part Four, p. 18; Davis FBI File Part Five, p. 336.

[3] Flynn's involvement is curious because he was the national chairman of the Democratic Party in 1940. Perhaps his inclusion came from his friendship with John Hastings, whom he had known from their days working in Mayor Jimmie Walker's administration of New York City in the 1920s (*National Cyclopedia Supplement Three*, p. 227).

[4] Federal Bureau of Investigation, "Axel Wenner-Gren Investigation File #65-8857," pp. 4, 6; Higham (B), p. 168.

[5] Davis FBI File Part Four, p. 30; *Current Biography*, 1942, p. 884; Davis FBI File Part Three, p. 48. The forty-four-year-old Hastings had lost his Senate seat in 1932 as a result of his involvement in financial scandals surrounding New York mayor Jimmie Walker. Hastings was also linked to Senator Burton Wheeler through Hastings's transit plan to reduce railway fares, which Wheeler was promoting in Congress (*NYT*, December 11, 1964).

[6] Pye, p. 72; Riess, p. 236; Krauz, Enrique, *Mexico: Biography of Power: A History of Modern Mexico 1810–1996* (New York: Harper Collins, 1997), pp. 493–494; Kirk, p. 180.

[7] Pye, p. 100; Higham, Charles (C), *Duchess of Windsor (C): The Secret Life* (New York: McGraw-Hill Book Company, 1988), p. 303; Wenner-Gren FBI File, pp. 4, 6.

[8] *NYT*, Nov. 25, 1961; *Current Biography*, 1942, p. 885; Wenner-Gren FBI File, p. 60.

[9] *Time*, June 29, 1942, p. 31; *Current Biography*, 1942, pp. 884–885.

[10] *NYT*, Jan. 11, 1942; Wenner-Gren FBI File, p. 17; Higham (B), p. 166; Higham (C), p. 303.

[11] Morgenthau, 1938–41, pp. 326–327.

[12] Dangerfield, Royden, and Gordon, David Livingston, *The Hidden Weapon: The Story of Economic Warfare* (New York: Da Capo Press, 1976), p. 143.

[13] Pye, pp. 58–60.

[14] Hyde, H. Montgomery, *Room 3603: The Story of the British Intelligence Center in New York During World War Two* (New York: Farrar Strauss and Company, 1962), pp. 52–53.

[15] Higham (B), p. 167; *Current Biography*, 1942, p. 884; Pye, p. 73.

[16] Higham (B), p. 167; Pye, p. 100.

[17] Higham (B), p. 168; Pye, pp. 98–99.

[18] Higham (B), p. 168; De Marigny, Alfred, *A Conspiracy of Crowns: The True Story of the Duke of Windsor and the Murder of Sir Harry Oakes* (New York: Crown Publishers, 1990), p. 298.

[19] *Current Biography*, 1942, p. 884; Davis FBI File Part Four, p. 230; Davis FBI File Part Three, p. 174.

[20] The FBI may not yet have been aware of Flanley's espionage activities because it did not object to granting him a passport to travel to Brazil. More deviously, the FBI may have granted Flanley a passport so FBI agents could follow him and find out who he contacted in Brazil (Davis FBI File Part Three, p. 101).

[21] *Current Biography*, 1942, p. 884; Davis FBI File Part Five, p. 136.

[22] Davis FBI File Part Five, p. 41; *Current Biography*, 1942, p. 884.

[23] Pye, p. 103.

[24] Pye, p. 72; Higham (C), p. 311; De Marigny, p. 297.

[25] West, Nigel, *A Thread of Deceit: Espionage Myths of World War Two* (New York: Random House, 1985), p. 130.

[26] FO Papers FO371/24212 35696, p. 131; Higham (C), p. 311; De Marigny, p. 297; Hyde, p. 52.

Chapter Thirteen: Strange Death

[1] *Newsweek*, Jan. 20, 1941, p. 12; Davis FBI File Part Five, pp. 65, 78; *Oil and Gas Journal*, Jan. 2, 1941, Jan. 30, 1941; Wehrle interview one, p. 3.

[2] *Newsweek*, Jan. 20, 1941, p. 12.

[3] *Who Was Who in America*, vol. 3; Davis FBI File Part One, p. 117.

[4] *NYT*, Feb 5, 1944; *PM*, May 4, 1941, p. 19.

[5] *Valley Morning Star* (Brownsville), Jan. 29, 1941.

[6] Williams, p. 340; *Houston Post*, Aug. 2, 1941, Aug. 3, 1941; Davis FBI File Part Five, pp. 41, 206; Wehrle interview one, p. 22.

[7] Wehrle interview one, p. 6; Davis FBI File Part Five, pp. 138, 141, 151; Wehrle interview one, p. 25.

[8] Davis FBI File Part Five, p. 331; *NYT*, Jan. 29, 1942.

[9] Wehrle interview one, p. 22.

[10] Davis FBI File Part Five, p. 61.

[11] Wehrle interview one, p. 24.

[12] Wehrle interview one, p. 2; Davis FBI File Part Five, p. 292.

[13] *Houston Post*, Aug. 2, 1941; Wehrle interview one, pp. 22–24; Texas Department of Health "Standard Certificate of Death for William Rhodes Davis."

[14] Davis FBI File Part One, p. 433; Wehrle interview one, p. 23.

[15] Wehrle interview one, p. 23.

[16] Dr. Mark Dallow interview, Feb. 29, 1996.

[17] Stevenson, p. 295.

[18] Bond, Raymond T., *Handbook for Poisoners* (New York: Rinehart & Co.; 1951), pp. 70–71.

[19] Wehrle interview one, pp. 23–24, 27–28.

[20] Wechsler, p. 112; Davis FBI File Part One, p. 417.

[21] *Congressional Record*, vol. 87, part 8, p. 8498.

[22] Wehrle interview one, p. 14.

[23] Berle Papers, p. 2; Davis FBI File Part Five, p. 121.

[24] Davis FBI File Part Five, p. 121.

[25] Bratzel, p. 55; Stevenson, p. 295.

[26] Stevenson, p. 295.

[27] Ibid., p. 129.

[28] Gentry, p. 265.

[29] Summers, Anthony, *Official and Confidential: The Secret Life of J. Edgar Hoover* (New York: G. P. Putnam's Sons, 1993), pp. 118–121.

[30] Gentry, p. 267.

[31] Summers, pp. 118–121; Gentry, p. 266.

[32] Berle Papers, p. 2; Gentry, pp. 265, 268–269; Schwartz, p. 172; Hyde, pp. 2–5.

[33] West, p. 130; Gentry, p. 271.

[34] Stevenson, p. 129.

[35] Gentry, p. 271.

[36] Stevenson, p. 129.

[37] Dallow interview. For a discussion of the problematic nature of Stevenson's biography of Stephenson, see West.

Chapter Fourteen: Collapse and Cover-Up

[1] Davis FBI File Part Five, pp. 151, 292, 349; Wehrle interview one, p. 25.

[2] *NYT*, Sept. 4, 1941, Sept. 6, 1941; Wehrle interview one, p. 22.

[3] Davis FBI File Part One, p. 417; Wehrle interview one, p. 23.

[4] Davis FBI File Part Five, p. 144; *NYT*, July 29, 1942.

[5] Davis FBI File Part Four, p. 60; Davis FBI File Part One, p. 433; Davis FBI File Part Five, p. 299.

[6] Davis FBI File Part Five, p. 299.

[7] *Washington Post*, June 27, 1952.

[8] Wehrle interview one, pp. 25–27, 29.

[9] Rogge, pp. 257–259; Davis FBI File Part Five, p. 352.

[10] Davis FBI File Part Four, pp. 192–193.

[11] *NYT*, Jan. 29, 1942; Higham (A), p. 71.

[12] Higham (A), p. 74; *NYT*, Jan. 29, 1942.

[13] *London Times*, Oct. 23, 1941; *Current Biography*, 1944, p. 140.

[14] Higham (B), pp. 168, 169; *Current Biography*, 1942, p. 883; Wenner-Gren FBI File, p. 3; *NYT*, Nov. 25, 1961.

[15] *Current Biography*, 1942, p. 885; Wenner-Gren FBI File, pp. 3–4.

[16] Wehrle interview one, pp. 5, 28–29; Davis FBI File Part Five, p. 121.

[17] Wehrle interview one, p. 17; *Houston Chronicle*, June 23, 1943.

[18] Telephone conversation with Thomas Hertslet, son of Joachim Hertslet, on June 3, 1997.

[19] Letter from Heinz Hertslet, brother of Joachim Hertslet, Apr. 28, 1997.

[20] *PM*, Oct. 28, 1946, p. 5.

[21] Kahn (A), p. 256; *Current Biography*, 1948, pp. 533–534.

[22] Rogge, O. John (B), *Our Vanishing Civil Liberties* (New York: Gaer Associates, 1949), p. 19.

[23] Rogge (B), pp. 21, 23.

[24] Ibid., p. 26.

[25] *PM*, Oct. 28, 1946, pp. 3, 6.

[26] Curiously, this report is no longer in the Justice Department's files. It is listed in the file index, but the Justice Department told the author that personnel "located no records" related to the Rogge report in the associated file. What happened to the missing file is unknown (letter from U.S. Justice Department to the author, January 7, 1997).

[27] *NYT*, Oct. 27, 1946; *Seattle Post-Intelligencer*, Oct. 27, 1946.

[28] *NYT*, Oct. 23, 1946, Oct. 26, 1946.

[29] *PM*, Oct. 28, 1946, p. 3; *NYT*, Oct. 26, 1946; *Des Moines Register*, Oct. 31, 1946.

[30] *PM*, Oct. 28, 1946, p. 3.

[31] *Des Moines Register*, Oct. 31, 1946; *NYT*, Oct. 27, 1946; *Seattle Post-Intelligencer*, Oct. 27, 1946; Kahn (A), p. 259.

[32] *Current Biography*, 1948, pp. 533–534; Hamby, Alonzo L., *Beyond the New Deal: Harry S. Truman and American Liberalism* (New York: Columbia Univ. Press, 1973), p. 80; *PM*, Oct. 28–29, 1946, pp. 3, 6, 7; Higham (A), p. 75; *NYT*, Sept. 4, 1943, May 31, 1985; *National Cyclopedia*, vol. 49, p. 85; Williams, Ben, p. 402.

[33] Berle, p. 707.

[34] *London Times*, Sept. 15, 1955, Sept. 24, 1955; *NYT*, Nov. 25, 1961.

[35] *Who Was Who*, vol. 3, p. 248; Wehrle interview one, p. 30; Wehrle interview two, p. 4.

[36] Telephone conversation with Thomas Hertslet, June 3, 1997; Heinz Hertslet letter, Apr. 28, 1997; Wehrle interview one, p. 30; Heinz Hertslet letter, Nov. 20, 1996.

[37] Wehrle interview one, pp. 9, 15, 30.

[38] Ibid., pp. 17, 19.

Bibliography

Public Documents

Great Britain. Public Record Office. Correspondence of the Foreign Office. 1936–1941.

U.S. Bureau of Census. Fourteenth Census of the United States: 1910. Population.

U.S. *Congressional Record*. Vol. 87, Part 8.

U.S. State Department. Documents on German Foreign Policy 1918–1945: Volume Five, Series D, Poland, Balkans, Latin America, The Small Powers 1937–1939. 1953.

U.S. State Department. Foreign Relations of the United States, 1938, Volume V: The American Republics. 1956.

U.S. State Department. Foreign Relations of the United States, 1939, Volume V: The American Republics. 1956.

Unpublished Materials

Berle, Adolf Augustus Jr. The Diary of Adolf Augustus Berle Jr. 1939–1941. Yale University.

Federal Bureau of Investigation. "William Rhodes Davis Investigation File # 65-1128."

Federal Bureau of Investigation. "Axel Wenner-Gren Investigation File # 65-8857."

U.S. Military Intelligence Department. File 10602-207.

Morgenthau, Henry F. Henry F. Morgenthau Presidential Diaries. Stanford University.

U.S. Department of State. File 812.6363 W. R. Davis & Co.

U.S. Department of State. File 800.20211 Davis, William Rhodes.

U.S. Department of State. File 800.20211 Hertslet, Joachim/59.

Books

Alinsky, Saul. *John L. Lewis: An Unauthorized Biography.* New York: G. P. Putnam's Sons, 1949.

Ashby, Joe C. *Organized Labor and the Mexican Revolution Under Lazaro Cárdenas.* Chapel Hill, N.C.: University of North Carolina Press, 1963.

Barnard, Ellsworth. *Wendell Willkie: Fighter for Freedom.* Marquette, Mich.: Northern Michigan University Press, 1966.

Barnes, Joseph. *Willkie: The Events He Was Part Of—The Ideas He Fought For.* New York: Simon & Schuster, 1952.

Bates, L. M. *The Thames on Fire: The Battle of London River 1939–1945.* Lavenham, United Kingdom: Terence Dalton Limited, 1985.

Belknap, John. *American Appeasement: United States Foreign Policy and Germany 1933–1938.* Cambridge, Mass.: Harvard University Press, 1969.

Berle, Adolf Augustus Jr. *Navigating the Rapids 1918–1971: From the Papers of Adolf A. Berle.* Edited by Beatrice Berle and Travis Beal Jacobs. New York: Harcourt, Brace, Jovanovich, 1973.

Beschloss, Michael R. *Kennedy and Roosevelt: The Uneasy Alliance.* New York: W. W. Norton & Company, 1980.

Bond, Raymond T. *Handbook for Poisoners.* New York: Rinehart & Co., 1951.

Bratzel, John F., and Rout, Leslie B. *The Shadow War: German Espionage and United States Counterespionage in Latin America During World War Two.* Frederick, Md: University Publication of America, 1986.

Breuer, William B. *Hitler's Undercover War: The Nazi Espionage Invasion of the U.S.A.* New York: St. Martin's Press, 1989.

Buhite, Russell D. *Patrick J. Hurley and American Foreign Policy.* Ithaca, N.Y.: Cornell University Press, 1973.

Camp, Roderic Ai. *Mexican Political Biographies 1935–1975.* Tucson, Ariz.: University of Arizona Press, 1976.

Carroll, Bernice A. *Design for Total War: Arms and Economics in the Third Reich.* The Hague, Netherlands: Mouton, 1968.

Chase, Allan. *Falange: The Axis Secret Army in the Americas.* New York: G. P. Putnam's Sons, 1943.

Childs, Marquis W. *I Write from Washington.* New York: Harper and Brothers Publishers, 1942.

Churchill, Winston Spencer. *The Gathering Storm: Volume One The Second World War.* Boston: Houghton Mifflin Co., 1948.

Cole, Wayne S. *Charles A. Lindbergh and the Battle Against American Intervention in World War Two.* New York: Harcourt, Brace, Jovanovich, 1974.

Cole, Wayne S. *Roosevelt and the Isolationists 1932 45.* Lincoln, Nebr.: University of Nebraska Press, 1983.

Cronon, E. David. *Josephus Daniels in Mexico.* Madison, Wis.: University of Wisconsin Press, 1960.

Cumberland, Charles C. *Mexico: The Struggle for Modernity.* New York: Oxford University Press, 1968.

Dallek, Robert. *Franklin D. Roosevelt and American Foreign Policy 1932–1945.* New York: Oxford University Press, 1979.

Dangerfield, Royden, and Gordon, David Livingston. *The Hidden Weapon: The Story of Economic Warfare.* New York: Da Capo Press, 1976.

Daniels, Josephus. *Shirt-Sleeve Diplomat.* Chapel Hill, N.C.: University of North Carolina Press, 1947.

De Marigny, Alfred. *A Conspiracy of Crowns: The True Story of the Duke of Windsor and the Murder of Sir Harry Oakes*. New York: Crown Publishers, 1990.

Derks, Scott, ed. *The Value of A Dollar: 1860–1989*. Detroit: Gale Research, 1994.

Donahoe, Bernard F. *Private Plans and Public Dangers: The Story of FDR's Third Nomination*. South Bend, Ind.: University of Notre Dame Press, 1965.

Dubofsy, Melvyn, and Van Tine, Warren. *John L. Lewis: A Biography*. New York: Quadrangle Books, 1977.

Eggleston, George T. *Roosevelt, Churchill, and the World War Two Opposition*. Old Greenwich, Conn.: Devin-Adair Company, 1979.

Farago, Ladislas. *The Game of the Foxes: The Untold Story of German Espionage in the United States and Great Britain during World War Two*. New York: Donald McKay Company, 1971.

Fisher, David E. *Race on the Edge of Time: Radar—The Decisive Weapon of World War Two*. New York: Paragon House, 1989.

Fodor, Denis J. *The Neutrals*. New York: Time-Life Books, 1982.

Freeburg, Russell W., and Goralski, Robert. *Oil and War: How the Deadly Struggle for Fuel in World War Two Meant Victory or Defeat*. New York: William Morrow and Company, 1987.

Friedlander, Saul. *Prelude to Downfall: Hitler and the United States 1939–1941*. New York: Alfred A. Knopf, 1967.

Frye, Alton. *Nazi Germany and the Western Hemisphere 1932–1942*. New Haven, Conn.: Yale University Press, 1967.

Gallup, George H. *The Gallup Poll: Volume One 1935–1948*. New York: Random House, 1972.

Gentry, Curt. *J. Edgar Hoover: The Man and the Secrets*. New York: W. W. Norton & Company, 1991.

Gilbert, Martin, and Gott, Richard. *The Appeasers: The Decline of Democracy from Hitler's Rise to Chamberlain's Fall*. Boston: Houghton Mifflin, 1963.

Gleason, Everett, and Langer, William L. *Challenge to Isolation 1937–40*. New York: Harper and Brothers, 1952.

Goodwin, Doris Kearns. *No Ordinary Time: Franklin and Eleanor Roosevelt—The Home Front in World War*. New York: Simon & Schuster, 1994.

Green, David. *The Containment of Latin America: A History of the Myths and Realities of the Good Neighbor Policy*. Chicago, Ill.: Quadrangle Books, 1971.

Guerin, Daniel. *Big Business and Fascism*. New York: Pathfinder Press, 1973.

Guffey, Joseph F. *Seventy Years on the Red-Fire Wagon: From Tilden to Truman through New Freedom and New Deal*. Privately printed, 1952.

Hamby, Alonzo L. *Beyond the New Deal: Harry S. Truman and American Liberalism*. New York: Columbia University Press, 1973.

Hearden, Patrick J. *Roosevelt Confronts Hitler: America's Entry into World War Two*. DeKalb, Ill.: Northern Illinois University Press, 1987.

Hecht, Marie B., and Parmet, Herbert S. *Never Again: A President Runs for a Third Term*. New York: Macmillan, 1968.

Higham, Charles. *American Swastika*. Garden City, N.Y.: Doubleday, 1985.

Higham, Charles, *Duchess of Windsor: The Secret Life*. New York: Mc-Graw-Hill Book Company, 1988.

Higham, Charles. *Trading with the Enemy: An Expose of the Nazi-American Money Plot 1937–1949*. New York: Delacorte Press, 1983.

Hoke, Henry. *It's a Secret*. New York: Pamphlet Press, 1946.

Hyde, H. Montgomery. *Room 3603: The Story of the British Intelligence Center in New York during World War Two*. New York: Farrar Strauss and Company, 1962.

Ickes, Harold L. *The Secret Diary of Harold L. Ickes: Volume Two 1936–1939 and Volume Three 1940–1944*. New York: Simon & Schuster, 1954.

Johnson, Donald Bruce. *The Republican Party and Wendell Willkie*. Urbana, Ill.: University of Illinois Press, 1960.

Josephson, Matthew. *Sidney Hillman: Statesman of American Labor.* Garden City, N.Y.: Doubleday & Co., 1952.

Kahn, Albert Eugene. *High Treason: The Plot Against the People.* New York: Lear Publishers, 1950.

Kahn, Albert Eugene, and Sayers, Michael. *Sabotage!: The Secret War Against America.* New York: Harper and Brothers, 1942.

Kennedy, Paul. *The Rise and Fall of the Great Powers: Economic Change and Military Conflict from 1500 to 2000.* New York: Random House, 1987.

Kirk, Betty. *Covering the Mexican Front.* Norman, Okla.: University of Oklahoma Press, 1942.

Krauz, Enrique. *Mexico Biography of Power: A History of Modern Mexico 1810–1996.* New York: Harper Collins, 1997.

Laquer, Walter, ed. *Fascism: A Reader's Guide: Analyses, Interpretations, Bibliography.* Berkeley, Calif.: University of California Press, 1976.

Lash, Joseph P. *Roosevelt and Churchill 1939–1941: The Partnership That Saved the West.* New York: W. W. Norton and Company, 1976.

Lee, Albert. *Henry Ford and the Jews.* New York: Stein and Day, 1980.

Leuchtenburg, Wiliam E. *Franklin D. Roosevelt and the New Deal 1932–1940.* New York: Harper & Row, Publishers, 1963.

MacFarland, Charles K. *Roosevelt, Lewis, and the New Deal.* Fort Worth, Tex.: Texas Christian University Press, 1970.

Mallison, Sam T. *The Great Wildcatter.* Charleston, W.Va.: Education Foundation of West Virginia, 1953.

Martin, James Stewart. *All Honorable Men.* Boston: Little, Brown and Company, 1950.

McCormick, Donald. *Peddler of Death: The Life and Times of Sir Basil Zaharoff.* New York: Holt, Rinehart and Winston, 1965.

Metcalfe, Philip. *1933.* Sag Harbor, N.Y.: Permanent Press, 1988.

Meyer, Lorenzo. *Mexico and the United States in the Oil Controversy, 1917–1942.* Austin, Tex.: University of Texas Press, 1972.

Meyer, Lorenzo, and Vazquez, Josefina Zraida. *The United States and Mexico.* Chicago, Ill.: University of Chicago Press, 1985.

Meyer, Michael C., and Sherman, William L. *The Course of Mexican History*. New York: Oxford University Press, 1979.

Millon, Robert Paul. *Mexican Marxist: Vicente Lombardo Toledano*. Chapel Hill, N.C.: University of North Carolina Press, 1966.

Moffat, Jay Pierrepont. *The Moffat Papers: Selections from the Diplomatic Journals of Jay Pierrepont Moffat*. Edited by Nancy Harvison Hooker. Cambridge, Mass.: Harvard University Press, 1956.

Morgenthau, Henry F. *From the Morgenthau Diaries: Years of Urgency 1938–1941*. Edited by John Morton Blum. Boston: Houghton Mifflin Company, 1965.

Moseley, Leonard. *Reich Marshall: A Biography of Hermann Goering*. New York: Doubleday, 1974.

Powell, J. Richard. *The Mexican Petroleum Industry 1938–1950*. Berkeley, Calif.: University of California Press, 1956.

Pratt, Julius W. *Cordell Hull*. New York: Cooper Square Publishers, 1964.

Pye, Michael. *The King over Water: The Scandalous Truth about the Windsors' War Years*. New York: Holt, Rinehart and Winston, 1981.

Rhodes, Anthony. *The Vatican in the Age of the Dictators 1922–1945*. New York: Holt, Rinehart and Winston, 1973.

Riess, Curt. *Total Espionage*. New York: G. P. Putnam's Sons, 1941.

Roberts, Andrew. *Holy Fox: A Biography of Lord Halifax*. London: Weldenfeld and Nicolson, 1991.

Rogge, O. John. *The Official German Report: Nazi Penetration 1924–1942 Pan-Arabism 1939–Today*. New York: A. S. Barnes and Company, 1961.

Rogge, O. John. *Our Vanishing Civil Liberties*. New York: Gaer Associates, 1949.

Salvemini, Gaetano. *Italian Fascist Activities in the United States*. New York: Center for Migration Studies, 1977.

Sampson, Anthony. *The Seven Sisters: The Great Oil Companies and the World They Shaped*. New York: Viking Press, 1975.

Schewe, Donald B., ed. *Franklin D. Roosevelt and Foreign Affairs: Second Series January 1937–August 1939 Volume Five: April–June 1937 and Volume Twelve: November–December 1938*. New York: Clearwater Publishing Co., 1969.

Schmidtz, David F., ed. *Appeasement in Europe: A Reassessment of U.S. Policies*. New York: Greenwood Press, 1990.

Schwartz, Jordan A. *Liberal: Adolf A. Berle and the Vision of an American Era*. New York: Free Press, 1987.

Shirer, William L. *Collapse of the Third Republic: An Inquiry into the Fall of France in 1940*. New York: Pocket Books, 1971.

Stevenson, William. *A Man Called Intrepid: The Secret War*. New York: Harcourt, Brace Jovanovich, 1976.

Sulzberger, C. L. *World War II*. New York: American Heritage Publishing, 1966.

Summers, Anthony. *Official and Confidential: The Secret Life of J. Edgar Hoover*. New York: G. P. Putnam's Sons, 1993.

Tansil, Charles Callan. *Back Door to War: The Roosevelt Foreign Policy 1933–1941*. Chicago: Henry Regnery Company, 1952.

Townsend, Peter, ed. *Burke's Peerage: Baronetage and Knightage*. London: Burke's Peerage Limited, 1970.

Tunney, Gene. *Arms for Living*. New York: Wilfred Funk, 1941.

Ward, Geoffrey C. *First Class Temperament: The Emergence of Franklin Roosevelt*. New York: Harper and Row, 1989.

Watkins, T. H. *The Great Depression*. New York: Little, Brown and Company, 1993.

Weber, Eugen. *Varieties of Fascism: Doctrines of Revolution in the Twentieth Century*. Princeton, N.J.: Van Nostrand Company, 1964.

Wechsler, James A. *Labor Baron: A Portrait of John L. Lewis*. New York: William Morrow and Company, 1944.

West, Nigel. *A Thread of Deceit: Espionage Myths of World War Two*. New York: Random House, 1985.

Weyl, Nathaniel, and Weyl, Sylvia. *The Reconquest of Mexico: The Years of Lazaro Cárdenas*. New York: Oxford University Press, 1939.

Whelan, Richard J. *Founding Father: The Story of Joseph P. Kennedy*. New York: New American Library, 1964.

Williams, Ben Ames Jr. *Bank of Boston 200: A History of New England's Leading Bank 1784–1984*. Boston: Houghton Mifflin Co., 1984.

Williams, E. T., ed. *Dictionary of National Biography 1951–1960*. London: Oxford University Press, 1971.

Williams, William Appleman. *The Tragedy of American Diplomacy*. New York: Dell Publishing Co., 1972.

Wood, Bryce. *The Making of the Good Neighbor Policy*. New York: Columbia University Press, 1961.

Yergin, Daniel. *The Prize: The Epic Quest for Oil, Money and Power*. New York: Simon & Schuster, 1991.

Articles and Periodicals

Boston Evening Transcript. 1938.

Chicago Tribune. July 30, 1939.

Christian Science Monitor. 1938–1939.

Current Biography. 1940, 1941, 1942, 1944, 1947, 1948.

Des Moines Register. October 31, 1946.

Fortune. January 1941.

Houston Chronicle. August 1, 1941, and August 23, 1943.

Houston Post. August 1941.

Life. January 1941, pp. 26–27.

London Times. 1936–1941.

Moody's Manual of Investments. 1934–1938.

The Nation. November 1940.

National Cyclopedia of American Biography. Vols. 32, 37, 49.

The New Republic. May 13, 1940, pp. 628–629.

Newsweek. January 1941.

New York Herald Tribune. 1940–1941.

New York Times. 1920–1946.

Oil and Gas Journal (Dallas). 1933–1941.

Overacker, Louise. "American Government and Politics." *American Political Science Review* (October 1933), pp. 770–781.

Overacker, Louise. "American Government and Politics." *American Political Science Review* (June 1937), pp. 480–491.

Overacker, Louise. "American Government and Politics." *American Political Science Review* (August 1941), pp. 701–725.

Petroleum Times (London). 1933–1947.

PM (New York). 1940–1946.

Railway Age Gazette (New York). 1910–1917.

Ross, Hugh. "John L. Lewis and the Election of 1940." *Labor History* (Spring 1976), pp. 160–189.

Scroggs, William O. "Mexican Anxieties." *Foreign Affairs,* vol. 18, no. 2 (January 1940), pp. 270–273.

St. Louis Post-Dispatch. 1939–1940.

Saturday Evening Post. July 29, 1939.

Seattle Post-Intelligencer. October 27, 1946.

Time. 1940–1942.

Washington Post

Who Was Who in America. Volumes Two and Three.

World Petroleum (New York). 1938.

Other Sources

Harrington, Dale. Interview with Erna Frieda Wehrle. November 11, 1995. Available from the author.

Harrington, Dale. Interview with Erna Frieda Wehrle. February 19, 1996. Available from the author.

Harrington, Dale. Interview with Dr. Mark Dallow. February 29, 1996. Available from the author.

Harrington, Dale. Interview with Colonel Juan Ortiz, New Mexico National Guard. March 22, 1994.

Intergenerational Genealogical Index.

Massachusetts Department of Public Health Marriage Records.

National Archives and Records Administration. National Personnel Records Office. "Statement of Military Service for Davis, William R."

Texas Department of Health. "Standard Certificate of Death for William Rhodes Davis."

Whealey, Robert H. Interviews with Helmuth Wohlthat. Lloyds Neck, N.Y., January 3, 1970; New York, N.Y., March 23, 1970; Düsseldorf, Germany, July 6, 1971. Available from Professor Whealey at Ohio University, Athens, Ohio.

Index

About the Author

Dale Harrington has worked in the banking industry for many years as a financial analyst. His investigation of business transactions (many of them with fraudulent aspects) has given him an insider's understanding of the complex relationship between American corporations and the federal government. He has an M.B.A. in finance from Golden Gate University and an M.S. in political science from the University of Wisconsin–Madison. Mr. Harrington lives in Oakland, California.